I left
my hat
in
Andamooka

I left
my hat
in
Andamooka

Clifford Austin

wren

WREN PUBLISHING PTY LTD
33 Lonsdale Street, Melbourne
© Clifford Austin 1973
First published 1973
National Library of Australia Card Service Number
and International Standard Book Number ISBN 0 85885 024 9
Registered in Australia for transmission by post as a book
Text set by Trade Composition Pty Ltd, Melbourne
Printed and bound by Wilke and Company Limited,
Clayton, Victoria

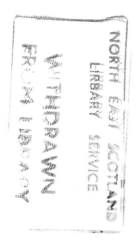

To
SHIRLEY AND BILL
whose practical help and encouragement
smoothed the path of transition from
city-dweller to nomad.

1.74

Contents

Grateful acknowledgements

to Thea, who fertilised the 'idea' to bring it to fruition; to Joy, whose fortitude was an inspiration; to John and Lorraine, the 'Chesneys', Bluey and Blanche, Murray and Fay, Ken and Lillian and many other old friends in the various cities through which we passed; to Leo, the Dependable, and to the many new friends we made, some named and some un-named, who did so much to make this book possible.

List of illustrations

List of colour plates

Author's note

This is not a story of high adventure and heroics against terrific odds.

Nor is it a technical treatise on opal mining. It is a simple account of a sixteen-month tour of a large part of Australia, the people we met and the things we did.

The people described are real people, but, in a few cases, their names have been changed for diplomatic reasons.

We didn't explore any new territory, nor did we make any startling discoveries, but we enjoyed ourselves—the sort of enjoyment any ordinary man or family could have, and many have dreamed about.

C.A.

I

The Road goes North

One big bump, followed by a shaking, as if we were fixed to the end of a jack-hammer, showed that we had come to the end of the bitumen for the next thousand miles or so.

I knew it was coming, but that didn't help to soften the effect of that nerve-wracking vibration. The noise was alarming. Every loose item aboard rattled. I could hear the crockery, cutlery and tins of provisions carrying on a war behind me as they tried to batter themselves to pieces.

I cannot go on, I thought. Neither human nerves nor man-made machine can possibly stand much of this! The Kombi will fall to pieces, I shall be raving mad and Jasper will probably be sick.

I suppose it was natural to feel like this after having been pampered for close on two thousand miles by good, smooth roads. The corrugations were so even and deep, the frequency of the hammer blows so constant that I was sure every screw must work loose and even the toughest metal must become fatigued, to say nothing of the strain on human endurance.

I consoled myself that, after all, this *was* the main highway up through the Centre and the only road link between Adelaide and Alice Springs. Perhaps this was just a short section due for repairs. The only information I could get in Port Augusta on the state of the road was "Not too bad"— a description I came to interpret as meaning "If it were any worse, you couldn't drive over it!"

The six hundred odd mile trip from Brisbane to Sydney had been quite uneventful.

We spent a month in Sydney before pushing on to Melbourne, where it took three weeks to see all my friends there and get some advice and encouragement from the V.W. factory at Clayton.

It was only after careful consideration that I chose a Volkswagen Kombi for this trip. There were several specific reasons for this. It is independent of water for cooling, the rear engine gives greater traction to the back wheels, it has excellent ground clearance, a good reputation for reliability and also a good coverage of service stations where spare parts are readily available. Finally, it is fairly economical to run.

A search round the used car yards had revealed one which had done only fourteen thousand miles. It was of the right colour—white for coolness and visibility (in case of trouble). I probably paid too much for it, but I clinched the deal quickly because I felt that, once I had committed myself to the temporary debt in which it involved me, the die would be cast and there would be no second thoughts.

We followed the coast road through Mt. Gambier to Adelaide where I procured a used two-way radio complete with a telescopic, thirty-five foot antenna.

I installed these myself in the caravan park, and was granted a licence to operate on the Royal Flying Doctor range of frequencies and was given the call sign of 8SHC—spoken as "Eight Sugar How Charlie".

After less than two weeks in Adelaide, we had our first taste of outback travel. I was lucky in having many friends whose combined experiences covered most of the phases of outback living, in country which varies from forest-covered mountains to barren, waterless desert with only faintly distinguishable tracks and occasional landmarks to show the way.

It was impressed upon me that it doesn't do to get yourself lost by taking a spurious track because, in some parts, you might travel a hundred miles or more without seeing any habitation or human being. Further, that water is all important and mechanical trouble must be avoided at all costs.

They told me, when leaving a township or lonely homestead, I must be sure to tell someone reliable where I was headed and when I expected to arrive. If I got hopelessly lost or had a breakdown, I should stay with the vehicle, conserve my water and wait patiently for a search party to come out and find me. I should be prepared for two weeks' lonely vigil and not, under any circumstances, wander away from the comparative security of the car, with its shade and sustenance.

This all sounded very exciting, and it remained to be seen whether or not I should have to follow this advice.

By the time we reached Port Augusta I had had a small sample of the barrenness and monotony of gibber plains—vast areas of undulating land strewn with large and small rocks interspersed with stunted bushes, and unrelieved by any features which could be regarded as landmarks. Although only in small doses, it was the shape of things to come and I was not impressed—at least, not favourably.

A look at my maps strengthened the feeling of being on the edge of civilisation. The Trans-Continental Railway which crosses the vast Nullarbor Plain to Kalgoorlie and Perth terminates here. The surrounding countryside is flat, dull and depressing.

Port Augusta itself is hardly the place I would choose in which to spend a holiday. It has only one street of any consequence and most of the buildings are old and shabby looking.

I was relieved when we pulled out and headed north.

Then came that enlightening bump!

After about twenty minutes of agony I found myself getting used to the constant hammering. I decided to try putting my foot down and accelerated to about 45 m.p.h. This seemed utter cruelty to the vehicle, but it certainly had the effect of smoothing out the corrugations.

I was able now to pay a little more attention to the scenery, such as it was, and noticed what I thought was a thick pall of smoke on the road ahead. As we approached, I realised that it was another vehicle coming towards us. My rear vision mirror showed visibility at the back to be nil and I became conscious for the first time of what dust can be like.

The other vehicle was getting close, so I slowed down to avoid plunging headlong into the fog which it was creating. It was a large truck and as it passed the driver gave me a friendly wave and a grin. Perhaps he thought I was a mate of his.

About half-an-hour later a car came into view through another cloud of dust. Again the friendly wave! When it happened a third time I woke to the fact that this was the camaraderie of the outback roads. Forthwith I entered into it with a feeling of warmth and enthusiasm. I tried to be the first to wave and, on the rare occasions when it was not returned, I muttered to myself "You miserable so-and-so!"

As the miles rolled by there was no improvement in the state of the road. The two hours I gave us to last out in one piece had passed and we were still going, averaging roughly thirty miles an hour. By now, Jasper was bored and settled himself down for a sleep.

I looked down at him and knew that he had complete confidence in me. I was happy in my decision to get him and with my choice.

I had been told many times that I was a fool to tackle such an extended trip on my own. I knew this to be true, but one cannot pick a suitable companion out of a hat. There was one place, however, where I could be sure of finding a mate who would be affectionate, loyal and willing to accept cheerfully whatever might come along.

The trip to the Dog Refuge was a sad experience.

How I wished I could have helped them all. I could have had a fully-grown Alsatian, a bull-dog, a poodle or a pom, a cattle-dog or corgi. Whilst they all appealed to me, the one which attracted me most was lying quietly with his head on his paws just watching rather than using up energy leaping and barking. Maybe he was tired. Perhaps he was weak. He was extremely thin and hungry-looking, but there was a certain aloof dignity about him which attracted me particularly. He had the head of a Boxer but he was not slobbery. His colour and body shape were those of a Golden Labrador. He just gave me one look and my problem was solved.

The attendant got him out and I paid the two-dollar fee. I led him out to the Kombi and opened the door. He needed no persuasion but just leapt in and on to the passenger seat, sat upright but quite relaxed as if he knew it was his place and always had been. During the drive home he maintained this position looking from left to right and observing all there was to see.

I don't know just why I decided to call him Jasper. Perhaps it was because his expression recalled the Sir Jasper of melodrama fame. But when I said "Come on, Jasper," he responded.

The following morning, after a good de-lousing bath which rid him of a few fleas and revealed half-a-dozen small ticks, I took him to a vet. He said he was probably about two years old and had the makings of a fine, healthy specimen, so I certainly hadn't been 'sold a pup'.

He was always ready to jump into his seat and settle down for a drive. In fact, he appeared to be more at home there than in the house, where he was unable to relax for long. He used to come to me frequently, put his paws on my lap and look at me as much as to ask "When are we pushing off?" Whilst he was always quite friendly and sociable by day, at night he became very possessive, and heaven help any stranger who might approach suspiciously.

It was about three in the afternoon when we arrived at the 'Pines', which was the turnoff for Arcoona Homestead and Andamooka.

Suddenly, bitumen! But my hope of a break from the corrugated gravel was short-lived. It was the road to Woomera and I could see ahead that a barrier and guard-house were there to enforce the large "Prohibited Area" sign.

We turned off this lovely road on to a rough, narrow track which I could see winding away for many miles over the barren, featureless but slightly undulating countryside. The only difference between this and the 'highway' we had previously travelled was the width. It was quite narrow with barely room for two vehicles to pass. Not that it mattered much. I had seen nothing of human life for the past two hours and didn't expect much for the rest of the day.

Over to the left I could just see the houses of what I assumed to be the residential area of Woomera. There, no doubt, would be shops and showers and bitumen roads and all the trappings of civilisation, but for all the good it was to me it might just as well have been a thousand miles away.

I pulled off the track for a light lunch. Jasper had a run and chased lizards until he came back panting for a drink of water. I had a good look round the Kombi to make sure that nothing had fallen off. No serious displacements had occurred and it was with a much lighter heart that I got going again, on the seventy-mile stretch to the Andamooka Opal Fields.

Sandhills were now becoming much more evident but the track, except for an occasional patch, was reasonably clear. Then, about half past three, I got my first experience of deep sand on the road. Only tyre tracks showed me which way to go. I didn't do what I should have done, but kept in top gear. Suddenly I was in it—up to the hub caps.

12

I changed down, but the back wheels spun, digging themselves in well and truly. I got out my shovel, and two rolls of chicken wire and started to dig. As I did so, threading its way through the dunes, came a Landrover containing five men and a girl. They pulled up alongside and, before I could even say 'hello', they all piled out and clustered round.

They were not Australians and, as they all started talking at once, I couldn't recognise their accents. Their dress was a conglomeration. Some wore old shorts and nothing else. One was in jeans and boots and a T-shirt. The girl was dressed in slacks, thongs and a bikini top. She spoke very good English, with what I believed to be a Polish accent. She barked something to the others and they all shut up, much to my relief.

"Don't worry about those," she said to me pointing to the shovel and the chicken wire. "Put them away. We'll get you out." A sharp word of command and the five men got to the back of the Kombi. Their combined pushing had it clear of the deep sand in no time.

I was very grateful and said so and ventured to ask where they were going.

"Port Augusta" she replied. "Just for the weekend. I suppose you are going to Andamooka?"

"Yes! What's it like there?" I asked.

"Quite a good place," she answered, "but you need a change once in a while."

"How's the road from here?" I queried.

"Could be worse. There's one very bad place you'll have to watch out for."

"How do you mean—bad?" I asked. "Rough?"

"Sandhills! It's about twenty-five miles from the opal fields. Sand has built up right across the road. When you get there, don't follow the tracks. Take the detour to the right. You'll see our tracks going up through the trees. Follow those and you should be all right."

"I will. Thanks for your help."

By this time the others had resumed their places in the Landrover—four in the back. The driver pressed the starter and she jumped up beside him. Then, with a cheery wave and a "See you in Andamooka" they were off in a cloud of dust and we were alone again. I couldn't help wondering about this party—who they were, how they were doing and what was the relationship between those five men and the quite young girl with the dark hair, the Polish accent and the authoritative tone.

I checked the speedometer and made a rough calculation when I should strike the bad patch. As I had reckoned on a twenty-five miles per hour average, I anticipated being in Andamooka Opal Fields around about five-thirty. Therefore, between four and five should be the critical period.

Four o'clock came and we still hadn't encountered the hazard. At four-fifteen I could see a line of sandhills ahead—a low, orange-coloured wall stretching away to the left and right as far as the eye could see. I approached timidly as the sand got thicker and thicker. Then it seemed

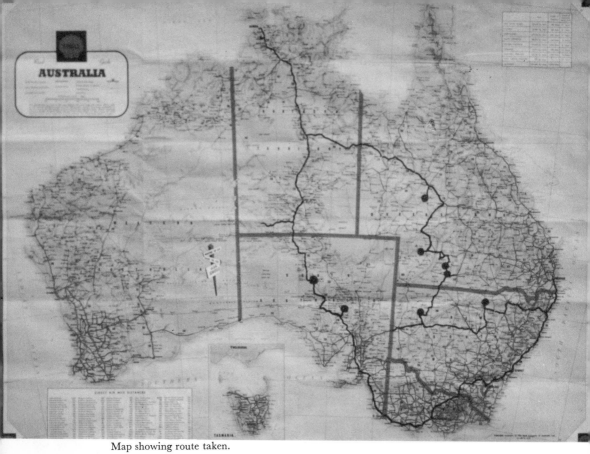

Map showing route taken.

'Come on, let's get moving!'

that there was a solid wall of sand ahead. But the track turned to the right, then left and wound its way deeper and deeper into the maze of dunes.

Then I saw it! The track didn't turn away this time but led straight over a slight depression in the crest of the red wall in front. Something had gone over it. That was obvious. The ground I was on was still fairly firm so I pulled up. Stunted trees and saltbush abounded and I walked round looking for the 'detour'.

Sure enough, there it was, but to my dismay this seemed even more formidable than the original track.

My dilemma was now which track to take. The girl had said take the detour to the right but whose right? Did she mean my right or their right? I cursed myself for not making sure what she meant. In the meantime, I just had to get over this, the first real difficulty I'd had.

I decided to try the left-hand track, as this looked a far easier gradient and had many more wheel marks. I approached gingerly and could feel the resistance of the sand building up until finally the engine stalled and I came to a stop. I started the engine again and slipped into reverse. Being on a fair slope, I managed to get back to where I had started. All right, I thought, let's try the detour.

This was equally unsuccessful, so I had another go at the first one with the same result.

After several more abortive attempts I decided to call it a day and camp for the night. A firm patch of ground just off the track would serve as a campsite. I drove carefully on to it by keeping to the gibbers and spinifex showing above the layer of sand. I was hot, tired and dusty. I peeled some potatoes, put them in a saucepan and lit my cooker. On the top of the saucepan I put an enamelled plate on to which I emptied the contents of a tin of peas and a tin of braised steak which would steam-heat as the potatoes boiled. I then prepared Jasper's dinner ready for the time when he should return from hunting lizards and an exploratory tour of the immediate surroundings. By the time he came back and my dinner was ready, it was dark.

I put Jasper's dinner plate, together with his water bowl, on the ground outside, closed the door of the Kombi and settled down to have mine in comfort. Now as never before I had cause to bless my foresight in screening every openable window. Moths and nocturnal insects came in clouds towards the light, but I was able to eat peacefully.

The water in which I had boiled the potatoes had to serve for washing up. I made a pot of strong tea, filled the vacuum flask and topped up the pot for immediate consumption.

Jasper's dinner plate, which he had cleaned up in record time, was covered with large black ants, so under the waste pipe it went and I let go the hot washing-up water. How I would have loved a shower before turning in! But I had to be content with a sponge down in less than a gallon of water. It was too hot to get into my bunk. A strong breeze had blown up but it was a warm one and gave no relief.

15

I just flopped on top of the bunk in my short pyjama trunks and switched off the light. Jasper settled down on the other bunk. I wound my watch, put my head on the pillow and was away.

After about four hours of deep, restful sleep I was suddenly awakened by a low growl from Jasper. I sat up in bed and looked out of the window. I could see the silhouette of the sandhills against the starlit sky. There was no moon but the brilliance of the stars made the night anything but dark.

"What is it, old man?" I asked. He was standing up on the bunk, hackles up and ears alert. He answered with another low growl, looking in the direction of the road we had come along.

I strained my eyes in that direction but could see nothing but the shadowy shapes of the clumps of saltbush.

"There's nothing there," I told him, but he knew better and continued growling, his body tensed.

I was beginning to get a bit nervous so I took my rifle from its rack, clipped in a magazine and 'shoved one up the spout'.

Again I strained my eyes in the same direction and there suddenly appeared two dim shadows moving slowly and silently towards the depression in the sandhills. They continued over the top and were lost from view. Jasper stopped growling and I started speculating. What possible reason could two people have for walking along a desert track in the early hours of the morning? As I looked towards the depression in the dunes, the figures appeared again going back the way they had come.

I kept quiet and watched until they were out of sight again. As I was debating what move I should make, the silence was shattered by a metallic 'clunk' and a roar as the motor of some heavy truck was started.

It came into sight and proceeded slowly up the sandy incline. It got as far as I had done and stopped. My eyes were now accustomed to the darkness, and I could see that it was a fully loaded truck with a small trailer. It backed off the same as I had but went much farther back. Then, with a roar, it went forward again. Up, up, almost to the crest and with the engine still roaring it lurched to a standstill. The engine was cut and I could hear faint voices. I saw the flare of a match as cigarettes were lit. Ten minutes went by before the engine again roared into life. I heard it slow down as it tried to take the load. It laboured and shuddered and finally stalled.

Again the truck started but this time backed down. Back, back, so far back that it was almost out of earshot, then silence. I thought they had given up. This proved my ignorance of the outback truck driver.

After another lapse of about three minutes I heard the roar again. This time it had a different sound. It was clear that it was moving fast. As it came into view, I estimated its speed at forty miles an hour, its trailer bouncing about like an old shoe tied to the back of a bridal car. Straight into the sand it plunged, and the battle between sand and wheels was on.

16

Up the incline it staggered, getting slower all the time. It reached the scene of its previous defeat and kept going, but only just. Now the truck was near the crest but the speed had dropped to less than five miles an hour. Still it managed to keep going and, at last, the crisis was past. The speed gradually increased and I saw the trailer bump over the crest. The roar of the engine became steady and then lessened until all was silent again.

Making sure that the safety catch was on the rifle I put it back in its rack and once more lay down on my bunk. I made a resolution that I would be up again at dawn to have another crack at that sandhill.

I awoke as the first glow of the rising sun appeared over the sandhills. The breeze had dropped and the first flies had come to take over from the night insects in their duty of harassing the traveller.

After breakfast I decided, rather reluctantly, to let the tyres down to about a third of their normal pressure. I had just completed this when I heard the sound of a vehicle approaching from the direction of Anda-mooka. Now we're going to see some fun, I thought. If it is a four-wheel drive job, I may get a tow.

Imagine my surprise when over the crest sailed a Kombi looking as if it had come straight from a wrecker's yard. Down it came, turned off the track and pulled up alongside.

"Having trouble, mate?" asked the driver as four hefty-looking blokes leapt out. Once again, obviously none of them was Australian born.

"Just about to have another go," I replied. "Gave it up last night and camped. How did you manage to get through so easily?"

"Simple really," he replied. "Keep your wheels straight, put your foot down and GO!"

I wondered how they'd get on coming back from wherever they were going because the gradient they had come up was far less severe than that on this side.

"Would you like me to take it through for you?" he volunteered.

"Please, I'd be glad if you would."

He jumped in and drove off down the track. A few seconds later he was coming back at a fair speed. At the foot of the incline I heard him change down to first and she roared as he put his foot down. Away she went, straight over the top as sweetly as you could wish.

I heard him stop and he soon appeared over the crest with a grin on his face.

"There you are, mate. No trouble at all!"

I was surprised, pleased and grateful and said so. We chatted for a few minutes and I was assured that there were no more serious hazards this side of Andamooka Opal Fields.

I mentioned the incident of the truck in the night. "Oh, yes. That was the Co-op truck bringing in the week's supplies. They warned us about this but they couldn't have noticed you or they would have told us."

Of course, these helpful lads were, like the other party, opal miners going off for the weekend. I had heard that Andamooka was a mining settlement in the old tradition inhabited by tough men of the roughest type, who, in their drunken brawls, indulged in shootings and stabbings at the drop of a hat.

If these men with their courtesy and helpfulness were a sample I felt more hopeful of a pleasant and productive stay. I bade them goodbye and wished them a happy weekend.

I whistled up Jasper who was having a marvellous hunt somewhere around and walked over the hill to the parked Kombi. I got in and was about to press the starter when I remembered the deflated tyres. Although I have a fairly good foot pump, it was hot and hard work getting those four tyres back to normal pressure.

The next twenty miles or so was winding and rough with a few sandy patches but, by now, I was feeling excited and thrilled at the thought that possibly beneath me lay pieces of stone of fabulous beauty—just waiting to be found.

As we topped one slight rise I caught my first sight of the 'diggings'— piles of whitish mullock peeping up through gaps in the undulating road. Down a dip and up another slight rise and the road swept round in a wide arc to reveal a motley collection of buildings. Half a mile nearer, I was greeted by a crude sign which said Welcome to Andamooka. I was there! I looked at my watch. It said 7.30.

2

Andamooka Opal Fields

Opals had always fascinated me and, although I had never before been nearer than four hundred miles to an opal field, I have worked many rough pieces into attractive gems after learning something of lapidary with the Gemmological Association of Australia.

For me, the fascination of opals is in their variety as well as their beauty. Like fingerprints, there are no two exactly alike.

A tour of the opal fields appealed to me for several reasons: their remoteness, the variety of their yields and the chance to try my luck actually digging in the virgin earth in the hope of finding the elusive gem.

Maybe I should meet a lone miner who would be glad to have, even for a short period, an extra pair of hands to 'pull dirt' or scratch at the promising clay and sandstone.

I had an intense desire to experience the feel of a miner's pick and, if I were fortunate, to hear the characteristic 'clink' of steel on opal, to know the thrill of the moment when great care is needed to avoid ruining a possible fortune.

Hitherto, my idea of a mining town had been coloured by the memory of Western movies—a wide, stony street lined by two-storey wooden buildings of mixed architectural features: one pub complete with a verandah and an elevated wooden footpath, a general store with merchandise piled up around the doorway, a sheriff's office and a jail.

Andamooka quickly shattered this idea.

There was no main street that I could detect. The buildings were neither two-storey nor wholly wooden but a mixture of wood, asbestos-cement, corrugated iron and rock—that is, those which weren't partly dug like caves into the hillside.

Obviously the buildings came before the 'roads', which has been formed by vehicles getting to and from and between them. There was no sign of a pub in the accepted sense, or of anything which looked official, such as a police station or a jail.

My first thought was to replenish my almost empty petrol tank and drove on to a concrete slab with a bowser, in front of one of the better constructed buildings. A big, blond, cheery fellow came out and greeted me. I imagined him to be of Scandinavian stock, and the proprietor not only of the bowser but also of the adjacent self-service grocery store, general store and tool shop.

Everything was open for business. Quite near was another self-service store and motor service station. This was the Co-op, whose truck I had seen in the early hours.

My first view of Andamooka Opal Fields had given me an impression of little activity but now, vehicles of all kinds, makes and ages were careering about, churning up the dust and generally defying all the rules of the road.

As my tank was being filled I enquired about water, which was my next major concern. My blond friend pointed to a windlass near the centre of the clearing which I shall, in future, call the City Centre.

"You can get water from the well," he informed me, "if you've got a bucket or, you can buy a hundred gallons from a truck when they bring it in."

"Ten gallons will be enough for me to be getting on with," I replied.

"Then take my tip and get it from the well," he advised, "but make sure you boil it before you drink it."

"Why?" I asked. "Is it that doubtful?"

"Oh it's sweet enough when it seeps in, but all the local abos use it and they're not too particular about the utensils they use to bring it up in. Besides there are no trees around here and the abo dogs find the windlass supports a convenient substitute."

"I see what you mean," I said, "but I'll chance it."

The well was about fifty feet deep and I could just see the water at the bottom. I got out my small plastic bucket, hooked it to the wire cable and let it go. It hit the water, turned on its side and stayed there. I had hit bottom!

I estimated the depth of the water to be about six inches. This didn't look very hopeful but I hauled it up. It was barely half full and, I suppose, represented less than half a gallon. However, I persevered and filled my storage bottles one by one until I had acquired about five gallons. Then I noticed that several people were waiting—some with jerrycans, some with 5-gallon drums and some just with old kerosene tins with the tops hacked off and a wire handle added.

In the circumstances I decided that five gallons would suffice for the moment.

I drove around making a mental note of what was where—the Post Office on the left of the track leading up a hill where there was a conglomeration of semi-dugout dwellings, sheds, tents, caravans and stores.

The roadway was unplanned and uncared for. Deep ruts and lumps of rock were distributed in the most awkward places and, to a stranger to the place, negotiating these required the maximum concentration.

Around the corner I was able to get a better view of the layout of this township which had just 'growed up' since opal was first found there in 1930 by two hands from Andamooka Station. They made their find after they had had to shift camp to higher ground during a sudden flash flood.

Over to the right, one building stood out as a fairly pretentious modern home which, I subsequently learned, belonged to an opal buyer. Further up on the crest of this low hill was the hospital, with its two radio masts which maintained contact with the Royal Flying Doctor Service.

I had no wish to go further in this direction just yet so, finding a place where I could turn safely, returned down the hill.

At the Post Office I noticed nailed to a couple of posts on the opposite side of the road a map painted on a large sheet of fibro. It showed the location of every place of note, including the groups of diggings with such fascinating names as Gunn's Gully, The Yarloo, Lunatic Hill, Black Boy, The Horse Paddock, German Gully and a host of others.

After taking a picture of this map, I decided to call in at the Post Office just to make my presence known and to see if, by any chance, there was any mail for me.

As I introduced myself, Gordon, the Postmaster, said, "Your mate's looking for you. He left a letter."

For a moment I thought he had made a mistake but the letter he handed to me had my name on it. I was delighted to see that it was from an old friend whom I hadn't seen for many years. I had heard that Mike was in Adelaide and connected in some way with the opal business. I had believed him to be on his way home to Brisbane, but had written to him at his P.O. box number telling him of my intention of leaving for Andamooka that day.

The letter simply said that he was in Andamooka, was driving a green Falcon station wagon with a roof rack and a Queensland number plate— look out for him and he'd look out for me.

I immediately tried to work out what would be Andamooka's equivalent to 'under the clock at Victoria Station' and decided that it would be somewhere between the well, the P.O. and the Co-op. I chose a spot where I could see all three and could easily be seen from each.

I went into the Co-op, bought some bread, bananas and one or two other things which I was surprised to see so far from their source of supply. I was even more surprised to find that the prices were generally up only a few cents above those charged in the cities.

By now it was past midday and I was both hungry and thirsty, so I 'camped' in this spot and had lunch, all the while keeping an eye open for a green Falcon with a roof rack and a Queensland number plate.

There were plenty of Falcons, Zephyrs, Prefects, Jeeps, Landrovers, ancient Humbers and Holdens, some probably twenty years old and I wondered how some of them ever managed to get there and if they'd ever get back to wherever they came from.

21

It wasn't long before I realised that my position was ill-chosen. The hot wind which is characteristic of this near-desert country had sprung up with a vengeance. Not only the wind but the local population seemed to wake up together. Vehicles were dashing about madly, tearing down the tracks, stirring up clouds of dust and pulling up suddenly with a squeal of brakes when the driver realised he was at his destination. It was clear that the mail was in.

I wanted to move to a quieter spot, but surely the green Falcon would turn up if I could manage to stick it out a little longer. Jasper was quite unconcerned and sat up in the passenger seat surveying everything and everybody in his lordly manner.

I was lighting my pipe when I heard a female voice with a marked Sydney accent say: "G'day, just arrived?"

I looked up to see the face of a quite attractive woman of about thirty peering in at the nearside window. Before I had a chance to reply, she went on, "Isn't he lovely. Can I stroke him?"

"Yes, we've just arrived and you can stroke him," I replied, rather guardedly because I had heard stories of the many and varied occupations and hobbies of certain women on the opal fields.

She put her hand in through the open window and fondled Jasper's head. "You're a lovely boy," she cooed. Then, to me "He's a Boxer, isn't he?"

"Part Boxer, part Labrador," I replied, "at least that's what the vet. said and I believe him."

She continued fondling and Jasper yawned with feigned embarrassment, but I knew he was enjoying it.

"I hope you don't mind me coming up to you like this," she said, "but I do love dogs and besides, it's nice to see a new face around the place. My name's Elsie Donovan and we've been here for six months."

"We?" I queried.

"Yes," she explained, "my husband and I came here to try our luck with opals. Are you in the opal business?"

"No, Mrs. Donovan. I'm after pictures and stories. I'm Cliff Austin and this is Jasper. Have you had much luck?"

"No," she answered wistfully, "not yet." And went on to explain that she had been a barmaid in a pub in Redfern, Sydney, before and for a time after she had married Jeff Donovan. They were paying an exorbitant rent for living in a bug-infested terrace house and, instead of putting their savings into buying a decent home, had decided to invest it in a second-hand utility, a tent and mining tools. They had come to Andamooka full of hope and enthusiasm. They had staked many claims, dug many shafts and, in six months of working like slaves, had produced less than a hundred dollars' worth of opal. Now they had reached the stage where their money had all but run out. If they didn't find something worth while in the next three weeks they would have to pack up and head back to Sydney.

"It all sounded so easy," she explained. "They said the whole area was loaded with opal and all you have to do is to stake a claim, dig a shaft till you reach the 'Level', scratch out the opal and sell it for a good price for cash to a local buyer."

"Then it doesn't work out that way," I suggested.

"Like hell!" she ejaculated bitterly. "But at least we are both fitter than we've ever been in our lives before. I suppose that's something to be thankful for."

With that she smiled, and I felt warmly towards her. In spite of the locale, she was well dressed in brightly coloured blouse and lightweight slacks. A large straw hat kept the sun from her face and neck. Her complexion was clear, but well tanned. Her hair—what I could see of it— was short and practical, but very blonde. Without doubt, she was an attractive woman. Her blue eyes showed a slight trace of hardness but this, I felt, could be excused in the light of her previous dealings with the hard drinking types of Sydney's Redfern. Her brief bitterness had quickly evaporated with her philosophical acceptance of her present plight.

I imagined she could be a very good friend to anyone worse off than her.

"Are you coming to the barbecue tonight?" she asked.

"What barbecue?"

"Tonight's the night of the year. Everyone will be there. Free beer, free steaks and dancing. You mustn't miss it".

"Where?" I asked, "and what's it all in aid of?"

"Right there!" She pointed over to the A.P.A. Hall where I had noticed a certain activity taking place. Trestle tables were being erected and fuel collected to supply the fires to cook the steaks. Crates of bread rolls were being unloaded from a Co-op truck.

"The Andamooka Progress Association puts on the show and everyone is invited." She sounded quite excited. "There's games and competitions for the kids in the hall, and dancing afterwards."

"Sounds good. Maybe I will come," I remarked, "but I've yet to find myself a camping site."

"That's easy", she assured me. "Just stop anywhere you fancy. We're camped just up the hill on the left. Why not call in for a cuppa about half past three? My husband will be back by then and he'd like to have a yarn. Look for a big brown tent."

I said I might, but couldn't promise as I had a friend to find. Once I'd found him, anything might happen.

"If you don't come, I'll see you at the barbecue," she said. "Must go and see if there's any mail. Hooray for now!"

And with a parting pat for Jasper she went off.

To find a camping site was now my main concern and, seeing no sign of Mike's Falcon, I again drove past the Post Office and up the hill towards the hospital. Keeping my eyes to the left I soon spotted the big brown tent surrounded by boxes, oil drums, old tyres and all manner of junk. On one side was a dilapidated iron shed which could have been a habitation, past or present. On the other side was a caravan without wheels and supported on oil drums. A very rough canvas awning over the door was intended to give some protection from the sun. There was no sign of life. Beyond was some bare ground, then some old diggings no longer active from the opal angle but, judging from the primitive sentry-box type erections above the shafts, serving a useful purpose in another direction.

I drove on up the hill. I am not unsociable, but when I can choose my own camping site I prefer to be away from other people—to be able to sing at the top of my voice or gaze at the stars, listen to the silence and enjoy the peace of the outback, away from the man-made jangle of voice and radio.

A couple of miles or so farther on, the track turned to the right. On the left was a wide slope of spinifex and gibbers leading up gently to the top of the ridge. Apart from some sandhills with mullock heaps beyond, there was nothing to suggest human habitation, so I turned off the track up the slope till I found a level patch of ground. This was visible from the track, but far enough away that I should be undisturbed by any vehicles which might come along.

This will do for now, I decided.

I parked facing roughly south so that, as the sun gradually got lower, it would not stream into the open doorway. With the offside curtains drawn and back window wide open I could obtain a little relief from the intense heat of the afternoon.

I was feeling sleepy. Maybe I'd call on Elsie Donovan for a cuppa tomorrow. I lay on my bunk clad only in a pair of shorts and before long I was sleepily reminiscing.

Yes, this little home of mine was cosy and convenient. The fitting out of the Kombi had been a matter of keen enjoyment both in planning the layout and the practical construction.

Although I had anticipated travelling alone so far as human companionship was concerned, I incorporated two single bunks in case I changed my mind.

One friend of wide experience gave me several tips. He said "Don't live rough unless you have to. Have as comfortable a bed as you can accommodate. Make sure you have a good-sized table of the right height to eat, write and read off. Be prepared for but not resigned to discomfort. Don't allow flies or mosquitoes to drive you 'round the bend'. Don't rely on always being able to 'boil the billy' over an open fire. Get your head down at dark and get up with the sun. Have one good, solid, cooked meal every day."

With these thoughts in mind I had planned to be able, at the end of a day's tiring driving, to get myself a quick but substantial meal, flop down on a sponge rubber mattress and go to sleep with all windows open yet quite unworried by flying insects.

Fly screening had been a relatively simple matter. Both bunks were

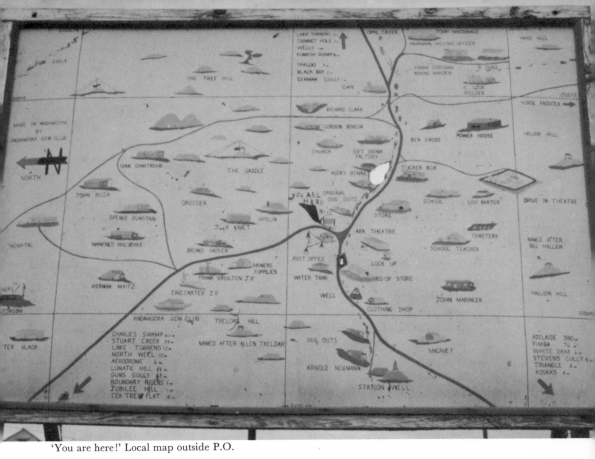

'You are here!' Local map outside P.O.

'Desirable residence'? Some of the original dugout dwellings.

very comfortable though a trifle narrow, but I quickly got used to that. I couldn't afford the time or money to make mistakes, and spent hours planning and scheming to avoid waste of space and material. It is one thing to fit a cupboard into your kitchen at home and quite another to fit up the interior of a moving vehicle, allowing for the stresses of rough roads and the need to keep the contents from spilling out each time you turn a corner, hit a pothole or brake suddenly.

Before building or installing anything, I tried to anticipate as far as possible how it would fit into my daily routine. For every half hour's practical carpentry, one hour was spent looking, thinking and imagining the result in actual use under mobile conditions. It was time well spent.

It may seem that the goods compartment of a Kombi is rather small to turn into a home that is somewhere to sleep, somewhere to eat, somewhere to work and somewhere just to relax. Admittedly, it has its restrictions, and I had to decide on what components and units of furniture I should need in order of importance and work through the list until there was no more space left.

As I had one bunk fixed longitudinally down one side and the other transversely behind the driving compartment, the table presented quite a headache. It had to be a decent size, firm and strong.

To make one was no problem, but how to support it and what to do with it when it was not being used was a mighty one.

As sleeping and eating do not normally occur at the same time, some bunk space could be covered up during the day, so I used a piece of 24″ by 34″ plywood, mounted on a dowelled frame of 1″ by 1″ pine. This was hinged to the wall over one end of the longitudinal bunk. When in use it still allowed sufficient clearance for mattress and bedding to remain in place. The free end was supported by two pieces of aluminium tubing forming a "V". This folded up flush with the underside of the table top which then lifted up clear of the bunk and clipped to the roof— out of the way yet instantly available without trouble when required.

I fitted up a small plastic sink with a wastepipe going through the floor. Over this sink is a 5-gallon plastic jerrycan with a tap and water-gauge.

I settled for using methylated spirit as a cooking fuel. I acquired two units and mounted them alongside the sink unit with a cover to form a draining board.

I had a substantial roof rack built to carry all my personal possessions which I couldn't bear to part with. A bull-bar in front not only offered us some protection in the event of a collision with cattle or a kangaroo, but also carried a second spare wheel and a water-cooling bag.

I also had the glass removed from the window in the back panel and a hopper type window substituted. This meant that I could get rear ventilation without having to open the whole of the back panel.

Then I designed an annexe, comprising a sheet of 'Kordux', which stretched right over the top to protect the luggage and equipment on the roof rack. The actual annexe portion rolled up on its long aluminium pole and straps to the side of the rack. When unrolled, two five-foot aluminium poles supported the long pole and outside edge whilst four tent pegs and guy ropes held it in position. End pieces hooked on to form a snug, roomy shelter. I was particularly pleased with this, as I could erect it or strike it in less than five minutes.

It is not always convenient to go to bed and get up with the sun and so lighting required serious thought.

I acquired a second-hand 12-volt generator, regulator, ammeter and battery of large capacity and had an extra pulley welded to the fan-belt pulley of the engine. The generator was mounted, the other things fixed and wired up including a small fluorescent bar for general illumination, individual bunk lights, a cooker light and two power points for my vacuum cleaner and two-way radio.

This got over the disadvantage of only having a 6-volt system, which is standard on the Kombis. I now had no fears of flattening my starter battery by sitting up late or reading in bed and if I should have starter trouble, I could always use half the 12-volt battery to get me going.

I was almost asleep when I was jerked back to full consciousness by the sound of a car horn and the crunch of tyres on the gibbers. I looked out to see a green Falcon pulling up alongside.

Mike had spotted the Kombi from the main track and decided to investigate. He introduced me to his partner, a large, deeply tanned and smiling Yugoslav.

Mike and George were prospecting in this very area and had pegged out a claim within a quarter of a mile. It was known as Gunn's Gully and, whilst there were one or two abandoned workings quite near, it had certainly not been worked out.

They were on their way back to the main settlement, where they were camped in a corrugated iron garage owned by an Adelaide opal buyer with whom they were working on a partnership basis.

They were very tired and greeted my suggestion of the barbecue without enthusiasm as they intended to have an early night in preparation for a busy day tomorrow. We had much to talk about but agreed to postpone this until tomorrow when they would call on their way up to their claim.

By the time Jasper and I had eaten it was getting near seven o'clock and the sun was well down. I listened to the news on the radio, then followed my strict rule of writing up my journal.

In noting the day's events I came to the point of meeting Elsie Donovan and realised that I had forgotten all about my expressed intention of going along to the barbecue.

I felt more like turning in, but I had to make the effort. After all, it could be fun and I would meet all sorts of people. The idea of wearing a shirt didn't appeal to me but I managed to find a clean one and a fresh pair of shorts. That will have to do, I told myself. I don't suppose they'll throw me out for not wearing a tie.

When on the move I carried a lot of stuff like my spare jerrycans of petrol, buckets, plastic garbage container (in which I did my ablutions and clothes washing) and spade loose inside the vehicle.

As soon as I camped for the night, all this stuff was thrown outside until I moved off again. I couldn't be bothered to load it all on again just for a trip to town, so I just drove off after making a mental note of its location.

It was now quite dark, but the track was sufficiently defined to enable the headlights to pick it up. Even so, it needed quite an effort to avoid the many deep ruts and dodge the lumps of rock scattered around everywhere.

When I arrived, the township was still a hive of activity. The stores were still open and cars coming and going. The piece of ground in front of the A.P.A. Hall was located easily by the light of the fires and the shadowy shapes moving around. The only other light came from the hall itself, from which music was emanating.

There is no parking problem in Andamooka. You just drive to a place nearest to where you want to go and stop—this way, that way, on an angle or across—it just doesn't matter.

I drove to a point where I could keep the Kombi in sight, shut Jasper inside and made my way through those shadowy shapes which, on closer acquaintance, proved to be a very mixed collection.

There were obvious miners, some with shirts, some in singlets only and some with nothing above the waist except the hair on their chests. Some wore beards, some were clean shaven and some were just unshaven.

Details were hard to see in the flickering light of the fires which were kept fed with charcoal from sacks, but I did notice one man who was dressed in well-creased slacks, white, long-sleeved shirt and a tie.

The most fully dressed were the Aboriginals, much to my disappointment and disgust. They should have been naked, or nearly so, with paint on their faces and bodies—brandishing spears or woomeras or whatever it is that they brandish.

Instead of that, they nearly all wore shabby trousers, shirts, pullovers and coats—even overcoats! Instead of spears they brandished bottles, the contents of which were rapidly inducing a state either of animosity towards their womenfolk and fellow natives or stupor, which had left some lying prone around the edges of the gathering.

Their women were as bad, and quite oblivious to the antics of their children who were rushing madly around with ice-cream covered faces. Even their dogs were there. There were dozens of them, all scavenging around for the odd piece of barbecued steak or bread roll which had been dropped.

I wandered over towards a trestle table, a helper looked up as I approached, grinned and shoved a bread roll loaded with steak and sausage into my hand.

"Here you are, mate. Try that for size!"

I grinned back and said "Thanks".

Having not long had a big meal I was not too anxious to sink my teeth into that steaming hot steak, so I continued my wandering with the roll in my hand.

It seems that I had inadvertently got myself into a line-up because a shove in the back brought me up to another trestle table, where I was almost forcibly presented with a bottle of beer.

With that I backed away to a small clearing in the mass of humanity. I took a bite at the roll and through the steak. The sausage popped out and fell to the ground where it was quickly snapped up by a lean black mongrel from the Aboriginal collection. The steak was delicious though slightly overdone.

I continued to wander around, the roll in one hand, the bottle in the other. I took a swig at the bottle of beer and as I did so, felt the roll being snatched from my hand. I whipped round thinking it was an Aboriginal child, only to come face to face with—a horse!

I accepted the fact that it would be a pretty motley gathering but, really, this was a bit much. After the first shock, I couldn't help laughing at the sight of this young horse calmly standing there and eating my roll and steak. I heard later that it was a brumby which had become a local pet and was entitled, perhaps, to feel at home.

I clutched the bottle of beer tighter, half imagining that a kangaroo or even an emu might be in the party and have designs on that.

I strolled around looking for Elsie just to show that I had kept my promise to attend. The firelight made it difficult to see anyone without going right up to them, so I made for the hall.

The noise was appalling. The music was coming from loudspeakers and two couples were trying to dance on the bare wooden floor. Children were rushing about shouting in some sort of semi-organised game which had got out of control.

Several women were in evidence and following the Australian tradition of gossiping in a group while their menfolk clustered together round the source of alcoholic beverage. Elsie was not among them.

I strolled around once more and decided that I had had enough.

When I got back to the Kombi I began to regret the lack of organised parking regulations because I was completely hemmed in. I hated the thought of having to wait there until someone left me enough room to get out. There would be a general exodus when the beer ran out, but not before. I had no desire to be on any of the tracks at night with that crowd, in the state most of them were in.

I looked around. If I could shift that Jeep a couple of yards I might just get out. I braced myself against it and it moved so easily and quickly that I nearly fell flat on my face. I was horror stricken to see it disappear into the darkness. I rushed to the Kombi and switched the headlights on. They were not pointed in the direction that the Jeep had gone, but I got sufficient reflected light to see it coming towards me again!

As it got nearer, it slowed down and finally came to rest at the bottom of a depression about 20 feet across. It had run into the hole, up the other side until the gradient had brought it to a standstill, then rolled back.

Feeling confident that it was now comfortably settled I pulled out and turned up the hill towards my campsite. It was a very dark night. But, although moonless, the stars were more brilliant and numerous than I had ever seen before, making it possible to pick out the shape of the landmarks as they were silhouetted against the speckled velvet of the outback sky. Even so, whilst I had no difficulty in recognising the sandhills and distant mullock heaps of Gunn's Gully, it was another matter to find a spade, a plastic garbage container and two jerrycans in that wide expanse of spinifex and gibbers.

I drove around and around, often having to pull up sharply to avoid plunging into a five-foot deep hole where someone had commenced a shaft and abandoned it.

Eventually, I came to the conclusion that either I was in the wrong place or someone had 'found' my spade, garbage container and jerrycans. I didn't need them tonight so the morning would be soon enough for a further search.

Within ten minutes of stopping, both Jasper and I were sound asleep.

Camped amongst the spinifex. The mullock heaps of Gunn's Gully are seen in the background.

30

3

Divining for Opal

I was awakened by the sun streaming in through the window in the door. Jasper was already awake, just sitting watching and waiting for me to open my eyes. I went outside, walked round the Kombi and there, about ten yards away on the off side, were the spade, the garbage container and the two jerrycans.

By seven o'clock our breakfast was over. The washing up was done—in the quart of water that I had used for my morning ablutions—my bed was made and some of the dust removed from the interior. I rolled a cigarette and had just lit it when the green Falcon arrived with Mike and George.

They had arranged to hire a bulldozer and try an open cut tomorrow. Today would be spent going round some of the abandoned open cuts.

Off we went in convoy to the top of the ridge. We managed to get within two hundred yards of their chosen site, then set out on foot through the deep, red sand to an area with one or two stunted bushes dotted about. This was adjacent to a long-since abandoned open cut into which the sand had blown. At certain points the 'level'—the strata in which opal might be expected to occur—was still visible below the band of 'kopi'—a whitish, earthy clay containing gypsum.

Mike explained that it was necessary to remove the overburden of sand and kopi which varied in thickness, from surface to fifty or sixty feet, before one could hope to find any traces of opal.

They estimated that, at this particular spot, the level would be found at about six to ten feet.

I asked if they had any special reason for choosing this particular site to stake their claim, as it was quite unknown whether the prospectors who had made the adjacent cut had had any luck or not.

George said nothing. Mike said "Opal is where you find it. One site is as good as another on the face of it!"

George wandered off with a pick saying that he was going to investigate

31

the level in the abandoned cut to see if there were any trace of 'potch'.

When he was out of earshot Mike asked me, "Do you believe in divining?"

"Well," I exclaimed, "I've had no experience but no one will deny that water has been located very successfully by diviners. I like to keep an open mind. Why do you ask?"

"George has got a thing about it," he replied. "He's almost convinced that opal can be found by divining. But he's very sensitive about it. That's why he clammed up when you asked why we had chosen this site. He thinks you might laugh at him."

"What rot," I assured him, "I think I know how I can put him at his ease."

"Go easy," Mike warned. "He's pretty touchy if he thinks you're taking the mickey out of him."

"Don't worry," I said, "I'll be back in a minute," and I went back to the Kombi.

A few years ago, during the height of my 'ratrace' days, a few special friends and I would occasionally find ourselves together for an hour or so in an atmosphere conducive to 'deep' discussion.

During one of these sessions, which often lasted into the small hours and never became heated, the subject of divining and similar phenomena had been discussed. Included in the latter was the 'pendulum' and its apparent ability to give positive and negative indications by its direction of rotation.

Here was something which could be demonstrated so the instigator of this trend in the discussion called for a piece of cotton and a small weight.

Our friend held the cotton about six inches from the weight so that it was free to swing. He then held it steady until it was in a state of rest.

Grasping the weight lightly between thumb and forefinger he pulled it about four inches out of plumb and released it. It then swung naturally backwards and forwards in a straight line.

Having let it swing thus for several seconds, he commanded "What is Positive?"

The pendulum now started to swing in an elliptical orbit which gradually increased to become a full circle in a clockwise direction.

He stopped it, started it again in the same manner and now commanded "Give me Negative!"

The motion immediately commenced again, but this time in an anti-clockwise direction.

We were not terribly impressed as it was obviously possible to control the direction by the minutest movement of the hand holding the cotton. We were each invited to try it in turn.

To me, it was a strange experience. Whilst I never succeeded in getting a perfectly circular orbit, the ellipses were definite. In my case anti-clockwise was Positive. Even when I closed my eyes the same thing happened, so I could not have been consciously controlling it.

Of the three others present, one had a violent reaction, one similar to mine and the third nothing at all.

This was all very interesting but not at all conclusive.

But I had made myself a pendulum 'to specification' from plastic and silver chain. It was in my collection of oddments in the Kombi, and I went to fetch it.

I had no intention of inviting my pendulum to tell me of the presence of opal but, at least, my actions would convince George that he could discuss his ideas freely without fear of ridicule.

It worked like magic!

George walked over and stared at me in amazement. I must have looked silly, kneeling in the sand and swinging a piece of plastic from the end of a chain. I didn't look up because my interest was revived. The plastic was giving me a very violent 'Positive'. For the first time it was spinning round in a perfect circle!

"What the devil are you doing," he asked.

I took no notice. I hardly heard him. I got up and moved about three yards to the right and repeated my actions. This time the pendulum swung in a normal ellipse in a clockwise direction. Back I went to the original spot and tried once more. Again the violent motion anti-clockwise.

"What's going on?" asked Mike.

"Of course, it could be the breeze," I muttered. "Hang on a minute."

Mike didn't say a word, but just looked on.

Now I moved to the left and got another 'Negative'. Then I moved back about the same distance from the original point.

Another violent 'Positive!' This was getting interesting so I explained my actions whilst moving back again and getting a further 'Positive'. These three were in a line. I was now so interested that I had forgotten all about reassuring George.

We were now all in it together, bound by a common enthusiasm. We plotted the 'Positives'. They formed a definite line!

It was now their turn to explain.

The previous day they had tried divining for opal with bent wires and had plotted the same line. They pointed out the markers which I had not noticed. That had decided where they would make their first cut. The bent wire method was a new one on me so they explained it.

Needless to say, it didn't take me long to produce two lengths of galvanised wire from the Kombi and make myself a pair of divining rods.

They worked the same as my pendulum had done. I then discovered that George had used a small piece of opal in the palm of each hand during his experiments. I had used nothing!

We then tried a forked twig which George broke off one of the little bushes. He got a reaction. I got nothing—neither with nor without opal in my palms. This was all very confusing!

33

Of course, by now, all three of us were convinced that we should find opal on that line beneath the sand and the kopi.

That night, we dined at one of the cafes, drank lots of beer, laughed, talked and expounded various theories on the art of divining.

My own theory—for what it is worth—is that the force which moves the pendulum, crosses the wires or bends the twig is purely a physical one supplied *subconsciously* by the diviner.

I can accept the existence of a sixth sense which varies in its development in each individual. Some have it strongly, others are not conscious of having it at all.

Believing this makes it easier to believe in the practicability of divining. Is it not reasonable to assume that, by its very atomic structure, any inanimate object like water, coal or opal could produce emanations on wavelengths to which the subconscious mind of those 'gifted' could be tuned? Accept this and the rest is easy. Anyway, this theory will do for me until someone offers me a better one.

The ice had now been well and truly broken and we were all keenly looking forward to tomorrow to see what the bulldozer would reveal.

Mike, of course, knew me well but George was a little cagey at first. Both of them, now knowing of my filming project and my obvious interest in opal mining for its own sake rather than making money out of it, accepted me as a mate rather than a competitor.

This was a very happy arrangement. I could give them a hand when necessary and they, in their turn, could help me with filming in colour the various phases of opal mining.

It was a casual thought that led me to taking a cine camera as well as a still camera which, of course, had been a 'must'.

It had been twenty years since I did any serious filming and my knowledge of 16mm work was out of date and mostly forgotten but, like riding a bicycle or swimming, one never forgets the rudimentary principles.

I bought an almost new, late model Bolex camera with a zoom lens, a substantial tripod and an exposure meter which I hoped would be reliable, and 2,000 feet of colour film.

Tomorrow, I should start filming in earnest, and it was in a very contented frame of mind that I returned to the campsite and turned in.

We were all on the site bright and early in the morning. Once again I parked the Kombi as near as possible to the claim and carried all the gear I thought I should need to the shade of a small bush. I loaded the cine camera with one hundred feet of colour film, assembled the zoom lens and tripod, then wrapped the lot in a piece of canvas to keep out the sand.

The temperature was creeping up, the flies were becoming very troublesome and the hot wind was beginning to blow quite strongly.

We sat around and yarned and smoked and sprayed ourselves with fly repellent until a distant roar announced the approach of a big bulldozer coming in a straight line from the direction of the township. The caterpillar tracks took all the obstacles with a clank and a roar.

When it arrived, I expected some immediate action but the driver stopped the engine, clambered down, took a swig from his water bag and, sitting down with us in the sand, rolled a cigarette and started yarning. This went on for the best part of half an hour before he got the message that he was there to make an open cut.

Mike gave him his instructions and once the machine was on the move, it wasn't long before the landscape began to change.

He dropped his blade about a foot into the sand and, within minutes it seemed, a new sandhill had been formed at the end of the run and the kopi was being disturbed for the first time in hundreds of thousands of years. George and Mike followed the dozer watching closely for traces of the level, while I took several shots of this operation.

At about eight feet the white of the kopi began to change to a brownish colour. The dozer was stopped and we all hopped in with picks and shovels probing for signs of the formation of opal.

Scraping six inch layers from the surface and keeping a constant watch, it was four o'clock before we found the first 'potch' which is common opal without colour or value.

From now on it was hand work, so the bulldozer was dispensed with for the day. The three of us got busy with picks, all the time looking carefully for traces of a lead to a seam from the chips that were yards away from our divined line and had probably been carried there by the blade. We went back to our line and started digging in earnest.

We found nothing! The sun was now well down. We were tired, sweaty and dirty and reluctantly agreed to call it a day.

I threw all my gear into the Kombi and drove back the short distance to our campsite. The other two went back to their garage for their evening meal and to sleep.

Next morning I left the Kombi where it was, chucked a few things in an old army haversack, picked up my pick and shovel and walked up to the site.

Mike and George were already on the job and, by the look of it, had been for some time. They hardly noticed my arrival. Their industry was explained when I saw, heaped on an old sugar bag several large pieces of opal.

"Strike it rich?" I asked.

Mike looked up with a grin and replied, "Looks hopeful but no colour yet. Have a look through that lot and see if you can see any colour".

I looked it over, applying liberal amounts of 'Scotch polish'. This is the name given to the process of wetting the stone by licking it to simulate the effect of polishing. It is effective if not a very hygienic method of evaluating the possibilities of successful lapidary.

There were some quite thick lumps of pale grey potch, but I could see not a trace of colour. Had all these hunks contained good colour a small fortune would have already been found.

However, where there's potch there could be colour, It's just a matter of following it up until it yields or peters out.

35

"George found most of that," Mike informed me. "I'm trying to find which way it runs. I'm working along our line. I've found a few chips. How about you trying over there?"

He pointed out a spot along our imaginary divined line. The temperature had now risen to a most uncomfortable level. I stripped off to my very brief shorts, sandals and giggle hat and started working on my hole.

Jasper was feeling the heat too, but solved his problem by digging himself a cubby-hole in the sand at the top of the shady side of the cut. He had chosen this spot strategically so that he could lie in the shade yet look down and watch all that was going on, like a gang foreman.

It was nearly an hour before I found my first little chip of potch. I was about to give up this hole when I found it, and it was encouraging.

In the meantime, both George and Mike had commenced new holes without much success.

I let out an excited "Ah!" Something had glinted in the sun and I knew I must be careful. I stopped digging and bent right down to have a closer look. The shining glass-like surface was opal all right. Perhaps I had found another 'Andamooka Queen'. I got out my penknife and carefully scraped away the surrounding dirt. The flake fell out, for it was only a flake of muddy-looking potch.

I was disappointed but not discouraged. Further digging produced more and bigger pieces. I was getting quite nonchalant about it now and made a small pile on the side of the hole.

My back was beginning to ache so I got up to stretch and have a smoke. As I did so, I looked at my spoils and thought I saw a tiny flash of green. I picked up the piece I thought it had come from, Scotch polished it and turned it in the sun.

Sure enough, there it was. In one corner a minute speck of brilliant green flashed and seemed to turn to blue as I turned it.

"Colour!" I yelled. "We're on it, lads!"

We were all excited and very optimistic now. We dug furiously for the rest of the day, but not another trace of colour did we find. Even the potch ran out.

At five o'clock we were all tired, dirty, hungry and disappointed so we decided to clean up at our respective camps and have a council of war over dinner at Raffai's Cafe, with lots of beer to wash it down.

Naturally, I was only an observer at this council of war. Mike wanted to abandon the cut and make another at a different angle. George was in favour of going deeper in the same cut. They turned to me for my opinion.

"Well," I said, "it's your money. A hundred dollars a day for the bulldozer makes it a pretty expensive gamble. Why not go deeper ourselves where we found the potch. Then, if we still draw a blank, we can have half a day chewing into the old cut from a different direction."

They didn't think very much of this idea but, after further discussion, decided to give it a go at digging deeper with the picks on the same spots where the potch had appeared.

'his is the spot!' Divining for opal with forked twig.

Just down to the 'level'. The same spot just after the bulldozer had been through.

ulling up kopi. The top of the shaft on Blackboy Hill showing windlass and wind-sock.

The following morning we got going again but soon found ourselves in trouble. A little more potch appeared but we were now into a layer of gypsum, which makes it hard going even with a jack-hammer.

"We shall have to blast!" announced Mike and without further ado went back to the Falcon for auger, gelignite and detonators.

This might be fun, so I hastily collected the filming equipment from the Kombi. When I got back, I found that George was already drilling the hole to take the charge with the auger. Mike was fixing the fuse and detonator into a stick of gelignite. I started filming the operations immediately.

I mentioned to Mike that I'd like a close-up of the fuse burning. Could he put a sufficiently long one in to enable me to do this and get myself and the camera away before it went up?

"Could do!" Mike agreed, "but I wouldn't like to risk it. You might trip up and break your ankle or something." He hesitated, then, "I know. We'll burn a dummy fuse for your close-up, then you can get well back and take a long shot when we put the actual charge in."

I saw the wisdom of this and took my shots.

Then they put the charge of gelignite in. The fuse was timed for two minutes. My camera would run for about twenty-five seconds before it required rewinding.

I saw smoke rising and George moving rapidly but steadily away. With my finger on the cable release I looked at my wrist-watch. It had stopped! I made a quick guess that about thirty seconds had elapsed since I saw the smoke. I guessed another minute and a quarter and pressed the button.

The camera whirred and the smoke kept rising. The camera whirred on and the smoke rose still lazily from the hole. It must be a fizzer, I thought. Then the camera stopped and half a second later—Thump! Up went the gelignite.

I was mad. What a waste of expensive colour film!

"Never mind," consoled Mike. "We'll have to blow one or two more. Let that be a lesson to you. Never wear a wrist-watch on this job. It's probably bunged up with sand."

Actually, this wasn't really a tragedy at all because, on looking at the camera footage indicator, it showed one hundred and fifty feet of film exposed and, as I only had a capacity for one hundred feet, I hadn't wasted any film at all—only time. That was another lesson I learned— always watch your footage indicator no matter how exciting the action.

I took the camera back to the Kombi to re-load, but this time I returned with a stop-watch which I'd had for years. I checked this. It was working perfectly.

We went through the routine again and now I was confident that I could get a little closer to the explosion without danger.

The first time, all the dirt and rock had gone straight upwards and landed within a few yards of the hole.

Unfortunately, this time I failed to notice that the charge was inserted at a slightly different angle.

I timed it beautifully. I pressed the button about four seconds before it blew. Then I got the fright of my life. Big lumps of rock and dirt were falling all around me. I ducked and took my finger off the button as one large chunk landed right beside me and a smaller piece hit the base of the tripod.

Luckily, no damage was done except that the shot had been cut shorter than I had intended. My third lesson for that day—always be sure which way the debris will go before deciding on how far away is a safe distance.

We did a little more digging but the wind, although hot, died down and we were completely at the mercy of the blistering afternoon sun. Even Jasper gave up and lay panting in his cubby.

We called it a day. I left my tools where I had dropped them, picked up the camera and tripod and staggered back to the Kombi. I was thankful that I had taken the few minutes necessary that morning to erect the annexe. I had also drawn the curtains so that my camp was comparatively cool.

I had been congratulating myself on picking a spot where the nocturnal insect life was small. But tonight, as soon as it was dark enough to switch the light on, all kinds of flying creatures descended on me in droves. I shut the door too late. They were everywhere—in my food, in my hair and even in my mouth.

Spraying with insecticide, normally most effective against flies and mosquitoes, had no effect whatsoever. They even seemed to enjoy it. I managed to reduce their numbers by lashing out with a fly-swat but still had to spoon them out of my tea and scrape them from my food.

Finally, in desparation, I switched the light off and turned in. The bigger ones had been accounted for but the tiny ones continued to torment me all night by crawling on my nose or my neck. They did not bite, but the tickling they caused nearly drove me mad. It must have been from sheer exhaustion that I eventually went to sleep.

In the morning, I felt that I should do some washing so we set off for 'town', where I did some shopping and filled every available container with water from the well.

A sudden urge to taste fresh milk took me to the Co-op where I bought a pint in a sort of pyramidal carton. At the exit, I again met Elsie Donovan who greeted me like an old friend and expressed disappointment that I hadn't turned up for the cuppa.

I, in turn, told her that I was disappointed that I hadn't seen her at the barbecue. She told me that she had been delayed and had arrived at about the time I was having my adventure with the Jeep.

This time, I made a solemn promise to call in the afternoon—as soon as I had done my washing.

For lunch, I planned to have slices of new bread, butter and honey. I made fresh tea in honour of the occasion.

I lifted out the pyramidal container of milk and read the 'Instructions for Opening'. It said "cut off a point."

My table knife made no impression apart from a dent, so I tried a pair of scissors. These worked and made an aperture about one eighth of an inch in diameter where the point had been.

So far, so good! I had the carton flat on my left hand during this operation and tilted it over my cup expecting the milk to come out under control. It didn't! Nothing happened!

Now, with my right hand, I grasped the carton firmly. Being in the shape of a pyramid I HAD to grasp it firmly. A stream of milk hit the roof!

Naturally I stopped squeezing and the stream died away but the carton fell from my hand with a thud on to the table. The impact caused another eruption, this time all over my bunk and the fly-screen on the side window.

Anyway, I enjoyed what was left in my tea!

After lunch and a brief siesta I drove down to the site of the Donovan's tent. It was well past the time that Jeff Donovan should have been back from his mine, but there was no sign of any vehicle.

As I walked up to the tent I called "Anybody home?"

Elsie's voice answered, "Come on in!"

I pushed aside the tent flap and stepped inside. It was quite a large tent and furnished principally with crates, some upside down as chairs and tables, some on their sides as open-fronted cupboards.

On an upturned crate were three pressure-operated kerosene burners. On one was a billy just coming up to the boil.

"I knew you'd come today." As she said this she sat up. She had been lying on a stretcher bed reading a magazine. She was clad in a sort of brunch coat and, as far as I knew, very little else.

As she got up she said "Sit down. Take the weight off your feet." She waved towards the stretcher she had just vacated. "Sorry there aren't any chairs."

The billy boiled over with a hiss and she threw in a handful of tea from a biscuit tin.

I now noticed that the stretcher she had invited me to sit on was one of two set closely side by side. A blanket covered both and peeping out from under it was a spotless white sheet and, at the head, two pillows both sparkling clean.

She turned off the burner and dragged another crate over to the stretchers. The top of this was covered with plastic of floral design and fixed with drawing pins.

Over this she spread a tablecloth of what looked to me like finest Irish linen. To add to my surprise she now produced two cups and saucers of English china so thin and delicate that, on this linen background, they could have been in some aristocratic country house.

At the best, I had been expecting enamelled mugs yet now, to complete the decor, plates, milk jug and sugar bowl from the same set were placed carefully in position.

To add to the incongruity of the whole proceedings, she placed the blackened billy next to the exquisite milk jug.

"Black, white, with or without?" she asked from the other end of the stretcher.

I was so confused that I could only stammer "Er, er, white without. Thanks!"

It seemed like sacrilege to pour tea from that old billy into those lovely cups, but she did it with a grace which would have done credit to a dowager 'at home'.

"This is beautiful china," I remarked hoping for a story.

"'Tis nice, isn't it," was all I got.

"How did you manage to get it here all in one piece?" I asked.

"Eighteen pieces to be exact," she answered with a laugh, "all wrapped in newspaper. Didn't chip a single piece. Here, have a cake! I baked them this morning—in that old camp oven. Tell me, what have you been doing with yourself? Where's Jasper?"

She seemed anxious to change the subject, so I thought it impolitic to pursue it at this time.

"To answer your questions one at a time," I replied, "we've been getting to know our way about and Jasper's outside in the Kombi."

"Bring him in," she commanded, "I want to have a proper look at him."

I went outside and opened the door. He needed no second invitation but leapt out and straight into the tent where, after a dignified but friendly greeting, stretched himself out on the ground, head on paws watching every movement I made and obviously hoping for some refreshment.

"Can I give him a plain biscuit?" she asked.

"Yes, if you like," I consented. I was pleased that she not only had the sense not to give him a cake but also that she asked my permission. I was beginning to like her.

She gave him the biscuit and fussed over him. He yawned with embarrassment. She lit a cigarette. I lit my pipe. Somehow, I felt more comfortable with a pipe going. She chatted on about Andamooka and the local characters until I was beginning to wonder what had happened to Jeff and what he might think if he suddenly walked in to find his wife sitting on a stretcher with a strange man.

This thought gave me a bit of a shock, so I got to my feet saying, "Isn't it about time your husband got back?"

"Yes. He is late today. Perhaps he's made a find," she replied, quite unconcerned.

"Well, I'm afraid I must go. I've got lots of things to do before dark. Thanks for the cuppa. It was most welcome."

"Pity you can't stop, but if you must go, you must. I'd like you to meet Jeff. "She sounded genuinely disappointed. I couldn't help wondering why exactly.

"Do come again, any time." She gave Jasper a big hug and we took our leave.

As I drove off I saw her in the rear vision mirror. She was holding up the tent flap. She watched us until we were out of sight up the hill.

I felt that there was an interesting story here and, if I were patient, I might hear it.

On the way back I met Mike and George. They told me they had decided to abandon the Gunn's Gully claim for a time, as the amount of precious opal we had found wouldn't pay the cost of the bulldozer. They had found another site which looked promising.

Eighteen thousand dollars worth of good opal had been taken out from nearby since April and the wires had indicated a good prospect. They suggested that I might like to join them in the morning and see if my crude attempts at divining agreed with theirs. They also told me that, if they decided to try their luck there, the level was a good fifty feet down, so it would mean digging a shaft.

I thought this might be interesting and more in keeping with my ideas of an opal mine. Up to now, I had only seen open cuts.

This new locality was known as Blackboy Hill. They said they would see me there and gave me directions.

Whilst in the Co-op this morning I had planned my evening meal. It was to be eggs and tomatoes fried in butter. To follow I would have a slice of spongecake and tinned apricots.

I had bought half-a-dozen eggs packed in a sort of papier mache container. I opened this packet and found that the first egg had got stuck. In trying to lever it out I put my thumb through it. The contents wasted no time in circulating around the adjacent eggs.

I carefully removed the other eggs and placed them on the table. I now got a teacup and poured the offending egg into it. So far, so good!

The container had to be washed. Keeping a wary eye on the table, I moved gingerly towards the door so as to get outside to a bucket of water. As I stepped outside, the sudden re-distribution of weight caused the Kombi to rock slightly. I turned quickly to see the five eggs all rolling towards the edge of the table. I managed to grasp two. One I caught using the container as a sort of net. Another I stopped with my knee but the fifth shattered to destruction on my kangaroo skin rug.

I put the survivors on the bunk and slung the rug outside. As I washed it and the egg container in the same water I noticed smoke curling slowly from the doorway.

The tomatoes had been frying nicely before I attempted to extract the eggs from the container, but I jumped inside to find a smoky black mess in the pan. The kettle on the other burner started whistling like an express train and spitting boiling water all over the cooker. This was not my lucky day! By the time I had cleaned everything up it was dark.

The battalions of moths were at action stations ready to move in to the attack, so the door had to be shut.

Cooking a meal on two burners in a partly closed vehicle on a tropically hot night is no joke. I was glad of that hopper window in the back to circulate what slight breeze there was. I realised now that I should have a fan and made a firm resolution to write to a friend in Brisbane to send me one by air freight.

In spite of the discomfort, I enjoyed my meal but resented having wasted an egg and a couple of tomatoes.

I switched on my little transistor radio. Crashes and crackles were all I could get. I went outside to find the sky was ebony black crazed by almost continuous patterns of forked lightning. No wonder the radio was so noisy.

As I stood there, a few spots of rain pleasantly shocked my sweating face. They increased their tempo and, before I could duck back inside, a deluge had started.

I hastily removed my shorts and groped on the lid of the garbage can for a cake of soap. In the darkness I knocked the can over and lost my morning's water but, who cares?

This was too good an opportunity to miss. I had craved a cold shower all day and now it was on. And was it cold!

Maybe it was the contrast but I shivered as I soaped myself all over. Then, as suddenly as it had started, it ceased, seemingly at the command of a clap of thunder. What a let-down!

There I stood covered in nothing but soap.

The empty garbage can and the bucket had collected a little water and I was able to rinse some of the soap off.

I had learned another lesson—never count your pints of water till you've filled the bucket—at least, not in a South Australian storm.

Jasper woke me at six a.m. wanting 'out'. When I got up at seven he was nowhere to be seen. My whistle would usually bring him back from quite a distance, but this morning there was no response.

At eight a.m. I began to wonder. At nine a.m. I was worried. At ten I was annoyed. I had promised Mike and George that I would see them at Blackboy Hill this morning and I dare not leave this site without Jasper. The heat was getting intense. There was not the slightest sign of last night's rain. I lay on my bunk and smoked.

At eleven o'clock precisely Jasper returned, leapt into the van and licked my face as much as to say, "Here I am. Sorry I'm late. Thanks for waiting." All my anger disappeared. I gave him a pat and his breakfast. I was only sorry I hadn't seen which direction he had come from.

I set out for Blackboy Hill and, by luck rather than good judgment, spotted the green Falcon and followed the easiest track to it.

It seemed quite high on the hill, although I doubt if the elevation was more than two hundred feet. On top of this escarpment it was flat and sloped gently down to the east.

The view was interesting. The fairly new diggings of the Yahloo could be seen to the right whilst in the far distance, shimmering in the heat, was a silver streak across the horizon. It was my first sight of Lake Torrens. I imagined a sheet of cool, clear water. Surely we could swim there!

Mike quickly disillusioned me. "Just a dried up salt pan," he explained. "Hasn't been really wet for years."

I must have shown my disappointment for he followed up his remark with "If you really want a swim, we were thinking of going out to a dam after lunch. I haven't been there but it's somewhere to the north past the airfield. We'll soon find it!"

They had been busy and had marked out a claim on the virgin ground. This consisted of four posts each three inches thick driven into the ground about one hundred and fifty feet apart to form a square. Mike's Miners' Right number and the date were roughly marked on each peg.

George explained that, as their time in Andamooka was limited, they had arranged to have the shaft dug mechanically. This would save time and labour but they couldn't get the use of this machine till tomorrow. Hence the idea of going for a swim.

Our directions had sounded simple enough but, once past the airfield, we got hopelessly lost because tracks went everywhere, often in circles and wide arcs.

The reason became clear when three kangaroos crossed the trail in front of us. They were followed by an old utility containing a driver and two other fellows with rifles. They were professional kangaroo shooters. They stopped when they saw our convoy.

It so happened that they, too, were ready for a swim and suggested we follow them. They set off at a smart pace. The Falcon quickly followed leaving me in the Kombi to bring up the rear.

This was one of the most hectic drives I have ever made. Driving into one car's dust is bad enough, but following two vehicles closely becomes a nightmare. At times I had to stop dead because visibility became absolutely nil.

Finally I gave up, hung back and then followed the trail of settling dust. I arrived at the dam only to find that I still had a very tricky sandhill to negotiate to avoid having to walk several hundred yards to the water. However, here was a chance to test my skill. I got into first gear, put my foot down and sailed over the top in grand style.

How we all enjoyed that swim! Although a trifle weedy, the water was cool and clear, except at the sides where the many bathers had stirred up the thick mud from the bottom. Jasper went straight in and swam round and round. His speed and endurance were fantastic. He retrieved sticks, wallowed in the mud and generally had a wonderful time.

Coming back was far easier. A well-defined track led straight back to the main road from the airfield.

That night, after our meal, Jasper took off! He had cleaned his plate up as he usually did, had a drink of water and then loped off in a straight line to the north-east—down the slope towards the track.

I whistled as loudly and as imperatively as I could, but he ignored me and went straight on across the track, through a clump of bushes and over a sandhill. Within seconds he was just a speck almost out of sight. I got out my binoculars and managed to pick him up.

He was still going but faster now—straight on and over the distant rise. With that I lost sight of him. I assumed that he had found himself a girl friend. I hoped that it wasn't a dingo or he might find himself in trouble.

When I retired to my bunk, he still hadn't returned. A sudden rocking of the van woke me up. He had returned and as usual, had taken a flying leap on to his seat in the front. The impact of thirty-five pounds of bone and muscle was enough to upset the equilibrium.

I sleepily got off my bunk and went outside. The first faint luminescence of a new day was showing in the east. I looked through the open doorway of the driving compartment. Jasper was curled up fast asleep on his seat.

"So you're back, you dirty old stopout," I exclaimed.

Not the slightest twitch of his tail nor the flutter of an eyelid did he offer in response. He was out cold from sheer exhaustion.

Later that day, I had my first contact with a 'willy-willy'. I had seen many of them at a distance since we left Port Augusta. They come in all sizes, from the little disturbance which just causes a small whirling pinnacle of sand to rise two or three feet from the road in front, to the great smoky-looking column several hundred feet high. They travel at various speeds on an indefinite course which can be likened to a drunken man trying to find his way home. It is the same sort of turbulence which causes a waterspout at sea.

The smaller ones I had actually passed through had caused me no serious inconvenience because I had seen them coming and braced myself accordingly. This was a big one and I didn't see it coming!

I was on the top of Blackboy Hill waiting for Mike and George to show up and, to avoid the heat, was lying on my bunk reading a technical book on opal.

The impact came from the back. It was as if a giant hand had tried to push us forward and the rear end lifted as the brakes held. The open door slammed so hard that it was a wonder the glass wasn't shattered. Then the back came down to earth again with a crash on to the shock absorbers.

For a moment, I thought we had been hit by another vehicle till I looked out to see this huge whirling column making its way towards the Yahloo.

It gradually thinned out and disappeared and all was peace again. Everything inside the Kombi was covered with fine, red dust. The violent closing of the door had burst open my medicine chest which was screwed to the inside and the contents were strewn all over the floor. A plastic 'vacuum seal' type of box containing flour had fallen from the rack and, while the lid had held, some contents had spilled on the floor. It took me half an hour to get ship-shape again.

45

The green Falcon arrived, followed by a big truck containing the drilling gear. Mike showed the operator where they wanted the shaft dug and the truck backed up. With a roar of a separate diesel engine, the rig commenced to rise from its prone position over the cab to a vertical angle over the back.

The long shaft terminated at the lower end in a huge auger bit. It was manipulated until a true vertical position was sighted from several different positions. Built-in hydraulic jacks were lowered to give the rear of the truck stability and it was all ready to go.

The big bit was lowered almost to the ground, then an iron collar was laid down around where the bit would cut in. The operator took his seat facing the rig where he could control the rotation speed and thrust of the auger.

A nod from Mike and the bit commenced to revolve, at the same time being driven downwards. The engine slowed as it took the load and churned its way into the sand and rock.

At about a foot deep it was stopped and the bit hydraulically raised until it was clear of the hole. The flats on the bit were loaded with the sand and rock it had excavated. Now, a sudden fast rotation created centrifugal force which scattered this debris around the hole. I now saw the reason for the iron collar. It was to prevent the debris from falling back into the hole.

This operation was repeated again and again as the hole gradually got deeper. Whilst the bit was actually drilling, Mike and George go busy with shovels keeping the immediate surroundings of the hole clear of the edge of the collar.

The drilling went on till about midday when the hole, which was now about fifteen feet deep, met a stratum of gypsum. The bit ground away but could make little or no impression.

Mike said "It's no good. We'll have to blast!"

While the truck was driving clear, Mike collected the gelignite, detonators and coil of fuse from the Falcon. In the meantime, George had driven an iron spike into the ground to secure a stout rope down which he climbed into the hole. After a brief inspection he came up and said "I think we'll need four!"

It took a long time for him to drill the holes to take the charges. On returning to the surface he remarked that it was very warm down there.

While George had a cool drink from the water bag, Mike went down to place the charges. Poor Mike! I think he suffered more than George because he had that type of skin which is particularly sensitive to the sun, with a consequence that he has always to wear full-length overalls, a broad-brimmed hat and shoes.

He came up soaked in perspiration to announce that all was ready. George insisted on going down to light the fuses. He reckoned he could shin up the rope quicker than Mike. They were ninety-second fuses!

Down he went, armed with a box of matches and a short length of fuse. It was more reliable to light the 'hot' fuses from a piece of burning fuse than to be dependent on the whims of matches—and he had four to light!

It seemed an age before we saw him start climbing steadily and unhurriedly up the rope.

"Better get back," Mike warned me. "It shouldn't spread much from that depth but you can't be too careful."

I didn't need telling twice after my last experience and retired about twenty yards. Mike joined me and was followed by George.

Thump!

"One," counted Mike.

Thump! Thump!

"Two, three," went on Mike. We waited for the last one. Seconds went by. Still we waited.

"Damn!" exclaimed George. "One's a fizzer!"

This was a real complication. He didn't relish grubbing about down a fifteen foot hole in the earth with a pick and shovel trying to find an unexploded stick of gelignite.

There was only one thing to do in my opinion, which wasn't worth much, and that was to abandon the hole.

But George and Mike were made of sterner stuff.

"We'll wait till after lunch," decided Mike. "I'll go down when the fumes have cleared away and see if I can find the detonator," he volunteered.

"No, I'll go," George dissented. "I set the charges. It's up to me. Besides, I know where I put 'em."

"That's a bloody silly argument," said Mike.

"Let's get some lunch," I suggested, "and argue about it later."

We had a leisurely lunch and I had a siesta. When I woke up they had settled their argument by the spin of a coin and George had already been down to test the air and have a reconnaissance. They were anxious to get going again as the shaft-boring equipment and operator were being paid for by the hour.

During my siesta they had been very busy and had erected a simple ventilation system in the form of a wind-sock.

This comprised a long length of fabric sewn at the edges to form a tube, the top of which opened out flat and was fixed to a pole supported on two oil drums. This was placed in such a position that the open top formed a funnel which, facing the wind, channelled it down the tube to the bottom of the shaft. This had proved most effective and George pronounced the shaft clear of fumes.

We attached a bucket to the end of a thinner rope, placed a light pick and shovel in it, and lowered it carefully to the bottom.

George went down again and immediately started sorting through the now loose debris. As I watched with a queer sort of feeling in my stomach,

47

I thought of the bomb disposal men during the war. Nothing would have induced me to go down that shaft!

We couldn't see what he was doing but after some ten minutes of suspence, three sharp jerks on the rope was the signal to haul up the bucket.

Mike slowly took the rope up very carefully hand over hand keeping the bucket clear of the sides of the shaft.

At first I thought it was empty but, as it came into the full sunlight, I saw the glint of the short piece of aluminium tube which was the detonator. Sticking out from the end was the fuse showing that it had gone out about three inches from the deadly fulminate of mercury which so readily explodes to fire the main charge.

Mike put the bucket down by the side of the hole and gingerly picked out the detonator laying it tenderly on the ground some distance away. He came back and called down to George, "Okay, George! Any sign of the jelly?"

George looked up. We could see his sweaty, grinning face in the light reflected off the kopi sides of the shaft.

"Nope," he answered. He seemed quite unconcerned about it and Mike explained that it was now probably all mixed up with the mullock and, even if not quite harmless, wasn't worth bothering about.

Ah well, I thought, I suppose they know what they're doing. Mike sent the rope down for the tools, the wind-sock was pulled clear and within fifteen minutes the rig was in operation again.

It went down to its maximum depth of twenty-five feet and it was hand work from then on.

We had all had enough by now, so the shaft digger was paid and dismissed and we called it a day—rather a disappointing day because we hadn't yet reached the 'level'.

We were about to leave when Mike remembered the detonator. Another short length of fuse tied to the piece that had fizzled out, a match and a sharp 'crack' and it disappeared. In the open it had gone off with no more fuss than a Guy Fawkes cracker but, at close quarters in a confined space, it could have been deadly.

'City Centre', Andamooka Opal Fields, showing community well.
Opal country. Typical opal-bearing hills on the road north of Coober Pedy, near Wellbourne Hill.

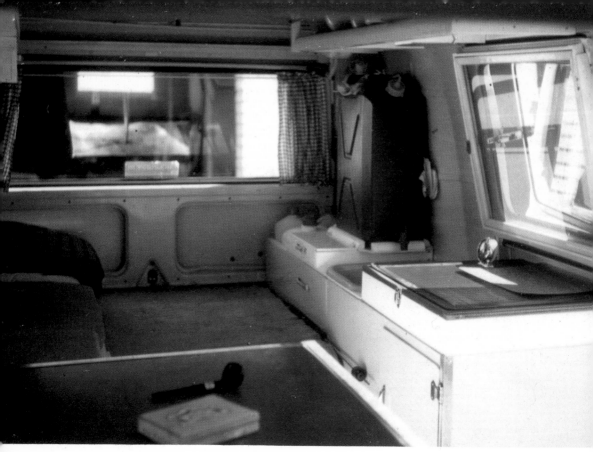

Inside the Kombi—before the trip started.
Inside the Kombi—after à few weeks.

4

The worst dust-storm in thirty years

When we got back to our campsite, the sky to the north-east was ominously blackening. It was not cloud, as one would expect from an impending electrical storm, but rather a yellowish haze gradually darkening to a deep grey on the horizon.

I had not yet experienced a dust-storm of any consequence but this had all the makings of a real sizzler. Jasper was getting restless and seemed impatient to get his dinner.

I read the signs and knew that he was intent on having another night out. But, much to his disgust and disappointment, I tied him up to a long length of clothes line and told him in no uncertain terms that he was not keeping his appointment.

He settled down just out of my range of vision and pretended to sleep. I finished my dinner and noticed that the line which previously had snaked past the door was now stretched taut.

Looking along the line I saw him at the end sitting upright, ears alert and gazing in the direction in which he had made off last night.

I called him. He condescended to look round then ignored me, so I hauled him in. As I was doing this the wind started to blow.

I got him inside, hastily battened down and closed all the windows. This was no cooling breeze but a hot searing blast. Although it was well over an hour till sunset it might have been midnight. The heat inside was unbearable.

I had expected to be enveloped in driving, choking dust but, apart from that which the wind was whipping off the ground, the main body of dust seemed to be in a belt above.

I opened the side windows and, although it only reduced the temperature by a few degrees, it kept the air moving and relieved me of that feeling of suffocation which was almost frightening.

The wind increased in force and the Kombi rocked rather like a small boat in the wake of a destroyer.

I got used to it after a couple of hours and turned in. Jasper had resigned himself to missing his night out and was sleeping. I would have loved to have known what he was dreaming about, because his back paws twitched as he emitted silly little falsetto yelps—such a contrast to his normal deep-throated bark.

In spite of the noise, the motion and the temperature, I slept quite well. When I woke up the wind had eased a little. I looked at my watch. It had stopped again. My built-in alarm clock said ten past seven. Outside was the gloom of a London fog.

Later in the morning I ventured into 'town'. The wind was still blowing hard, there was a lot of dust in the air but visibility, being about one hundred yards, made the general light very bad.

I called at George and Mike's garage and was surprised to find them both lying on their stretcher beds reading by the light of a pressure lamp.

It was no day for work on Blackboy Hill. I left them to it and called at the Post Office for my mail.

Gordon was a mine of information on the field and the people working on it. With so many Europeans and the preponderance of mechanisation I asked him about any miners of the old school, and if any of the originals were still alive.

"There's one character you should go and see," he told me. "He's been here since the field was discovered."

I asked him who he was, where he was and what he did now, but Gordon answered "Best thing to do is to ask him yourself. There he is, just going in to his camp."

I looked in the direction he indicated and saw the back of a man just disappearing through the open doorway of a semi-dugout dwelling almost opposite the P.O. He was rather stooped but had moved briskly during the brief glimpse I had of him.

"What's his name?" I asked.

"Albertoni," Gordon replied. "Francis Albertoni or Franko."

"Think he'll talk to me?"

"He'll talk to you all right. It's stopping him that's the trouble. He's a grand old man of eighty-five and likes to be known as the 'Mad Black-smith'. That was his original trade before he came here in the first opal rush. But don't get the wrong idea. He's one of the sanest men around here."

I walked over to the semi-dugout. It is called a semi-dugout because it is not actually a tunnel in the hillside but rather a cutting with a roof on it. The walls are natural rock, partly sandstone and partly kopi.

Timber is in short supply in Andamooka. There are few trees of any size within miles and the original builders of these dwellings had to make do with any materials they could pay hands on.

The result is a complete hotch-potch, without any of the beauty of a patchwork quilt. It seems that nothing was wasted in those early days. Old packing cases and sheets of corrugated iron were precious to the old prospector who wanted to build himself a shelter from the relentless sun and occasional rainstorms.

The roofs were sometimes a crude form of thatch made from the coarse grasses which grow in this barren terrain. Canvas hoods from long-since abandoned trucks, the remains of old tents and sacking are all used to augment the protective quality of the twigs and branches which are the backbone of the roofs.

The floors are earth, uneven and as hard as concrete. A fire-place is hewn out of the rock walls with a hole above for the smoke to escape and create a draught. Cupboards are recesses cut into the walls.

Such was old Franko's home or 'camp' as he preferred to call it and it was typical of the many other similar ones scattered around the City Centre of Andamooka.

I stood at the open doorway and peered into the gloom within to see the old man with scraps of paper starting up a fire in the alcove on the left-hand side.

I rapped on the rough wooden door jamb. He took no notice.

I called out "Anybody home?"—as if I didn't know!

With this, he turned round. "Mr. Albertoni?" I enquired formally and politely.

"That's me," he answered. "Come in!"

Once inside and out of the glare of the sun which had re-appeared during the last few minutes I could make out more details.

I introduced myself and he offered me a firm, steady hand. I saw his face for the first time and was impressed by his warm, friendly grin.

"Sit down. Sit down," he invited, removing an old shopping basket which he had just brought in from an upturned box covered with what could have been a piece of blanket, "while I put the billy on".

I removed my giggle hat and put it on the floor beside me as I sat down on the box.

The fire was now well alight. Most of the smoke went up and out but much of it hung about and I started to cough.

"Mustn't mind the smoke," he apologised. "It keeps the flies out."

While he was filling the billy with water from a can and arranging it over the fire, I told him what I was doing in Andamooka. I felt that, with this old man, my best chance of getting his co-operation was to put all my cards on the table. As I talked, I looked at him. Could this man really be eighty-five?

He had taken his hat off to reveal a full head of dark hair which, with his beard, was only flecked with grey. The skin on his face was smooth and far less wrinkled than mine. His eyes were bright and twinkling, his voice young and clear.

The billy set, he eased himself down on to the floor with his legs stretched out. He leant against another upturned box which served as his table. He found this position most comfortable and practical for, with his back to the door, he could read a little by the light from the open doorway.

He admitted to being a bit short-sighted and having a slight hearing loss. But, apart from these he said, he was very fit and active. He didn't drink or smoke. Drinking was a mug's game and smoking was a dirty habit, but he had no objection to me smoking my pipe if I got anything out of it.

The billy hissed as it boiled over. He put some tea in it and replaced it on the fire to boil a few seconds more.

"Like a mugga tea?" he offered.

"Thanks, I'd love one," I replied.

"Got another cup here somewhere," he remarked groping about in a mass of cardboard boxes, tins and all sorts of stuff which I couldn't recognise in a dark corner.

"I've got one outside, I'll get it," I said as I hastily got up and went outside to the Kombi for a beaker. In the circumstances, I preferred my beaker and quite enjoyed the strong black brew as he told me how he lived on his pension, worked in his garden and sharpened picks for those miners who brought him wood for his fire or did other small services for him. He also told me that he played the accordion and the tin whistle.

Here, indeed, was an interesting and very likeable character but, as time was getting on, I excused myself saying that I'd like to have a further yarn with him some evening. He said I'd be very welcome any time. I was quite sure he meant it.

Now that the dust storm had passed I returned to the garage only to find that Mike and George had gone—presumably to Blackboy so, after doing a bit of shopping at the Co-op I made my way there.

I found them hard at work. George was down below with a short-handled pick while Mike was operating the windlass. Where he got it from I didn't ask but it was very crude. It consisted of a square of timber which straddled the hole. Two end pieces supported the spindle which went through the centre of a wooden drum. One end of the spindle was bent to form a winding handle and a wire cable was wound on the drum. The bucket was made from a 25-gallon oil drum. This had been fitted with an iron handle which looped on to a stout iron hook on the end of the cable.

Imagine the man at the bottom of the shaft. He has to dig the dirt and fill the bucket—swing his pick and wield his shovel whilst avoiding the obstacles of the bucket itself, the rope he climbs up and his own legs and feet—all this in a hole three feet six inches in diameter. It is not my idea of fun!

Even the man on the windlass has no easy task. A twenty-five gallon drum full of rock weighs every bit of one hundred and fifty pounds. When he has wound it to the top, he has to hold the winding handle with one hand whilst he heaves the full bucket away from the hole and on to the ground with the other. He now has to lift or drag the full bucket well clear and empty it.

To let go the handle of the windlass accidentally could mean death or serious injury to the man below. If the bucket is not dragged completely clear, it could tip over and precipitate the contents down the shaft with equally disastrous results.

Mike suggested I might like to go down. Without thinking, I said I'd like to and as soon as George came up for a rest I prepared to go down the rope hand over hand.

Mike didn't like the idea of this because he knew that I had a mild attack of fibrositis in my right shoulder. "I'll lower you down in the bucket," he suggested. "It's quite simple. Just stand in the bucket and hold the cable."

This seemed quite okay to me so, making sure that he had a firm hold on the handle. I stepped off the edge into the bucket. One leg in, the bucket immediately listed violently and crashed on the side of the shaft.

"Go on, put the other foot in and straighten up," commanded Mike.

I put my whole weight on the bottom of the bucket and clung desperately to the cable. I was now hanging at a ridiculous angle and tried hard to straighten the bucket with my feet. Another crash on the side of the shaft and another shower of rocks went down the hole. I was glad I wasn't below.

After thrashing around like this for several seconds, I managed to establish some sort of equilibrium.

"Okay," I said. "Lower away!"

The windlass creaked and the bearings squeaked and down I went. Although it was less than thirty feet it felt like half-a-mile before the bucket bumped on the bottom and the cable went slack. I put one foot out and cracked my shin on the shovel. I lifted my other leg out, stepped on the pick head and its handle came up and hit me on the side of my knee-cap.

I didn't seem to be doing too well but I was determined not to be beaten. Keeping my aching knee-cap and my smarting shin well out of the way, I swung the pick. It hit the bucket!

This was an impossible situation, so I yelled up to Mike to raise the bucket a few feet. This was better and I succeeded in loosening some rock.

When I thought I'd got a load I called for the bucket to be lowered. Down it came, but I wasn't quite quick enough in pushing it to the side. It clipped my ear and shoulder.

My admiration for my two friends was growing every minute. I appreciated their patience as I slowly scooped the mullock up with the shovel and only managed to transfer about a cupful at a time because, in the confined space, the shovel caught the edge of the bucket, tipped it and shot the contents back where it had come from.

By the time that one bucket was full and I triumphantly yelled "Haul away!" I was dripping with perspiration, smarting in some places and aching in the remainder.

But I hadn't finished yet. When the bucket came down again. I yelled that I was coming up and stepped confidently in. I gave Mike the signal to start winding and waited.

I overlooked the fact that the bucket was not central and, as soon as it was free of the ground, it swung like a pendulum and my bare back hit the side of the shaft. Being on the move, I left a lot of skin behind before Mike realised what was happening and stopped winding.

When I eventually stepped out on the surface I felt that I had been well and truly 'blooded'. I believe that I should have done better going down the rope and resolved that it was the first and last time I'd do it this way.

I spent the rest of the afternoon nursing my wounds and watching the others work.

After an early dinner that evening I forgot to tie Jasper up. By six o'clock he was away. There was nothing I could do about it. It wouldn't have been any good telling him to be in by ten although he seemed to be able to tell the time with remarkable accuracy with his biological clock—meals, walks and things of that nature. I took my aches and bruises to bed and was very soon asleep.

I was awakened at six by the rocking of the van. He was back! I turned over and went to sleep again. He would have to wait for his breakfast.

At seven-thirty I was again awakened by the rocking of the van. This time it wasn't Jasper—he was out for the count—it was the wind. A complete reversal of wind direction was bringing the sand back, thicker and even more violent. I heard a clatter and the hollow thump of plastic hitting the ground.

I had left all my odd things outside as usual. These included my cooler containing butter, milk and half-a-pound of sausages left over from last night.

I looked out to see my red plastic bucket skipping over the gibbers at a good fifteen miles an hour. Visibility was down to about a hundred yards and the bucket disappeared.

The cooler had also vanished but I found the butter box upside down in the sand several yards away. Of the milk and the box containing the sausages there was not a trace. I retrieved the butter box. The lid had stayed on and the oily contents were intact.

As I was getting back into the Kombi, a kangaroo came hopping round as if looking for shelter. He was a sitting shot for my rifle but, not being that sort of a person, I just said "Sorry, mate, there's no room for you!" and slammed the door.

The wind got stronger and hotter. The van rocked so much that I was glad that it was parked nose-to-wind, otherwise it might even have blown over.

I lay on a towel on my bunk exuding gallons of perspiration. My thirst was raging but the black tea was a great comfort. It was impossible to do anything useful, even if I'd had the energy.

I closed my eyes and imagined I was in a train travelling at sixty miles an hour. It was easy to do this because everything was there—the roar of the wind, the swaying and even the rhythmic puffing of the engine because Jasper was panting noisily and his whole body was pulsating. Only the clackerty clack, clackerty clack of the wheels was missing.

It was nearly eleven before the force of the wind eased. At noon, I made a reconnaissance. The wind was still strong, but visibility had increased to several hundred yards. I needed bread, milk and something to replace the lost sausages which I had planned to warm up for dinner.

It was a good opportunity to call on old Franko again. He was pleased to see me and told me that this dust storm was the worst in his thirty years experience here.

I suggested that he might entertain me with his accordion and whistle, but he said he only played at night because the music attracted the Aboriginals who then came too close to his camp for his liking. According to him, the majority of them were dirty, lazy and likely to steal anything removable. They kept well away at night.

I said I would return that evening, weather permitting, then called at the Post Office. Gordon had radioed the pilot of the mail plane and warned him of the storm, so we had to wait for our letters.

Although it was still overcast and very dull, visibility had now increased to a quarter-of-a-mile or so. I drove back to the campsite. I remembered that my cooler and bucket had taken off earlier and I should do something about finding them. I set off in the direction I had seen the bucket skipping merrily along. Some distance off I found the bucket, hooked by its handle to a bush. There was no sign of the cooler, and I wrote it off.

By late afternoon the weather was almost clear again and, after dinner, we set off again for Franko's.

Again, I left my odd stuff on the ground but, this time, I took the precaution of putting in markers in the form of sticks tipped with strips of white reflective paper which would be picked up by my headlights when I was returning.

The old man, as usual, proved an entertaining host, keeping me enthralled with tales of his early life. His father was Swiss, his mother Irish and his grandfather Italian.

He had worked on the Transcontinental Railway from Port Augusta to Perth. The stories he told me of these times were colourful and amusing. In a dissertation on the making of 'damper' his enthusiasm for the 'camp oven' ran away with him. He rushed to a corner and produced an elongated, cast iron pot and proceeded to dance a little jig, at the same time beating the bottom rhythmically with his closed fist.

"This is what you want to make a good damper, my boy!" he cried. "I've had this old oven longer than I can remember and it's still as good as new."

To convince me of its soundness, he continued to beat out the rhythm and dance around. I was convinced that this performance of a one-man percussion band must attract all the Aborigines in Andamooka to gather for a corroboree.

While he was finding his accordion I put a new reel of tape on my little portable recorder. I had set it going when he had started telling me about damper. I hadn't drawn his attention to it for fear of either making him nervous or encouraging him to 'put on an act'. I told him about it now.

The old man was enthusiastic and wanted a playback which I promised him after he had played his accordion and what I had believed to be a tin whistle but which was, in fact, made of wood.

Some of the old melodies he played I knew, others I hadn't heard before. Many of these he had picked up on his travels or had composed himself.

After the playback he told me more yarns of his early days on the opal field and also many lurid stories of some of the characters in Andamooka—past and present.

It was after eleven when we got back to the campsite after a most enlightening and entertaining evening.

Next morning we went up to Blackboy to see how Mike and George were getting on. They had struck the level at approximately forty-five feet but had found no trace of opal—not even a little potch.

They were both rather depressed. It was getting near Christmas. Mike had promised to be home in Brisbane and George had planned to spend the holiday period in Adelaide.

A few more days and they would both have to be off. Already a number of the miners had departed, and many of the workings were deserted.

All this made me consider my own position. I wasn't concerned just *where* I should spend Christmas, but the wet season could start anytime in January. The track north to Coober Pedy and Alice Springs might be cut for weeks by flood waters and I had no wish to get myself stranded before reaching 'The Alice'. I would need a couple of weeks in Coober Pedy to film shots I required so I, too, had to be thinking about moving on. I had already been in Andamooka just on a month and was thoroughly enjoying myself.

I decided that when Mike and George pulled out I would do so too, but in the opposite direction.

On the way back from Blackboy it was reasonably early and I thought it a good opportunity to call on Elsie and meet her husband.

I drove off the track and made for her camp. I thought for a moment that I had turned off at the wrong place. The familiar brown tent should have been straight ahead but there was no sign of a tent of any sort.

There was the dilapidated iron shed and there was the caravan without wheels but the space in between where the tent should have been was bare except for some empty wooden crates—one with the top covered with floral plastic fixed with drawing pins. It gave me quite a shock.

Then I remembered that she had told me if they found nothing worth while in the next three weeks, they would have to pull out. The three weeks had gone and so had she.

56

I thought of all the hard work they must have done and all the money they had spent—all to no avail. But was it?

The money had bought experience and physical fitness unobtainable in the 'Big Smoke'. I shall always remember her smile and her philosophical outlook when she had told me of their battling.

But, that is opal mining! The 'finds' are not always restricted to the lovely gem. Some strike it rich and drink themselves to death. Some strike it rich and lose it all trying to strike it richer. Some strike it rich and, if they are wise and have sufficient experience, leave the mining to others and become buyers. Very few men have made lasting fortunes working with pick and shovel.

They say 'opal fever' is worse than 'gold fever' if you get a bad attack. I can believe this because I have experienced that feeling of compulsion once you have found *something*, however small.

I felt a little depressed as I drove thoughtfully back to our campsite. My chances of getting Elsie Donovan's story—if there was one really worth getting—had vanished.

Today's mail had brought me back my first batch of processed film and I was most anxious to examine it to get some idea of the performance of my camera under these tropical conditions. I could not project it and had to be content with seeing it frame by frame.

The exposures seemed correct and the colour values excellent, but it would be many months before I could get any idea of the action.

I was awakened next morning by an early visit from Mike and George. They had had a telephone call from their Adelaide business associates and were leaving immediately. They were already packed and ready to go.

When they had gone, I felt very lonely. My time with them had been very pleasant and, if not productive of opal, had taught me a lot about the practical side of opal mining.

It was Friday. I was still short of one hundred feet of processed film and was expecting it to arrive tomorrow. I was most anxious not to leave without it, therefore I decided to move off on Sunday morning. That would give me the rest of today and all day tomorrow to get the remaining shots and say goodbye to the few friends still in Andamooka.

Firstly I had to get water. Again I was lucky. The well was deserted.

I had managed to stock up with about eight gallons of water when an old man approached. He told me he was a pensioner and was waiting for the mail to arrive with his cheque. In the meantime he said he was broke and hadn't even had a drink of tea for nearly two days. He showed me a condensed milk tin containing some opal chips and several pieces of processed opal matrix which, he said, no buyer would give him a dollar for.

I realised that it could be a 'take' but this old man had a certain dignity which appealed to me. He had neither asked me for money nor tried to sell me the opal.

I had a loose dollar note in the top pocket of my shirt. I put it into his hand saying "Get yourself some tucker, old timer," and turned to put the last water bottle back in the Kombi. I wasn't particularly interested in his opal, but he placed the tin on the driving seat. I shook my head saying "Keep it!"

"I'm not a beggar, mate," he insisted. "A deal's a deal and I'm grateful." With that, he shuffled off towards the Co-op. I put the tin in a box with my other few bits and pieces.

When I got to the Post Office the mail had arrived and had mostly been distributed. There was nothing for me and Gordon had time for a chat. I told him I was moving off on Sunday and how much I had enjoyed meeting old Franko. I also asked him about Elsie Donovan. Of course, he knew Elsie. Everybody did. She came in regularly for her mail.

Strange to say, he had never seen her husband nor did he know where his mine was. He knew they had pulled out but nobody seemed to know exactly when. Elsie had not left a forwarding address, which was all very mysterious but not particularly unusual with such an ever-changing population of different nationalities. I then remembered that I had seen nothing of either of the parties who had helped me when I had been bogged.

From the descriptions I gave him, Gordon couldn't help me here either. There were many such groups of European migrants.

I had 'bush biscuits' and honey for a light lunch and called on old Franko again. He had just had a load of wood dumped outside his camp. This consisted of branches of dead trees which some kind person with a utility had collected for him, no doubt in return for his skill in sharpening some picks.

He was struggling to get the straggly pieces through the narrow space in the wire fence which was his front gate. I took some movie shots of this operation then gave him a hand clearing the rest and stacking it in his 'garden'.

When it was all ship-shape, he showed me round proudly. It was a pathetic attempt to get something to grow in the dry, sandy dirt which made the soil. Here, struggling desert peas and tomatoes were tended lovingly and consumed the last drop of waste water after it had served every other purpose down the line.

He showed me his own private well which he had dug himself many, many years ago. It was about twenty feet deep and, looking down after he had removed the cover, I could see the sky reflected in water. There was about six inches in it, he said, but it was his last reserve and, until rain came again and filled it, he would not touch it unless he were desperate.

We now came to his open-air workshop which was screened from the wind by a rough wall of large pieces of rock in the form of a 'U'. Inside was his blacksmith's forge and anvil.

The forge was powered by an ingenious device he had constructed thirty years ago and was still operating faultlessly. This was an old bicycle turned upside down. The main gear wheel had been stripped of one crank leaving the other to form a handle whereby to turn the chain and back wheel. He had constructed a blower comprising a fan and a tube leading to the furnace.

The blower was driven by belt from the bicycle wheel and the high gear ratio supplied sufficient speed to the fan blades to give him all the forced draught necessary to heat the furnace to the required temperature.

Leaning against one wall were several picks awaiting to be collected by their owners. I could see that Franko was a real craftsman of the old school.

On taking my leave of the old man, I noticed that a weld on my roof rack had broken away. This was most disconcerting and I had to have it fixed before tackling the rough road north.

I knew there was a welder in town somewhere so I set off to find him. His name was Szuc and he lived in a neat little dwelling alongside his 'shop', where there was the usual collection of iron and steel, some all rusty and some new, mixed up with old car parts such as gear boxes and back axles.

He was busy under a truck when I arrived but promised to do the job for me the next morning. The afternoon now had nearly gone. I was hot and tired. I got back into the Kombi and whistled Jasper.

No response! I walked up and down whistling. I drove around between the shacks, but he had vanished. For twenty minutes I waited, walked, drove and whistled.

By this time I was getting very testy. I was not only hot and tired, but hungry and thirsty as well. There was only one thing to do—go back to the campsite, have my dinner and bed down for the night.

I arrived back and got the potatoes ready for the pot when I spotted him coming up the slope from the same direction in which he had gone off previously. He arrived quite unconcerned, had a long drink of water and looked at me as much as to say "Here I am. Where's my dinner?"

I was too relieved to be cross with him so I obliged.

From then on, however, I had no fear of him getting lost and ceased to worry when he went off. Even so, it was often very inconvenient to have to wait on his pleasure to return before I could move away.

After dinner he made no attempt to leave me again, so we both settled down for our last night but one in Andamooka.

I had arranged with Mr. Szuc to do the welding early so we were up and about just after dawn but, in spite of this, he was already out when we arrived. His wife said he would be half-an-hour. She was a friendly type and seemed quite ready for a chat. In fact, she seemed to welcome the opportunity of letting off steam.

They had been here in Andamooka for six years and had never had a holiday in that time. I suppose the thought of approaching Christmas made her all the more conscious of it.

They also had a mine in which her husband worked. All the morning and well into the afternoon he worked. Then back to the welding shop to be open for business by four p.m. This was their bread and butter. Any jam was put back into the mine, with the result that there was never any spare cash for luxuries like holidays.

They seemed to live reasonably well on the proceeds of the welding business, but the mine only yielded sufficient opal to maintain the fever.

Initially, they had agreed to live this sort of life for only two years. Now it had extended to six and, quite obviously, she was getting near the end of her endurance.

I wondered what the final outcome would be.

I cannot help feeling that the luckiest ones are those who find nothing but stay long enough to get the fever out of their systems. To find a little can be like a drug beckoning you on with a hollow promise. Find a little more, and it takes a strong character not to get completely 'hooked'.

The one redeeming feature is that it is a healthy life. For those with no particular ambition there are worse ways of living to a ripe old age, even if you only find enough opal to 'make tucker'.

The weld fixed, I called in at the Co-op service station to get oil and tyres checked and fill up with petrol ready for tomorrow's long drive to Kingoonia.

After that I visited the store where I stocked up with tinned milk, meat, fruit, green vegetables and five pounds of potatoes in a plastic bag.

The mail was now the only thing lacking. Gordon said it wouldn't be in till four o'clock, so I spent the afternoon making a round of my remaining friends and acquaintances.

I found five in all. In each case I asked about Elsie Donovan. Yes. They all knew her and were unanimous in their opinion that she was a 'good type' as opposed to a 'good sort', which, in Australian parlance, means a woman whose morals are distinctly doubtful. None had a bad word to say for Elsie yet, strangely enough, no one with whom I had discussed her had ever seen or met Jeff or even knew of the location of his mine.

At half-past four I collected my mail and was relieved to see the film amongst it. I filled in a re-direction form to Coober Pedy and bade farewell to Gordon whose efficiency and willing help did much to confound my low opinion of the Australian P.M.G.'s department.

I had hoped that my last evening in Andamooka would have been spent in the stimulating company of Mike and George, but as that was impossible I checked the film and turned in very early. Jasper made no attempt to go a-wooing so I assumed that he, too, had concluded his goodbyes.

At eight o'clock on Sunday morning I took my last look around the campsite to make sure that nothing had been left behind.

The last item to go aboard was my plastic garbage container. As I went to lift it in, I was accosted by an appalling stench as though twenty dead rats were rotting in the sun. I unclipped the lid and stood back wondering what I should see. 'Twas only my bath water!

Last night I had strip-washed in a bucket of fresh water. This I had also used to wash and wash up with this morning. I had forgotten all about the water in the garbage can. It had been used for two nocturnal baths and twice to wash clothes and had been standing, sealed up in the container, in the heat of the sun for two days. No wonder it stank!

It was nine o'clock before I pulled up to say goodbye to my old friend, Franko. I went in, sat on the usual box and put my hat on the floor beside me.

Over the inevitable 'cuppa' he gave me a message for an old mate of his in Coober Pedy—one Jack Brewster who had a mine and ran a motel.

"See Jack. Tell him you're a friend of the Mad Blacksmith and he'll see you right."

At a quarter-to-ten I had to drag myself away after promising to try to find a book written several years previously about Andamooka in which he figured prominently. He gave me the title, but was doubtful about the name of the woman who wrote it.

He said he wanted it for his kid brother who was in an old men's home!

As I waved goodbye I hoped I should see him again some day. I was both sorry and glad to be leaving—sorry to leave so many friends and so many stories of human interest untold—glad to be on the move again.

5

We nearly came to grief

Even at this time in the morning, the heat was blistering. Whilst I had the driving windows wide open, the living quarters were all closed up and sealed as far as was possible.

In spite of this, I still found that after a day's run there was a layer of dust over everything.

Having left Andamooka Opal Fields well behind, I remembered the stretch of sandhills which had caused me so much delay on the way there.

The speedometer mileage showed me that I must be getting close to it so I watched anxiously for the first signs. The sand was certainly getting thicker and a few minor dunes were in evidence on both sides.

On we went without trouble and still there was no indication of any impending sand barrier. We covered mile after mile of normally sandy track, then we were passing Andamooka Homestead which is twenty-six miles from the opal fields. I then realised that we had long since passed the crucial spot without encountering anything which could be classified as a hazard.

In a way, I was a little disappointed. This showed me very dramatically just how quickly road conditions can change. The wind had constructed that barrier and, presumably, the wind had removed it just as easily.

I was travelling in short-sleeved shirt, shorts and sandals. The shirt was sticking to my back, so I decided to remove it. I stopped, opened the door and got out. It was like stepping into an oven. The almost incessant wind of this desert country had taken time off.

The sun was so powerful that I hastily reached inside the Kombi for my hat. It wasn't there! I thought back. As usual, I had put it on the floor beside the box I sat on in old Franko's place. I could only think it was still there. It wasn't worth going back thirty miles for the sake of a dilapidated, stained, ex-army, jungle headpiece so I took my shirt off and got back to the shade of the Kombi. Even Jasper didn't need a second invitation to leave the lizards in peace and return to his seat.

I switched on the radio to get a time check. Radio Australia came in strongly on the short wave and the record being played was 'I left my heart in San Francisco'. I started to sing. Jasper looked at me in disgust so, by way of apology, I parodied the words to 'I left my hat in Andamooka'. This seemed to satisfy him as an explanation for my sudden outburst, so he sat back with a look of resignation on his face.

This was very much 'mirage' weather, and they were many and interesting. It is a common sight in Queensland to imagine a layer of water across the road ahead. So realistic is it that approaching vehicles are clearly reflected in it. A small car approaching may look like a double-decker bus at a distance of a quarter-of-a-mile.

Way out in this type of country it was on a much grander scale. I got quite used to seeing what looked like huge expanses of cool, glistening water on the horizon and thinking how lovely it would be to drive right up to it, strip off and plunge in. Unfortunately, of course, you never get there!

Approaching Woomera, I experienced the most interesting mirage I had seen. Going to Andamooka in the opposite direction, I had passed the prohibited area on the left and I had looked hard and carefully at the little I could see—just a few buildings and what looked like an aircraft hangar. But they were too far away to see any detail.

Coming to this area I noticed this hangar affair again. I thought I must have taken a different track because it was so much closer, so close in fact that I could see it in detail.

But I *couldn't* have taken another track. I hadn't passed a single fork. Then I saw that this building was apparently surrounded by water. As I drove on towards it, instead of getting closer, it started to recede and was soon back to the tiny size I had first seen it.

This telescopic effect was new to me and I wondered what the security people at Woomera would do to counteract it if they knew.

We now joined up with the northern 'highway', the only road between Port Augusta and Alice Springs, and also with the railway line linking Port Augusta with Perth. Nine miles further on we were at Pimba, the first of many tiny railway settlements comprising one or two houses and little else.

The road follows the railway all the way to Kingoonia. When I say 'follows', I don't mean that it goes parallel. Far from it! It makes its way along with it and crosses the tracks six times. At every crossing there is a warning stop sign announcing heavy penalties for any transgressor. I wondered how many travellers paid serious heed to these signs because it is quite an event to see anything or anybody on this lonely road and you would both see and hear a train in plenty of time to take evasive action.

I saw by my strip map that another thirty-nine miles would bring us to the shores of Lake Hart. The hot red sand and the blazing sun were making me almost delirious and I kept imagining hearing a voice asking "What can I get you? How about a lager?".

I had visions of a cooling dip in the lake. I could see it now glistening silver in the sunlight. This was no mirage. We were nearly there. The shore came to within a couple of hundred yards of the road and the railway, which, for once, was running parallel. There were some kind of buildings here so I stopped.

We both jumped out and made for the shoreline. The buildings were a disused and abandoned saltworks. The 'water' was solid salt and stretched as far as the eye could see. About a quarter of a mile out there appeared to be real water. Whether there was or not I never found out. I had learned to mistrust my eyes in this sort of country.

Hot and sweaty, I called the panting Jasper who was quite ready to return to the shade of the Kombi. I gave him some water and had a generous swig of tea. Then we pushed on again through mile after mile of gibber plains and sandy wastes.

The only relief from the monotonous colour of the red sand was an occasional clump of paddy melons. The green stems and bright yellow fruit looked so inviting that I was tempted to stop, pick one up, cut it in two and taste the juice. It was the bitterest taste I have ever experienced. It seemed to last for hours in spite of drinking tea and sucking barley sugar.

It was quite late in the afternoon when we reached Kingoonia. I saw the pub and made straight for it. The bar was closed but I found my way to a small room where four men were sitting round drinking bottled beer. They were a party travelling south and told me that the lady who was responsible for serving refreshment was away for a few minutes.

Seeing my obvious disappointment—no doubt my tongue was hanging out—one of the young men found a spare glass and invited me to share his large bottle until such a time as I could buy my own. I accepted gratefully, introduced myself and was in turn introduced to the others.

When the lady of the house returned, I ordered two large bottles which I shared with my kind-hearted companion.

When the others had filed into the dining room for tea, I asked if I could have a shower. "Of course," I was told. "Help yourself. Down the alleyway and first on the left!"

It seemed too good to be true and I hurried outside to get my soap, sponge and towel from the Kombi. I found the showers and, to my delight, there were hot and cold taps which actually responded to manipulation. This was the greatest moment of my life. First of all, I had a cold shower to rinse the dust off, then a hot one and soaped myself liberally, then another cold one just for the joy of it.

What with the beer and the shower, I felt on top of the world and returned to the Kombi to get Jasper's dinner. I washed up his plate and saw that the time was nearly seven o'clock. I lay on my bunk for a few minutes and woke up ravenously hungry at nine-thirty.

I had my meal and didn't even bother to move the Kombi away from the front of the hotel before turning in and sleeping soundly till seven a.m.

Then I had another surprise. Instead of being awakened by the sun streaming in the windows on to my face, the sky was overcast. Outside it had obviously been raining because I was greeted with that delightful smell of parched earth responding to life-giving water. The radio news at

Ayers Rock about midday.

Late afternoon.

Sunset.   After sunset.

Ayers Rock at sunrise.
Last view of the Kombi during the climb up the Rock.

a quarter-to-eight mentioned an isolated fall of ten points recorded at Kingoonia.

However, it was short-lived and, by the time I had filled up with petrol and water and left this tiny township, the sun was blazing down again as relentlessly as ever. It was nine-fifteen.

The road was fairly wide with long stretches of sand and wicked corrugations. I had one hundred and eighty miles to cover this day and could have taken it easy, but I put my foot down and was soon doing fifty miles an hour. The monotony of the scenery and the corrugations made this the only sensible thing to do.

By midday I had covered one hundred and forty miles and had not seen any vehicle or human being. Once a herd of brumbies had scampered off from the side of the track at my approach. Apart from that there was no sign of life, and I was anxious to get to Coober Pedy.

I suppose I must have been dreaming a bit but even when you are fully alert, bull-dust holes are difficult to detect until you are actually upon them, particularly at fifty miles an hour.

The front wheels just dropped. Then, with a shuddering crash they hit bottom. I rose clear of the seat, my bare head hit the roof and I momentarily blacked out.

In a complete daze I realised that I had lost control as the Kombi was swerving across the track hitting the deep sand on each side and swaying dangerously as it was shuttle-cocked from side to side.

My returning senses told me I dare not brake but must accelerate to get back on to a straight course. I managed to correct the sideways sliding, only to find that now I was in really deep sand and just has to keep going, in spite of a splitting headache and a clanking, scraping noise so violent that I thought the Kombi was about to fall apart.

It must have been every bit of five miles before the sand thinned out enough for me to risk pulling up.

I was still feeling dizzy when I got out to inspect the damage. It was not so bad as it had sounded but quite bad enough. Two more welds had gone on the roof rack. One lug had cut right through the gutter and was scraping the side of the body. The whole heavily laden rack was at a crazy angle, and seemed ready for the decree nisi to become divorce absolute at any moment.

I took two aspirins with my mug of tea followed by a cigarette and a brief relax on my bunk. The aspirins took effect and I got to work with a length of rope to make the rack sufficiently fast to get to Coober Pedy. A few things had come adrift inside, but there appeared to be no other damage.

⁃ I don't know what happened to Jasper. He probably hit the roof too, but seemed none the worse for it and happily chased lizards while I was doing the temporary repairs.

It took nearly two hours to do the last thirty miles and it was two-thirty before I saw on the horizon the collection of buildings which was my first sight of the thriving mining township of Coober Pedy.

65

6

Coober Pedy

The name Coober Pedy is Aboriginal and, roughly translated means 'White men's holes in the ground', because of the popularity of habitations dug out of the solid rock in the early days when transport was a major problem, even for food and water. It was discovered in 1915.

Complete lack of standing timber suitable for building anywhere in the vicinity forced the early pioneers to find other means of protection from the burning sun in the daytime and the intense cold of winter nights.

My first impression of Coober Pedy came far nearer to my preconceived ideas of a mining township than had been the case with Andamooka. This had the main street with buildings on either side but, so far, no sign of any dugouts.

As usual, my first call was at the police station which I had difficulty in finding. I enquired if there were any special camping regulations and of the availability of water.

Again I encountered courtesy and a helpful attitude. "Camp where you like," I was told. "Water is at the still where you can make some arrangement with the chap who looks after it, to buy supplies."

There were three main stores, the biggest of which is the Miners' Store, which sells everything anyone is likely to need and incorporates the Post Office.

I went in and had a look round and bought the inevitable pyramid carton of milk from one of the well-stocked refrigerated counters. I put a twenty cent piece on the counter and waited for my change. I thought it would be eleven cents assuming that it couldn't possibly be dearer than at Andamooka. After all, this place is on the main highway and Andamooka seventy-five miles off the track at the back of beyond.

I got no change! Twenty cents was the price, take it or leave it. I took it this time, but left it thereafter. I found after a further look round that milk wasn't the only expensive commodity. Everything was far above what I considered reasonable prices and it was brought home to me perhaps for the first time, the very real advantages of a Co-operative movement.

Whilst Andamooka was populated mostly by Czechs, Yugoslavs and Poles, this place seemed to be dominated by Greeks, Italians and Germans, with just a sprinkling of Australians.

First impressions were not very favourable so I shaped my course towards Franko's old friend, Jack Brewster. I had no difficulty in finding his 'motel' and wineshop.

Franko was right. He and his wife were the souls of hospitality and made me feel much better. They gave me a great deal of useful information about Coober Pedy and advised me where to go and what to see. I arranged to camp for the night behind a tin shed at the side of the cluster of buildings which constituted the 'motel'.

This was not a very salubrious spot as it was littered with all kinds of rubbish, mostly bits and pieces of old motor vehicles. There were many old motor-car bodies scattered round the environs of the township and I was told that they were used by the aboriginals to sleep in after a night 'on the plonk.'

As I settled down for the night I noticed a fire burning in a hollow about three hundred yards away. Sitting around were ten or more Aboriginals of both sexes, complete with children and dogs.

A party was in progress and the noise of their laughing and quarrelling went on well into the early hours. However, I was not unduly bothered and, on the whole, had a very good night.

The next day dawned windy, cold and grey with dust—a most unpleasant combination.

However, I got to work early on the roof rack and blessed my foresight in bringing such a good selection of tools and bits and pieces.

This job took me all day but, when I finally repacked the tools, I felt proudly that this trouble was behind me.

Before dark, I explored the town on foot I walked up the main street past the Miners' Store. To the left was evidence of a road which swung to the right and vanished in the dusty haze. Straight on, the main street widened out in a sort of valley between rising ground on both sides and I had my first sight of the dugouts.

Away to the right was the Roman Catholic church, but the only evidence of this was the cross on the wooden door covering the entrance. A caravan was parked outside.

To the left were other dugouts and buildings all decorated with signs offering something ostensibly of interest to the tourist. There were signs everywhere to tell you how and where to spend your money—where to eat, where to sleep, where to get opals, artifacts and souvenirs—*but* there is absolutely nothing to inform the visitor that the police station is accommodated in the building housing the Regional Department of Mines. There wasn't even a sign simply stating Police.

The road to the left past the store happened to be the main highway to Alice Springs. Most travellers fail to make the sharp left turn and plough their way on into the dugout area.

The sign-post showing this left turn to the Alice fell, or was knocked down, several years ago. It was still lying on its face at the side of the road.

I enquired of one of the nearby shopkeepers why the sign had not been re-erected and received this priceless reply: "The bloody thing had been up for thirty years and by now everybody knows that that's the road to the Alice. Why bother to put it up again?"

The local police officer spoke to me of Ernest Renshaw who had come to Coober Pedy several years ago as a reporter and photographer working on a feature for a Melbourne newspaper.

Why he abandoned this in favour of opal mining did not concern me but he evidently had sufficient success to warrant making his home here. He is now a buyer of considerable repute, runs a small business and is a leading light in Coober Pedy society.

I found Ernie living in a neat semi-dugout residence adjoining his business premises. He was expecting me as the police officer had told him I should be contacting him.

He and his wife made me very welcome and my original antipathy to the township underwent a further process of evaporation. I left after this first visit feeling that I had made some real friends and with a stack of useful information.

On the way back from the Renshaws' place I passed the church again and, seeing that the caravan door was open and a Landrover was parked alongside, I assumed that the priest was present. It was a good opportunity to meet Father Cresp, whose virtues had been fully extolled by Ernie and his wife. He was a young man of great charm, Italian by birth, I should imagine, and rather shy.

He showed me his little church, hewn out of the rock by local voluntary labour. Inside, it was delightfully cool and peaceful, lit by electricity from a small generator which he insisted on starting up so that I could see it properly.

Although I had been given directions to find the still they had been very involved and I made no note of them. I asked Father Cresp and was told clearly, concisely and accurately. He also told me that many of the popular tourist show-places were closed for the Christmas period, their owners having gone to the capital cities or the ocean beaches for the annual break.

He himself was here for Christmas although his territory for administering spiritual comfort and guidance extends from Port Augusta to Alice Springs, west to the Western Australian border and to some undefined line to the east—he didn't really know—possibly in the middle of the Simpson Desert.

When he was not driving round his gigantic 'parish' in his Landrover he lived in the caravan by the dugout church.

At one time, water was the main obstacle to extended living at Coober

Pedy but, since the advent of the solar still, there is no longer any need to go thirsty or dirty.

The water comes from bores and, on reaching the surface, is so brackish that it is quite undrinkable. The still is composed of acres of channels into which the bore water is pumped. These channels are covered with gables of glass and the heat from the sun evaporates the water which collects in globules on the underside of the glass, then runs down into separate channels on each side of the main channel. This water, now sweet and drinkable, is directed to tanks where it is dispensed through overhead pipes to those with some means of transporting it on payment of a fee, in my case, of fifteen cents for ten gallons.

Compared with the price of thirty cents per thousand gallons excess water rate on the coast of Queensland, this seems very expensive but, to anybody who has experienced the value of water in the arid, semi-desert country, it is worth every cent charged.

This solar still is capable of producing three thousand gallons of pure water every day, and is constantly being extended to handle more.

Having topped up with water I determined to find a better campsite and set off up the track which leads ninety-two miles to William Creek. Less than a mile from the township I found a site which suited me. It was at the top of a depression which led down to the old water tank and the Aboriginal settlement. The view was particularly interesting.

Being on relatively high ground I could look out to the north-east and across a vast plain which extended featurelessly into the far distance. The heat haze made it difficult to pick out any detail so it was easy to imagine it to be the sea. From this point the horizon was entirely devoid of any prominence whatsoever—just a line separating the darker tones of the earth from the light, misty blue of the sky.

If I moved a little and looked to the left, I could see close 'inshore' an island formed by a hill typical of opal country—not more than a hundred feet high with a flat table-like top as if it had been cut off with a knife.

That night after dinner, Jasper disappeared. It was about six-thirty. I wasn't unduly alarmed. In due course I went to bed expecting him to wake me up by jumping into his travelling seat.

I woke at six a.m. He was still missing. I began to get a bit worried. I waited and waited and at eleven decided to go and look for him. I drove round the town but there was no sign of him so I called in to see the policeman, who was sympathetic and promised to look out for him. Ernie Renshaw suggested he might be out with the Aboriginals and their dogs 'noodling the dumps'. (This means sorting through the mullock heaps for small pieces of opal missed by the miners.) He said, "They all drift back to town by lunchtime. I should wait till then".

So I went back to the campsite for an early lunch. I returned about twelve forty-five and, sure enough, the Aboriginals were there in force sitting on the ground leaning against a wall or anything that would support them. Several groups were using the side wall of a store and consisted of men, women, children and dogs of all shapes and sizes. Amongst one such group sitting with two Aboriginals on each side of him was Jasper, lolling contentedly against the wall like his companions.

He didn't see me at first but as I pulled up he became devoid of his lethargy and pricked up his ears. As I opened the door he leapt forward, wagging his tail furiously and on to his usual seat just as if I had arranged to call for him.

I said nothing but he gave me a queer guilty look. The Aboriginals took no notice whatsoever, looking neither at him nor me.

I'm told that they are very fond of their dogs and always manage to feed and water them somehow. Being quite illiterate, they were incapable of reading his tag even if they noticed it.

My relief was unbounded but, in spite of his whinging, I resolved to keep him tied up for our remaining time in Coober Pedy. I was told that a pack of Aboriginal dogs will tear a white man's dog to pieces, but there's one white man's dog that got away with it!

That night I tied him up. Just before dark as I was writing up my journal, I was disturbed by the yelping of many dogs. It was more the sound of dogs at play rather than an attack in force. I heard no growling but, even so, looked out apprehensively.

Five dogs were romping round Jasper, who was standing quite calmly surveying them. As I emerged from the Kombi expecting trouble, they dispersed, then trotted off in single file down the gully which formed the depression leading to the native settlement at the bottom of the hill.

I assume that they were his newly-acquired friends who had missed his company and had come visiting. This happened for several evenings in a row.

During my talks with old Franko at Andamooka we had discussed the question of how many old timers were still working on the fields and in the traditional manner.

He told me of an old friend of his, one Vic. Williamson, who, to the best of his knowledge, was living in Coober Pedy and probably still gouging as he was a youngster of a mere seventy-five or thereabouts. He suggested that I might look him up.

On making enquiries I found that everybody knew old Vic., but he didn't come into town very often. Asking where he could be found I was told "Out at German Gully," but it was left to Ernie Renshaw to give specific and reliable instructions on how to get there.

It was quite a secluded area, set in a shallow gully between the low opal-bearing hills. It contrasted greatly with the other diggings which I had seen so far. There was no noise of bulldozers, mechanical shovels or electric generators and when I arrived in the early afternoon the place seemed deserted.

I parked the Kombi on the flat and followed a narrow footpath up the hill towards a windlass the top of which I could just see behind the great heaps of mullock.

Another camp amongst the gibbers at Coober Pedy. It is *not* the sea on the horizon.

German Gully—Vic Williamson's dugout is in the centre.

The path ended at the doorway of a dugout. The door was open and I peered into the cool, shady interior. To the right immediately inside was a rough table and chair. To the left was a fairly deep alcove at the side of which stood an old kerosene refrigerator. Another alcove was cut into the wall beyond the table and chair. This undoubtedly contained a bed, because I could see a pair of slippered feet on the blanket hanging over the end.

After I had knocked on the wooden door jamb, the feet slid off on to the floor and the old man shuffled out, rubbing his red-rimmed and rather blood-shot eyes.

I then realised that I had disturbed his siesta and apologised for my thoughtlessness.

As is typical of these old miners, he showed no irritation but welcomed me with the offer of a drink. He explained that he hadn't been feeling too well and was having trouble with his eyes, which were watering copiously. The glare of the sun from the open doorway seemed to make them worse so I cut this first visit short and was invited to come back any time, perhaps tomorrow, when he would no doubt be feeling better and would show me round and enjoy a yarn.

I asked him if there was anything he needed that I could bring with me next time. He suggested that I might pick up a chicken which he had ordered from the store for his Christmas dinner as tomorrow was Christmas eve.

Christmas eve dawned hotter than ever. It was the sort of heat that made starting any job difficult. Once on the move, soaked with perspiration, it didn't seem so bad.

We went into town and collected Vic.'s chicken, then on to German Gully. Vic. was feeling a bit better and we cracked a bottle of beer from his fridge. It was certainly old but it put a good chill on the grog.

We talked for about an hour then he took me up to the windlass at the top of his mineshaft. It was about thirty feet deep and I was relieved to see a ladder disappearing into the depths.

It was a 'chain' ladder consisting of two lengths of steel rod between which were welded rungs of the same material. Each rod was about eight feet long bent at the top to form a hook. The top 'link' was attached to a beam of wood long enough to bed firmly across the hole so that the ladder hangs down at the side of the shaft. Lengths can be added until the chain of ladders reaches the bottom.

Whilst this is far superior to going up and down by rope, until you get used to it, it can be quite tricky. Being articulated, it will sway to and from the side of the shaft. Unless holes have been cut in the side of the shaft, there is little room to get your feet squarely on the rungs.

However, I soon mastered the technique and we both went down with a candle each. At the bottom, the shaft widened out to form a cavern sufficiently high for me at least to stand upright.

Horizontal tunnels called drives had been made in different directions.

Those drives which had been worked out or proved barren had, in their turn, been filled with the debris cut from new drives to save the back-breaking labour of lifting all the dirt to the surface and disposing of it there.

This was truly an opal mine of the traditional kind—dug by hand by an old timer and still being worked by the same old timer using methods as old as the opal industry itself.

I wanted to start gouging right away but I had to curb my enthusiasm as the tools were on top and Vic. had already suggested that Wednesday would be a better time to start work again.

We climbed aloft again back into the broiling midday heat. Down below it was almost cool.

Back in the dugout we were joined by Vic.'s next-door neighbour, a young Englishman named Jimmy. With a partner, Jimmy was occupying a disused dugout constructed when this little field was producing large quantities of precious opal.

His partner was away for Christmas and Jimmy was holding the fort and carrying on single-handed. We had some more beer and before leaving I was invited to visit Jimmy's dugout on the next trip out.

Walking back to the Kombi I picked up several large pieces of opal from the surface of the mullock heaps. Much of this showed brilliant colour but, having been left exposed to the heat of the sun for so many years, had become crazed and utterly valueless as gemstones.

The fact that so much potentially good material (judging by present day standards), had been missed or disregarded by the original miners was a good indication of the beautiful stones which must have been mined when the field was first discovered.

Much of this useless opal I had picked up showed a predominance of brilliant green which, until quite recently, had not been a popular colour. Then, if it didn't show plenty of red, it wasn't worth bothering about.

Today, they tell me, whilst red fetches the best prices on the American market, the green is the most valuable for export to Japan. The Japanese for some reason regard red with disfavour and superstitition.

Many old, abandoned shafts are frequently worked on the chance that there may be much green opal at the bottom—thrown there by the bucketful in the old days when it was regarded as of no more value than colourless potch.

It was a bit too early to start dinner so, on the way back, I drove past our campsite and on into town as I needed more cooking salt. Having got it, and a few more small items, I turned for 'home'. As I passed Jack Brewster's place I spotted Jack outside his wineshop and pulled up to say 'hello'.

Jack was his usual cheery self and invited me to come along tomorrow and have Christmas dinner with them. Thinking this would be an evening function I accepted gratefully and asked what time it would be on. "Oh, about midday," he replied.

For the moment I was horrified at the prospect of attempting to

73

consume a hot meal, and all the grog which was bound to go with it, in the heat of the day which could be anything up to fifteen degrees above the century. But I could only say "Right, I'll be there!"

I consoled myself with the hope that at least I could spend the afternoon sleeping it off, and wondered just how much of a booze-up it would become.

As I was about to drive off I realised that Jasper was missing again.

He was still missing at eleven a.m. on Christmas morning so I went searching. I inspected one crowd of seven Aboriginals and nine dogs but he wasn't among them.

Two of the natives came over and said 'hello' so I asked them if they'd seen him. One told me he had seen him at the Reserve that morning. I drove over but there was no sign of him. I wasn't unduly worried now as I guessed he'd turn up sooner or later.

I returned to the campsite to clean up for the party and, on returning to the Brewsters', saw him calmly walking down the centre of the main street with two other dogs. I didn't say a word but just stood by the open door of the Kombi. He broke away and leapt into his seat as they came alongside and the other two continued on their way as if they had just escorted him home.

What could I say? What could I do? I just had to accept it.

When I went into the motel, the other guests were sitting around drinking beer, which was flowing freely. Some of them I already knew. Jack, who could never remember my name, introduced me to the others as the "Bloody Scribbler".

It was a friendly and gratifying insult for it made me feel that I was accepted. Many were the highly coloured stories I was told 'to put in my book', but most of them were quite unfit for publication.

When dinner was served, the many beers had the effect of making us all delightfully mellow and full of goodwill. Champagne was served with the poultry and after the Christmas pudding a very pleasant pink drink was just about the last straw. For nearly everyone the rest of Christmas Day passed in sleeping it off.

7

An ambition fulfilled

Wednesday was the great day for me to do my first underground gouging but, when we got to German Gully, Vic. was once again very much under the weather. His eyes were particularly bad, but he assured me that he was well enough to come down with me to get me going.

This time, as well as candles, we took a carbide or acetylene lamp. This has superseded the candle and is a useful source of illumination when no electric generator is available.

It is a simple device and comprises a can with two compartments. Into one you put the calcium carbide and the other is filled with water. A screw-down valve on the top controls the dripping of the water which, on contact with the carbide produces the evil-smelling acetylene gas which rises up a pipe to a burner. A lighted match applied to this ignites the gas and results in a bright white light.

We put the carbide lamp, the candles and a couple of picks into a bucket and lowered it down the shaft by the windlass.

When it touched bottom, Vic. swung himself over and on to the ladder with a warning to me "Don't come down till I'm clear of the bottom of the ladder". He disappeared into the shaft and I waited till I heard his muffled "Right-o!" before I followed.

When I reached the bottom he had already got the lamp going and I had a much better view of the small cavern by the brighter light. Although it was possible for me to stand up to view the drives, the headroom at the actual working faces was considerably reduced and it was a case of sitting, squatting or kneeling on the rough surface to do any actual work.

"Where shall I start?" I asked eagerly.

"Anywhere you like," Vic. replied, "it could be anywhere. It's all a matter of scratching away till you strike a seam, then follow it up till you strike colour."

It all sounded so easy, but I longed for a cushion. Kneeling on that rough floor was purgatory. Sitting was just as bad and squatting was impossible for anything but an inspection.

Vic. somehow made himself comfortable on the floor and watched me with amusement. He saw my difficulty and discomfort and threw me a hessian bag which he evidently kept down there for the purpose. I folded it and used it as a knee-pad. That was better! Then I had difficulty in fixing the lamp in such a position where I could see what I was doing. It wouldn't stand up where I wanted it. Where it *did* stand upright, I was in my own light.

I started with the heavier of the two picks.

"I don't think you'll find anything there," remarked Vic. "I've already worked round there. Still, carry on if you want to."

By now, I had got myself comparatively comfortable and managed to get the lamp to stand up so I determined to carry on right where I was.

I chipped and chipped and soon my sugar bag cushion was covered with sharp bits of rock which made it as uncomfortable as the floor itself. My back was beginning to ache and I was soaked in perspiration from the exertion.

A large piece of sandstone flaked off and knocked the lamp over. In my anxiety to set the lamp up again, I overbalanced and sat down heavily on the debris I had removed and pushed behind me. The impact of these sharp pieces of rock on my inadequately protected backside was excruciatingly painful and I was almost ready to give up.

I looked round at Vic. who had now lit the candles. The sight of his old face and his watering eyes made me realise what a marvellous spirit these old-timers must have had to work alone day after day, month after month, under conditions of such torture.

Suddenly I felt ashamed at my softness, grinned at Vic., shook the rocks from the sugar bag and settled myself down to continue.

Then I heard that 'clink'—the sound I had dreamed about! Vic. had heard it too. "Take it easy," he reminded me, quite unnecessarily.

I put down the heavy pick and raised the lamp, gazing at the spot with excitement. I scraped carefully with the chisel-like point of the lighter pick. The light from the lamp was reflected back as it struck the glass-like fragment. I scraped again and a small piece fell into the rubble beneath. I scrabbled around till I found it, examined it carefully and handed it to Vic.

"Potch," was Vic.'s verdict, "but it may be the start of a seam. See if you can follow it up."

I threw the heavy pick behind me and worked carefully along the face revealing a thin line of colourless potch which was gradually widening as I got farther into the drive.

It widened to about a quarter-of-an-inch then started to diminish and finally disappeared completely. I threw the light pick down in disgust and disappointment, but Vic. suggested that I cut into the widest part to see if it would open out *behind* the face.

This I did and was almost immediately rewarded with a trace of colour—a tiny flash of blue with a suggestion of gold.

I forgot my sore knees and aching back as I cut deeper and deeper into the sandstone wall. The seam now started to thin down again but didn't disappear until I had found one small piece of pin-fire opal about half the size of my little finger nail and a sixteenth of an inch thick.

This I knew I could cut and polish and possibly two other small pieces. I took my watch from my pocket. It showed that I had been working for over two hours and Vic., in spite of being far from well, had patiently sat and watched and given me advice.

It was time to call it a day although, by now, I could have gone on for hours. I offered my finds to Vic., but he insisted I keep all I had found. It wasn't worth much to a buyer but to me it represented the fulfilment of an ambition—to dig out with my own hands some precious opal.

We came up and Vic. retired for a rest in his dugout. I had a snack in the Kombi and half-an-hour on my bunk, then called on Jimmy who was also resting after spending the morning digging a new shaft.

We had a couple of bottles of beer and he took me up to his new site where he had dropped the pick and shovel, which were his only excavating tools.

He had marked out the dimensions of the hole—about four feet by three feet—and had sunk his shaft about eighteen inches.

Feeling full of goodwill, I volunteered to give him a hand. With a facetious "Don't go down more than thirty-five feet today," he handed me a heavy pick and broad shovel and sat down to watch.

It was unbearably hot just standing in the sun. Digging was sheer hell. A constant stream of perspiration ran into my eyes so that I couldn't see. My hands were so wet that I couldn't get a proper grip on the pick handle. Of course, the whole operation was utterly stupid in the hottest part of the day but, in spite of that, I managed to sink his shaft another twelve inches.

Jimmy said "Chuck it. Come and have a beer!"

I climbed out of the hole.

In the cool of Jimmy's dugout, the thermometer on the wall read 106 degrees, so it must have been somewhere between 115 and 120 degrees out in the sun.

No wonder the people who live and work out here consume so much beer. It is very pleasant, in spite of the fact that it seems to leak through the skin as fast as you drink it.

I slept in on the following morning after such a strenuous day and round about eleven a.m. called on Ernie again. When I arrived he was in the throes of grading and weighing a parcel of rough opal he had just bought for several thousand dollars.

I stared goggle-eyed at the table. I had never seen so much beautiful opal in my life. Where it had come from and how long it had taken to collect so much I didn't ask. One doesn't if one is wise. It is an unwritten law to refrain from asking questions which would only cause embarrassment and evoke an evasive answer.

Ernie had an overnight guest. He was Ray Weldon, a young Victorian schoolboy aged eighteen whose plan was to hitch-hike up through the Centre, to Darwin if he had time and then across to the Queensland coast at Townsville, then down the eastern seaboard to Brisbane, Sydney and back to his home outside Melbourne.

He was having difficulty in hitching a ride north to the Alice and time was passing too quickly because he was due back in about three weeks.

Ernie knew that I was leaving shortly and that I could accommodate him and suggested that he should ask me and wait if I were agreeable.

I took to Ray right away, partly because of his adult outlook and partly because he was a keen photographer and ardent 16mm enthusiast, although he had only a still camera with him.

My motives in agreeing to take him with me as far as the Alice were not entirely unselfish. He was delighted and enthusiastic when I suggested that he might help me with some continuity shots and 'cut-ins' featuring me, Jasper and the Kombi—shots which I couldn't possibly take myself.

I was waiting for some processed film to be returned in the mail and, if it arrived today, I should be prepared to leave in the morning, which was Sunday. There was no mail for me at the P.O. There should have been fourteen bags but only four had arrived. My film was probably in one of the missing ten and they could quite easily have gone to Darwin in error. I knew that Ernie could be relied upon to forward my film by Redline bus to Alice Springs as soon as it arrived. Therefore, I could now see no point in hanging about any longer in Coober Pedy. It was the end of the year. The 'wet' could come any time from now on, and the sooner I got to Alice Springs the better.

After lunch I found Ray and suggested he should stay with me from now on. Back at my campsite he helped me check the van. I cleaned the air filter, changed a tyre which had a nasty cut in one wall, then together we made the rounds to say goodbye via German Gully and the Brewsters.

Except for his brief stay with the Renshaws Ray had been eating out of tins most of the time since his departure, so we shared a meal of steak, potatoes, carrots and peas.

I erected the annexe where Ray made himself comfortable in his sleeping bag. By nine o'clock we were all sound asleep, including Jasper who had made no attempt to go visiting since he had sensed that a move was afoot.

I woke up at five-thirty on this last day of the year. After a light breakfast we struck camp, set up the movie gear and drove around to various local spots for Ray to take the continuity shots.

When the last foot of film had run through the camera, I unloaded it and packed the film for mailing. The camera I packed carefully in its case under the front bunk—the coolest and least dusty of all places in the Kombi.

As my film was to be specifically on the opal fields I didn't expect to unpack it again for several thousand miles, that is, until I had been right to the 'top end' and back to the opal fields of western Queensland.

By a quarter-to-nine we were ready to pull out. I stopped at the P.O. and dropped the film packet in the box. We took the left turn past the store and headed for the dusty plain which I had gazed across every morning for two weeks.

Down 18 inches. Another twenty feet to go! The author digging a shaft in 115 degrees heat.

8

The beginning of the 'Wet'

It was three hundred miles to the Northern Territory border and I had strong doubts whether we should make it that day. Everything would depend on the state of the track.

We made good time and managed to keep up a steady forty-five m.p.h. in spite of the sand and corrugations. I was now keeping a sharp look-out for bull-dust holes and had no time to get depressed by the monotony of the scenery. Even wildlife was in short supply.

As we had used a few gallons of water last night, I decided to replenish our supplies at Matherson's Bore, where a grisly murder had recently been committed. Ray was navigating and watching carefully for the windmill which would signify its presence. But saw no sign of Matherson's Bore.

We had covered one hundred and fifty miles when we came to the second Oodnadatta turnoff and the Hawk's Nest Well. The big, circular tank was full to overflowing with cool, sweet water and we filled every container we'd got, including ourselves.

Jasper got into the cattle trough, then rolled joyously in the mud around it. We washed him and we washed ourselves, then set off much cooler and happier to cover the next fourteen miles to Wellbourne Hill.

The scenery improved a little, but not so the road. We seemed to have returned to the typical opal country with its low, flat-topped hills.

Wellbourne Hill is not a township but a few buildings and a petrol bowser. I took on six gallons of fuel and enquired about opal in the area. I was told that opal had been found close by, but whoever had prospected had done no more about it, as there was no apparent mining activity.

I was also told that the road from here to Kulgera across the border had recently been graded and was good enough to belt along at seventy miles an hour.

This was so for the first couple of miles, but then it became even worse than the first hundred and fifty miles of the day's run.

It was very pleasant having someone to navigate and talk to. Of course, I talk to Jasper while we're travelling but, as his sphere of interest is chiefly in chasing things that run or fly, food and sex, our conversations are never very inspiring.

We passed Granite Downs and I was now hopeful that we might make Kulgera that night. Only seventy miles to go and it was still not four o'clock.

Suddenly the van swerved violently and hit the bank on the left. I tried to pull out of it but had little control over the steering and realised that I had had a back tyre blow-out.

Stabilising the jack in the loose sand proved difficult and, by the time we had put one of the spares on and stowed the other wheel, twenty minutes had passed.

We got going again and I became conscious of a hammering noise on the roof. Ray jumped out and announced that the complete roof rack had slid forward at least four inches.

I investigated and found that one of my brand new aluminium lugs had sheered through, allowing the bearer to sag and bang on the roof with the motion of the vehicle. I gathered that the crash into the bank when the tyre blew out was responsible for the rack shifting.

We made a pad out of an old inner tube which I always carry, packed it in place of the broken lug and lashed it down with rope. If only this would hold it would have to do till we reached the Alice.

After all this delay, we were still nine miles short of the border when we camped for the night at seven-thirty by the side of the track.

I opened the door and removed Ray's swag, comprising his rucksack, sleeping bag and bedroll. I stepped inside and was dismayed to find a thick layer of dust over everything.

At that moment I was thankful beyond measure for my independent 12-volt electric supply, the fluorescent light and vacuum cleaner.

In spite of these amenities it took a good half hour cleaning up before I could start to cook our evening meal.

I suspected that I had forgotten to shut the hopper type window but it wasn't that. A quick investigation revealed that the whole back panel was showing light from inside all round the rubber seal. I put my hand on the catch and found it loose. One retaining screw had fallen right out and disappeared. The other was only just holding and preventing the whole lock and catch from falling off. I tightened up the loose bolt as hard as I could and the panel sealed itself once again.

After that, we felt we had earned our soup, eggs and fried potatoes.

We got away again at eight-fifteen a.m., crossed the border and stopped to take a picture of the sign N.T. Border. This, like every one of the few signs we passed, was riddled with bullet holes.

We reached tiny Kulgera without further incident. I filled up with petrol and went over to the police station to check up on the state of the track north to the Alice. The officer on duty was, as usual, very co-operative and gave me an accurate but not very encouraging report.

I had heard that certain types of firearms had to be registered in the Northern Territory so, to be on the safe side, I casually mentioned that I was carrying a .22 rifle. Did I have to register it?

"My word, you do!" he replied. "If they find an unregistered rifle in Alice, they'll impound it for sure. Better bring it in and I'll give you a permit."

I took it to him for examination after which he noted the make, type and serial number in a book. Without further ado he made out the permit and handed it to me. He reckoned that the weather was about to break and that the 'wet' would be really on within a few days.

I had hoped that the roads might improve with a different administration taking over their maintenance once we had crossed the border, but I was disappointed. The only difference I noticed was that there were now more Caution signs.

This meant very little, because we'd come to one of these and slow down looking for trouble only to find there was none. Then conversely, without any warning whatsoever, we would plough into deep sand and a vicious curve which could easily mean disaster.

The only thing to do was to ignore these signs and be on constant alert, with eyes glued to the track and both hands on the wheel. My arms ached with the strain of keeping on course and dodging great boulders which I always seemed to meet in awkward places.

The only real improvement was in the scenery. Once we had passed Erldunda Homestead and the turnoff leading to Mt. Ebenezer and ultimately to Ayers Rock many promontories gave the landscape the long-awaited interest—the Mt. Sunday Range on the right and the Seymour Range in the distance. It was a pleasant relief when the track wound its way through the Chandlers Range past Henbury Station. We had heard that on this property were some huge craters several miles across which, it is believed, were made by the impact of giant meteorites.

Here the Finke River is crossed and, being dry for most of the year, the road simply dives down on to the riverbed and up the other side. A few weeks later this could become a raging torrent quite impassable for any road traffic.

The same thing can happen at the Palmer River crossing, which we had negotiated about twenty miles back, and the Hugh River another fifteen miles or so further on at Renner's Rock.

From the Finke River the James Range was dead ahead and Alice Springs a mere fifty seven miles away. A grey streak on the horizon ahead had now become evident. It was either dust or rain.

Suddenly I sniffed and looked at Ray. He sniffed and looked at me.

"Can you smell coffee?" I asked.

"Yes, good isn't it," he replied.

The grey streak had now become a wide band and a portion of a rainbow against the darker grey straight ahead. It was only a little bit of rainbow, as if someone had taken a pair of scissors and snipped it off top and bottom.

I wanted a picture of this so we pulled up. As we stopped, the coffee odour became stronger. I opened the back door to get the camera and was again dismayed to see a layer of brownish dust over everything.

"Oh hell," I muttered, "the damned lock's become loose again." I wiped the dust from my camera case with the side of my hand. It was sticky and the odour of coffee intense. Then I saw the jar on its side hanging over the edge of the shelf and the screw cap on the floor. It had been a full jar. I salvaged about a teaspoonful.

Out came the vacuum cleaner once again and, luckily, I was able to collect most of the 'dust' in the bag, but where it had settled in the sun, it had melted and had to be washed off.

When we started off again the sky was almost completely overcast and wet patches appeared on the track. About ten miles from Alice we ran into the tail end of that shower.

We hit the beautiful bitumen six miles from Alice and big pools of water signified that we had only just missed a very heavy shower.

The McDonnell Ranges now predominated the view ahead and it wasn't long before we passed the airport turnoff on the right and a very modern-looking drive-in cinema on the left.

In a few minutes we were passing through Heavitree Gap in the Ranges and into Todd Street, Alice Springs' main thoroughfare. It was still spitting with the monsoon season's first rain of the year.

The 'wet' was on.

9

Alice Springs

It was about six-thirty when I said goodbye to Ray. Had I been pushing on immediately I should have been glad to have kept him as a companion, but he was the one pushing on.

I was expecting to be here for three months at least, during which time I should have to find some sort of a job to keep us in food and petrol.

I had started off with my working capital tied up in ten travellers' cheques. I had already cashed six of them and my ready cash was now reduced to three one-dollar notes and some loose change.

I was due for a full service on the vehicle. I needed a haircut and wanted to spend some time in a caravan park for the sake of the amenities they offer.

I consulted my list of parks showing rates, facilities, locations and, most important of all, which would accept dogs. It was getting late and I was tired, dirty and very hungry so I picked on the nearest one to the Stuart Arms where I was having a couple of lovely cold beers.

This caravan park was the Wintersun and was situated just over a mile up the Stuart Highway next to the racecourse. It was a happy choice as it was not only reasonable in price but was well laid out with plenty of trees and lawns. The toilet and laundry block was clean and spacious. There were even electric shaver points under the mirrors over the wash-hand basins. It was also within a quarter-of-a-mile from a minor shopping centre. I booked in!

The air was completely still and the temperature was in the nineties all night. Although I awakened several times to try to cool off with a shower, I slept well in between times.

As a thirst-crazed man dreams of gurgling streams of cool, clear water, I dreamed of the gentle purr of whirling blades as they fanned my hot, moist body and billowed out the curtains. Each time I stood in the shower that night, I resolved to look around first thing tomorrow for a cheap fan that I could drive from my 12-volt system.

My next door neighbours had a caravan and a Holden station wagon. They, too, had come up the south road from Adelaide and needed extensive repairs to both vehicles. They had been in Alice some time and had established themselves firmly in their alloted position.

Lou Charles and his wife Edna both had jobs. Lou was a tall, rangy type—tough and wiry. He had temporary employment as a labourer with the Department of Works. It was hard work but well paid. Edna was a waitress in a cafe in town and worked shifts. Both were becoming very fond of Alice Springs and were not averse to settling here for good.

Lou had been a head groundsman on a large government institution in Melbourne before a chest X-ray revealed a slight shadow on one lung and he had to have treatment followed by a move to a warmer climate. They had agreed to take this working holiday to search for a congenial location to earn a living. He was hoping before long to find a groundsman's job again.

Edna had a wide experience as cook in hotels and convalescent homes and had taken the waitress job as a stop-gap until such a time as she could again use her skill to better financial advantage.

I found them a delightful couple and learned all these facts about them within one hour of speaking to them the following morning.

That first morning at the Wintersun Jasper had called to see Lou and Edna. They both made a big fuss of him and offered him a drink. Edna put down a bowl of water of which he politely drank about a thimbleful. Had they offered him biscuits, scraps or even a bone, I should have been annoyed. As it was, I knew that they were dog lovers and we had something in common. I went straight over and introduced myself.

After getting their story I briefly told them mine. Mentioning that I had to repair my roof-rack, Lou suggested I should call on Neil Watson who owns a service station. He has a well-equipped welding workshop and wrecker's yard. Lou said he was my best bet for the roof-rack job.

Neil was, as I found them, a typical Australian—friendly, casual, easy-going and helpful. I told him the tragic story of the incessant trouble with the rack. I wanted the job done immediately but he and his mechanics were busy so I suggested that I could do the job myself with only a little help from him and his organisation.

I told him what I proposed to do in order radically to alter the rack fixing arrangement.

"I shall need the use of your bench drill, power hack saw, electric drill and space to put the rack while I'm doing it," I told him.

"Be my guest," Neil answered. "No problem at all!"

These seemed to be stock phrases in Alice Springs and not once did I find them to have been uttered insincerely.

"Get rid of all that stuff off the rack and we'll give you a hand to get it off. After that you're on your own," he warned me.

I went back to the caravan park and borrowed a couple of old tables from the store. Although the rain of yesterday had cleared they told me that we could expect more at any time from now on. I stowed the mass of stuff off the rack on the tables and draped the 'Kordux' cover complete with annexe over them and lashed down, just in case of a sudden downpour.

I had already worked out a design for new steel lugs and, on Neil's recommendation, went along to an engineering works to purchase the steel. More willing co-operation!—they not only supplied the steel plate but also cut them to shape on their guillotine, so that I didn't need the power hack saw but just a file to finish them.

It was now well into the afternoon so I told Neil that I'd be back in the morning to use his workshop. I arranged with the V.W. people to service the Kombi while I was working on the rack so everything was working out beautifully.

Before going back for the evening meal, I toured round the Alice to get my bearings and get to know something of the geography of the place, making a mental note of what was where.

I was impressed by the many neat modern homes with their gardens of native flowers. In many gardens the trees, shrubs and flower beds were individually edged and surrounded by a sort of natural gravel which, in a less arid climate, would be green lawn. Where small patches of grass were in evidence, it was obvious that only the constant application of water from sprinklers was winning the fight against the dry heat.

A large percentage of the homes had solar hot water systems. Except for pumping your hot water up from a hot bore this must be the cheapest and most efficient way of obtaining a constant supply of really hot water.

The domestic system uses a convolution of copper tubing fixed to a flat plate and painted black. This absorbs instead of reflecting the sun's rays. It is mounted in a frame and covered with glass to retain the heat absorbed.

As the water flows into the tubing it is heated to almost boiling. Although not really unsightly, the solar hot water system can hardly be called a feature of architectural beauty. It has to be placed at the optimum angle for maximum absorption of the sun's rays. Some are placed on the roof, some beside the house. The principal snag is that the hot water storage tank has to be placed *above* the unit to be fed by the rising hot water as it is replaced by cold.

On the way back I detoured up the steep slope to the top of Anzac Hill. This memorial outlook offered an excellent view of the whole of Alice Springs and the McDonnell Ranges now tinted with that characteristic purplish-blue so delightfully captured by Albert Namatjira, the famous Aboriginal artist.

The late afternoon sun was still shining, but a bank of dark cloud to the north presaged further rain before nightfall.

On returning to the park I found that I had other neighbours. A young couple had just arrived after negotiating the south road from Adelaide with a station wagon and a caravan. Once again, the latter was a partial wreck from the hammering it had received on the horror stretch.

Reg. and his young wife Aileen were also 'Bloody Poms' and, all of us, having some knowledge of the environs of Peckham Rye and Catford, we were soon exchanging stories.

Reg. was a carpenter by trade and was frantically making temporary repairs to his caravan to keep out the impending deluge.

Darkness came and still it held off, until a terrific clap of thunder seemed to release the tons of bottled-up water which had been hanging over us like a sword of Damocles.

I had already turned in when it started and lay watching the almost continuous pink illumination of the tropical lightning. Then the wind got up and bedlam reigned. Two trees were blown down and tents were uprooted leaving their occupants exposed to the downpour.

According to the radio news in the morning, Alice Springs only had 106 points of rain in the night, but great pools of water lay in all the hollows of the camping ground.

I was lucky. I had inadvertently picked a spot where I was left high and dry.

By ten o'clock the sun was out hotter than ever. Lines were rigged and every inch of hanging space including trees and branches of trees was used over which to drape wet blankets and bedding which fortunately dried very quickly.

Humidity now rose to an uncomfortably high level and I hoped my friends in Brisbane would respond quickly to my telegram to air-freight a fan. I had tried to buy one locally without success.

I was thankful that I had left Coober Pedy when I did, because the midday news told of flash floods and the cutting of the south road by the Finke River. The Palmer and Hugh River crossings were expected to be out in a few hours. A mile or two north of the Alice the Charles River was over the bitumen to a depth of about six inches and rising.

For the first time I heard that the Alice might be cut off from supplies arriving by both road and rail. When the Finke is really flowing even the trains from Port Augusta are halted. It is then that everything has to come in by air and the prices of normal commodities skyrocket.

I drove down to Neil Watson's service station and immediately got assistance in lifting the roof rack off. I marked and drilled my new lugs and finished them off with grindstone and file.

It was quite late in the afternoon when I called on Neil to set the bearers correctly by heating with an oxy-acetylene blow-torch and bending them. This took at least an hour but when we finally lifted the rack back into position on the roof it fitted snugly.

It took me only a few minutes to secure each lug with bolts instead of welds and, this time, I was really confident that my troubles were over.

For all his time, trouble and the use of his tools, Neil only charged me for the oxygen and acetylene gas used.

I now started taking salt tablets regularly although I was not conscious of any loss of salt and the effects thereof. I realised that the rate at which

I was perspiring must be taking its toll. I must have shed gallons of moisture working on those lugs and the humidity was increasing to such an extent that even the 'Alicians' (or should it be 'Springers'?) were complaining. They'd never known it so bad, they told me. Their type of heat was a dry heat and this wasn't according to the book.

A Redline bus had managed to get through before the Finke had closed the road. Ernie Renshaw was as good as his word. My film was on it, so the evening was spent with white gloves and spyglass.

A week passed without much incident. The rain influence diminished and, having finished the minor repairs and amendments to the Kombi, we visited many of the local places of interest including the Pichi Richi Sanctuary, with its fascinating clay modelling of Aboriginal figures, and the museum of the early days in the original telegraph station.

I cashed my seventh travellers' cheque and knew that I *must* get a job of some sort to keep us in food and petrol and lodging in the caravan park and to build up more capital to carry on the trip when the 'wet' was over.

Lou. told me I could probably get a job as a labourer with the Department of Works or even as a wardsman at the hospital so I went along to the Commonwealth Employment Service office to see what was available.

A charming young lady was helpful but asked me what was my trade. Knowing that she would laugh at the futility of it if I told her, I countered with, "What have you got?", thinking I might bluff my way into something more congenial than shovelling dirt on the roads.

"Well," she answered, "there are vacancies for plumbers, electricians, bricklayers, plasterers—".

As she thumbed through the cards, I weighed up the possibilities. These weren't much good. I wouldn't last five minutes.

"There's one here for a temporary brush hand. Can you paint?"

"Of course," I replied eagerly, "I've been a painter. Had my own business once."

Which was technically true because immediately after the war, I had spent my gratuity from the R.A.F. on a hand-cart and ladders after being talked into the idea by a friend who believed that a fortune could be made at painting and decorating.

"Fine," she said. "I'll ring Mr. Jensen and get him to come over to see you."

Len Jensen explained that he was short of labour to complete his existing commitments on time. The job would probably last a fortnight or possibly three weeks. I could start when I liked.

Today was Friday and I promised to report for duty at 8 a.m. on Monday. The pay was good. They worked an eight-hour day and no Saturdays. Most importantly, nobody bothered about union tickets in the painting trade in the Alice.

I bought myself a putty knife and some paint scrapers, as these were the only personal tools a painting tradesman required. I didn't bother

Simpson's Gap.

The Pichi Richi Sanctuary. Clay modelling of aboriginal and symbolic motifs.

Alice Springs from Anzac Hill. Looking down Bath St. Heavitree Gap is in the background.

about overalls. I could never have worn them in that heat anyway and preferred to work in shorts, sandshoes and nothing else.

Although Alice Springs boasted a swimming pool, I was not encouraged by the sight of the crowds which flocked there from opening to closing time. Naturally, Jasper wouldn't have been allowed in so we set off for Simpson's Gap where I understood there is a good pool. Before leaving I told Lou. of my intention.

"You're mad," he said. "Nobody swims there. You'd be fished out a frozen corpse."

Having previously experienced the Australian antipathy to cool water and also having enjoyed a swim in the Thames estuary in early December, I was not deterred.

Simpson's Gap is only fourteen-and-a-half miles out of Alice and nine miles of that is on good bitumen. The remaining five-and-a-half miles is a sandy, gravel track. One small section of this had been washed away in the rain the other night, but it was quite easy to negotiate by driving carefully.

At the Gap, the normal parking place is about a quarter-of-a-mile from the cleft itself and it is usual either to walk along the river bed or scramble over the rocky path.

Seeing car tracks down on to the bed and a large sedan car along by the first pool, I lazily decided to drive down. I realised my mistake as the Kombi's wheels sank into that loose gravel. I kept going and tried to turn in a wide arc to return to solid ground.

This was, of course, a fatal procedure as the front wheels tried to bulldoze the gravel instead of riding over it.

Six young people having a picnic saw my predicament and offered their help. With the aid of my chicken wire and six broad young backs, I was soon returned to firm ground. I wouldn't do *that* again! With all the weight I was carrying, I couldn't compete with a relatively light sedan on that sort of loose stuff.

A series of small pools formed a chain which led right up to the deep cleft in the range. Jasper explored every one, chasing lizards up the bank and generally frolicking.

The sun reflected an orange light from the sandstone, and the deep shadow in which the main pool lay made it look black and almost sinister.

The sandy beach gave way to walls of overhanging rock and through the Gap could be seen another beach bathed in bright sunlight. The only way to get through was to swim. I tried the water with my foot. It was cool without being cold. From where I was standing I could see that the water was clear and deep.

I dived in! I got a mild but exhilarating shock from the cool water but struck out for the centre of the pool. Jasper joined me and swum alongside as if to say "Race you to the other end!"

In a few minutes we arrived at the other end neck and neck. I lay for a little while on the sand getting my breath back, but couldn't wait to get back into that deliciously cool water.

So much for Lou.'s frozen corpse!

On the Saturday night we went to the drive-in cinema. It is quite a drive to the other side of town and through the Heavitree Gap. I was advised to go early as this was Saturday and, apart from the pubs, the drive-in was about the only source of entertainment.

I enjoyed that evening and repeated it many times during my stay in Alice Springs.

Next morning I told Lou. of my pleasant swim at Simpson's Gap and also my intention of going again that very afternoon. Lou. nodded wisely. "You were lucky yesterday. It may not be so good today." He added pessimistically, "You want to watch out!"

I laughed at him and, after lunch, we set off once more. Once again I tried the water with my foot. It was just as warm. I dived in and settled down for the short easy swim to the other end. This time, Jasper didn't swim by my side, but kept to the edge under the overhanging rocks. I called him but he just kept going along the edge.

Suddenly I was in it—a belt of freezing cold water! I gasped as it took my breath away and my arms and legs went numb. I turned and made my way towards Jasper. The water became warm again.

So that was what Lou. meant! When we got to the little beach I tested the water as it tumbled in a cataract over the big rocks into the pool. It was quite warm! I could only assume that this pool in the chasm was additionally fed from an underground source which varied according to some natural phenomenon.

On the way back I was able to follow the course of this cold current by swimming alongside with one arm and leg in cold water and the other in warm. It was quite remarkable and obviously inconsistent.

Back at the Kombi, a Landrover was parked alongside. A man was leaning against the door smoking a cigarette and obviously not a tourist. I guessed by the sign on the side of the vehicle that he was waiting to drive a party of women back to Alice. We had passed them with their straw hats and cameras as we came out of the pool.

I said "G'day". I had learned that this was the acknowledged way of greeting a stranger or of opening up a conversation.

"How was it?" he asked seeing that I was still wet.

Thinking that, as a local he might enlighten me, I told of my experience with the different temperatures.

"What's the reason for it?" I asked.

"Aw well," he drawled. "It's like that. You never know from one day to another."

And that, I presumed, was all he knew or cared.

"Been to Wigley's?" he asked.

"Where and what is Wigley's?" I alliterated.

"Wigley's water hole," he explained. "Much nearer than this. Usually quite good, but it'll be a bit muddy after this rain."

He told me it was not a tourist place, although less than a mile off the

Stuart Highway on the right after you cross the Charles River. This was actually just up the road from the caravan park.

When we got back Lou. and Edna said they were having a bit of a party that night if I would care to join them. The guests would be four in all—a nurse who had been working in the hospital at Andamooka and . . . I sensed a slight hesitation before he told me this . . . a family comprising a full-blooded Aboriginal with his wife and little girl. They were mission-trained and spoke English.

He was pleased when I said how delighted I would be to meet an Aboriginal on a social level. I was keen to know more of them because I refused to judge them on what I had seen so far. One could so easily get the impression that they were lazy, dishonest and good-for-nothing. From what I have read, I have the highest regard for their culture, moral standards and loyalty before they were contaminated by contact with white man's doubtful standards of conduct, his greed and selfishness.

From my point of view, the party was far from a success.

The nurse, Doreen, tried to monopolise me and kept up a barrage of questions about Andamooka and the people there. The Aboriginal family were all very shy. The little girl said not a word. The wife was not talkative and never attempted to elaborate on the polite yeses and noes she gave to my questions on their life. The husband was more expansive, but really said very little. They were Christians, he told me, according to the teaching of the Mission, but I couldn't help feeling that it was politic to say that and, secretly, he still lived according to tribal law.

They all looked uncomfortable in their European clothing. He wore a collar and tie, carefully pressed trousers and shining shoes. Lou. suggested that he might like to remove his tie but he declined and continued to finger it nervously. The rest of us were all dressed as casually as possible.

I felt very sorry for these people so far removed from their natural environment. I longed to be transported with them to a river bank under the stars with a campfire burning and see them divested of these ridiculous clothes so that they could talk proudly of their ancestors, their prowess in the hunt and tell me stories of the 'dreamtime'.

Maybe they are illiterate and backward according to our standards but, I'm sure, there are many ways in which they are far in advance of us.

I left the party feeling depressed and totally inadequate.

IO

A working man again

My workmates were cheery lads and, seeing that I was not entirely
ignorant of painting technique, accepted me as one of them after our
first 'smoko'.

I nearly did the wrong thing. When the leading hand or foreman or whatever you like to call him shouted: "Okay, chaps. Smoko!" my natural
inclination was to finish to the end of the girder I was painting. I had
about three feet to go and it might have taken me a minute and a half.

Suddenly I realised that the others had put down their brushes, got off
the scaffolding and I was still painting. Someone yelled "Hi, Cliff,
smoko!" as much as to say, "What the hell do you think you're doing—
still working when it's smoko time?"

I hastily put down my brush.

It was not quite like that at the end of the day. At ten-to-five the call
was given "Okay! Square off!" This meant finish at a convenient point,
empty paint kettles, clean brushes, stack trestles and planks and be all
ready to leave the job on the stroke of five.

It took me a little time to get used to this working strictly according to
the clock. Had I followed my inclinations, I should probably have been
dubbed a 'scab' or a 'guvner's man', so I thought it better to play it
their way, remember that it wasn't my own home I was painting and
forget those nooks and crannies not seen from the ground.

That night I was desperately tired. Hopping up and down ladders,
balancing on planks and stretching to reach the high parts brought into
action muscles I hadn't used so strenuously for many years—and all in a
shade temperature of over one hundred degrees. But there's something
very satisfying about this sort of fatigue and I slept well, waking refreshed
and with little trace of stiffness.

Taking stock, I realised that I was feeling remarkably fit, all systems
functioning normally and regularly.

When I received my first pay packet I had completely settled down to
the physical and mental routine.

The following week I was assigned to an interior job in a private house working with two 'Poms' who had been in Alice for several years. Both were from the North Country and good mates to work with when I got used to some of the filthiest language I had ever heard. Every other word was a 'four letter' one used as a noun, verb, adjective, adverb or just as an ejaculation. It was terribly monotonous. I had to resist the temptation to express myself in similar vein in the belief that it was the only way to make myself clearly understood.

However, by using other words which I believe they had forgotten, I managed to communicate and even succeeded in persuading them, by example, to relieve the monotony of their expletives. Maybe it's the climate because I found this tendency with all the men I worked with to a greater or lesser degree in the Northern Territory.

I didn't care much for this interior job. The house was not air-conditioned, as were a large percentage of those in the Alice and, if I *had* to sweat, I preferred to do it in the open air. Jasper had to stay in the Kombi for several hours at a time, whereas with an outside job he'd roam around close by and always managed to find himself a shady spot to go to sleep.

Only once did he cause me any embarrassment. We were painting the outside of an Administration building. This was surrounded by well-kept gardens which included a lily pond complete with gold fish. The thermo-meter that day registered one hundred and five degrees, and we were all feeling pretty lethargic.

Jasper couldn't settle down so he decided to take a walk round to the back of the building where the caretaker's quarters were situated. I kept my eye on him just to make sure that he wouldn't take it into his head to wander in.

He stopped suddenly as he came face to face with one of the prettiest little kittens I have ever seen. The kitten faced him with arched back then, without further warning, she flew at him, a ball of fluffy, demoniacal fury. He leapt backwards as he turned and fled howling as if he had been severely injured.

I knew this wasn't the case because he had been too quick for her. However, I went in pursuit just to make quite sure.

I found him in the lily pond lying amongst all the fish with only his head above water. His howls had brought the caretaker, who was also the gardener, on to the scene. He looked in horror at the sight of a large dog in amongst his beloved lilies and goldfish and threatened me with terrible retribution for allowing my dog to desecrate his pool and contents.

I hauled Jasper out and admonished him after making sure that he really had escaped injury from that fiery she-cat. There wasn't a scratch on him!

Together, the caretaker and I examined the lilies and the fish but all was tranquillity again. The lilies still sat on the water and the fish still swam calmly round and round, so that he had to admit that no damage had been done.

We finished on quite good terms but, he warned me, dogs were *not* allowed to roam freely in the grounds.

We finished that job a couple of days later but not before Jasper had obviously made many more rapturous entries into that sacred pool to cool off. I often asked him where he'd been to get dripping wet.

Three weeks passed and I still had the job. I had considered leaving the caravan park and camping somewhere just out of the town, but life was very pleasant here. I had made a lot of friends and Jasper was very popular.

Being able to shower whenever I felt like it (and that was often), having the use of an electric washing machine (at 20 cents a time), an ironing room and clothes hoists to hang my washing on, I should have been foolish to 'live rough' when there was no real need to.

As opposed to the other places I had spent any time in, the police in Alice were very active and 'moved on' anyone camping in unauthorised spots within five miles of the town.

Also, I was now able to vary our diet and eat more fresh food, having the use of a community refrigerator. I could now buy meat, fish, butter, etc. in economical quantities without the inconvenience of having to consume it before it 'went off'.

Rain and thunderstorms were now very frequent, hardly a day passing without at least one downpour. The nights were unbearably hot and, with the dampness and pools of water everywhere, mosquitoes had become troublesome. I found it impossible to sleep with the door closed and only the insect-screened windows for ventilation. I even had to open the back panel and relied upon the smoke from mosquito coils to keep these pests away.

I had a letter from my friends in Brisbane saying that my fan had been air-freighted and should already be in Alice. My telegram had just missed them before they left for three weeks' holiday.

In the same mail I received a postcard from the airline company telling me that a parcel awaited me at the office.

This being Saturday morning, I collected the parcel and carried out my original plan of trying to find Wigley's water hole.

We drove up the Stuart Highway. The Charles was again about six inches over the road but we had no difficulty in getting through. A little further on I found the turn-off to the right. It was pretty rough with deep ruts and pools of muddy water. Sundry tracks branched off to right and left, so I stopped and armed myself with a scribbling pad on which I made a rough map as I went along. I hadn't a clue which way to go but just followed my nose, mapping as I went.

I must have had an invisible guide because, in a few minutes I found myself winding in and out of rocky hillocks towards cliffs at the base of which one could reasonably expect to find water.

I carried on and there amongst the trees I saw the glint of muddy water as the sun was reflected from it. It was quite clear that many cars had

95

parked here because there was a profusion of litter—beer cans, cartons and cigarette packets strewn on the ground.

We stopped and, as I opened the door, Jasper leapt to the ground and bounded into the muddy water. I had no idea how deep it was but it was very still and very dirty. Flies and ants were everywhere and I was not in the least anxious to sample it. Many large ghost gums and other trees were growing around, and great hunks of rock stuck out from the gravel.

I was not impressed with this as a place for a pleasant swim, but Jasper was having a marvellous time swimming round and round in circles snapping at water beetles, twigs and all sorts of floating debris.

I walked around and on the high side I discovered a rough track between the masses of rock. I followed this upwards until it petered out in a tangle of long grass on level ground clear of the trees. To my left, a jumble of rock piled up to a hundred feet or more. To my right was a line of trees which I took to mark the water course which fed the muddy pool.

Jasper now joined me, covered in mud. He made for the trees and I followed, stumbling over big boulders hidden by the long grass. Then I saw a gravelly beach backed by quite a long stretch of comparatively clear water. This was flowing and the light of the sun on the little ripples made it look inviting.

When I reached the edge, Jasper was already in and I called out "What's it like, mate?" Being so much alone with him as my only companion, I talk to him as to a human being. He seems to understand and answers with a look, a wag or a lick which I have learned to interpret as an intelligent comment.

He turned round and gave me a look which I interpreted as, "Come on in, it's great!" I wasted no time in stripping to my swimming trunks.

Although the water was fairly clear I couldn't see the bottom and wouldn't risk a dive. I stubbed my feet on several big rocks before reaching deep water, but the subsequent enjoyment made it well worth while.

We spent a good hour in this cool water bounded on one side by a wide gravel beach and on the other by overhanging rocks and trees. There was no litter here, so I assumed that few of the visitors took the trouble to come this far.

Back at the Kombi I had lunch before exploring in the other direction, where we found other pools among the rocks but none so good as the long stretch of water we had swum in.

Wigley's would see us often!

It did, in spite of reports from the locals that the ground was infested with snakes and the water with leeches. Of all the times we subsequently visited Wigley's I never saw a single snake, leech or offensive creature of any kind.

Back at the park, I unpacked my parcel. The fan was quite tiny but efficient. I checked its current consumption with my multi-meter and was very happy to find that I should be able to run it for hours on end without serious drain on the 12-volt battery.

Looking back during the climb up the 'Valley of the Winds'.

The Todd River flows . . .
. . . and dries up again.

At nine o'clock that night, the thermometer in Lou.'s caravan read ninety-four degrees. The sky was black with heavy cloud and lightning was flickering constantly.

I plugged in the fan and focussed it on my bunk. It was not very powerful but gave sufficient breeze to be noticeable. It was going all night and I slept well, being disturbed only by an extra heavy clap of thunder. The noise of the driving rain was soothing and I quickly went off to sleep again.

The morning was bright and sunny but last night's storm had been widespread. The radio said that the rail link with Port Augusta was cut several times between Alice Springs and Oodnadatta. The train with our food supplies had turned back, and the service was suspended indefinitely.

The Stuart Highway from Darwin had also been cut. The air was now our only link with civilisation and fresh food supplies were running low.

I imagined some storekeepers rubbing their hands with glee. They could now charge air-freight prices for everything. There were reported to be ample stocks of tinned food, but even that went up two or three cents without any justification that I could see. These stores relied solely upon the tourist to remain in business. The local residents knew their policy and restricted their custom to the stores which played the game.

The poor tourists were fair game for profiteering in towns like Alice. Whilst this was my experience with food and general commodities, I must record the other side which helped to restore the balance. I have nothing but praise for the treatment I received from other businesses.

One morning I found I had a flat tyre. I changed the wheel and took the offender in to a tyre specialist on the Stuart Highway for repair. They took the tyre off and examined the tube but could find no puncture. The trouble was a faulty valve which they replaced. They jacked the Kombi up and replaced the wheel in its correct position thus restoring the spare to the spare wheel compartment. They examined *all* the tyres, showing me cuts and places where trouble might occur. They didn't suggest that I should buy any new tyres or have any retreads, but told me that I should be quite safe on bitumen for at least two months.

When all was completed and at least half-an-hour had been spent on my vehicle, I asked what I owed them.

"That's okay," the manager said, "glad to be of help."

"That's very nice of you," I replied, "but what about the new valve?"

"Forget it, but please remember us when the time comes for *real* tyre service." He smiled as though he were really pleased to be of service.

I wouldn't have gone to anybody else for the two new tyres I *did* buy before leaving Alice for the north.

Fresh food was getting very scarce. Potatoes, green vegetables and bananas were quite unobtainable. Fortunately there were two good bakeries in town and bread was never in short supply. I could never reconcile myself to paying the price of rashers of bacon, but discovered that I could obtain a large packet of frozen bacon ends and pieces for 24 cents.

97

Milk, for those who had to have it, was 25 cents a pint but it could have been 50 cents for all I cared. I had now developed quite a liking for dried milk and always kept several tins in my emergency supplies.

A slight lessening of the rain influence allowed some of the roads to be re-opened. Two days later the Finke had fallen sufficiently to allow the 'Ghan', as the train is officially called, to get through.

This was followed by a buying spree from the population and another downpour from the heavens. The 'Ghan' was trapped in the Alice!

This sort of thing went on throughout my stay. It was now the beginning of March. The end of the month, they told me, would see the end of the 'wet'. Whilst my time in Alice Springs was interesting and enjoyable I was getting itchy feet and keenly looking forward to pushing on up the Stuart Highway to Darwin.

My job with Len Jensen had finished at last. It had gone on longer than I had dared hope and, although I had managed to get my bank balance to the convalescent stage, it had still a long way to go before I could pronounce it healthy.

I heard that another painter in the town was in need of a temporary hand so, after a quick interview, I found I had another week's work.

A church doing mission work with the Aboriginals had an old building adjacent to the presbytery. This was being used by the native women and children in some way, but exactly how I didn't know. The front of this building required a clean-up consisting of two coats of paint on the window frames and the door plus a rub-down and one coat on the weatherboarding. A newly-built canopy required full preparation and two coats. Normally this would have taken two men no more than three days but, as I should be working on it alone, my temporary boss, Luigi Busseti, reckoned it would take me a full week.

Working so close to the presbytery, I saw quite a lot of the officiating cleric, who kindly brought me tea and biscuits during the morning and afternoon.

Native women of all ages used this building and seemed to be coming and going or gossiping outside most of the time, whilst little children played around on the bare floors all day.

The windows were of the old sash type, the top sections of which had not been opened for years. The first one I attacked slid down without too much difficulty. The second one was stuck fast.

As I wielded my paint scraper to free the cracks I could see two tiny toddlers crawling around on the bare floor right under the window on which I was working.

The top sash yielded to my efforts and opened about four inches so I put my hand over the top to grasp it firmly in case the cord had broken and to prevent it from crashing to the bottom.

As I did so, a spider ran from between my fingers and dropped to the floor below. A glint of red had caught my eye and I looked closely.

There, on the floor, was unmistakably a red-backed spider and a large one! I closed the top sash and raised the bottom one so that I could put my leg over the sill and my foot on the spider but, by the time my foot touched the floor, the spider had disappeared.

The red-backed spider is venomous and a bite from one of these can make an adult quite sick for many weeks, so I've heard. To a little child, the bite has often proved fatal!

Now, there was one loose in a room with at least six small children and I felt that something should be done.

I hastened to the presbytery and explained what I had seen. I was shocked by the answer I received.

"Oh yes, the place is infested with them. There are so many we've given up worrying about them!"

After that, I killed all that I saw when I could catch them. What more could I do?

The rain having kept off for a few days, we set off for Standley Chasm at the week-end. The first twenty of the thirty-two mile trip was on good bitumen, then it deteriorated to a gravel track for the next six miles. The final stretch was very bad—deep ruts, boulders and treacherous mud.

The tourist literature describes this as a pleasant drive to the point where you have to leave your car. Then, it says, half-an-hour's walk brings you to the Chasm itself.

I feel sorry for any elderly people who fall for this. It could be more accurately described as one hour's rock climb. There is no path to follow. You just have to make for the gap in the range by scrambling over tree roots and rocks after pushing aside the scrubby bushes. The tourist brochure omitted to mention the advisability of wearing strong shoes with non-slip soles.

When we got there, I was very impressed by its rugged beauty. In places, the gravelly floor was only a few feet wide with towering cliffs of reddish sandstone rising sheer on both sides. The effect of the sunlight gave it an almost white-hot glow in contrast to the deep bluish-black shadows.

It wound its way right into the mountain rising all the time. At intervals, pools of crystal-clear water barred the way as we progressed far beyond the limits of the casual tourist.

Some of the pools were four feet deep and I had to go through holding camera and sandals above my head. Often the climb out up the sheer face of the rock was tricky with only one hand to pull myself up.

Whilst negotiating one of these, I heard a scuffle above. What I believed to be a large goanna slid down the ten feet of rock and hit the water with a big splash and then vanished into a deep fissure in the cliff before I could notice any details.

Jasper, who had evidently disturbed it, nearly followed but managed to turn so that only one of his back legs went over the edge. By a furious movement of his other three legs he succeeded in getting himself under control and staying on top. I don't know which got the bigger fright, the goanna or Jasper.

I I

Namatjira's Twin Gums

The art and tourist shops in Alice Springs all sold picture post-cards of this pair of similar ghost gums. I had seen them often as I passed them on the Hermannsburg Road on the way to Simpson's Gap. Compared with the picture post-cards these trees were a disappointment. They looked decidedly moth-eaten.

However, I was anxious to take a picture to compare the colouring with Namatjira's watercolour interpretation.

I called at every art shop in Alice in an endeavour to obtain a print of Namatjira's original work which had made the gums famous. Not one of these shops had a copy nor did the printers' catalogues list one but, I was assured, they could no doubt get me one if I could wait a week or two.

Then came the panic news on the radio. The famous twin gums were dying from some mysterious disease. An S.O.S. was broadcast for botanists with a special knowledge of eucalypt diseases to come forward with an explanation and a solution to save this tourist attraction from extinction.

I took the first opportunity to drive out, have a look at them and get my pictures before they finally succumbed to the mysterious malady.

About this time of the year after rain, several species of trees are attacked by a caterpillar. One gum tree in the caravan park was infested and campers were warned not to camp under it because this 'itchy grub' as it is called, on coming into contact with the skin, can cause intense irritation or even a serious infection.

By day, the insects live in silky net bags which hang from the branches. At night they come out to feed on the foliage.

I drove off the road and right up to the famous gums. A station sedan was parked nearby and I recognised it as belonging to Reg. and Aileen. They had had the same idea of getting some pictures.

We all stood gazing at the trees and the hundreds of dark objects hanging from the branches.

I said, "I shouldn't have thought it needed a botanist and an entomologist to tell them what's wrong with those trees."

Reg. answered, "It's quite obvious. Even *I* can see that those bloody bag-moth caterpillars are having a ball!"

The following day, the radio announced dramatically that the illness of the famous twin gums had, at last, been diagnosed. It was bag-moth caterpillars, or 'itchy grubs'. A full-scale programme of spraying with insecticide had been agreed upon. It was to be implemented immediately to try to save the precious gums.

A few days later, the 'Centralian Advocate' came out with the full story showing photographs of the trees with a man in a bucket dangling from the cable of a 35-foot crane and wearing protective mask and clothing. He was spraying the high branches with a mixture of dieldrin, HBC and DDT.

What was more interesting was the disclosure that, to the best of the experts' knowledge, Namatjira never had painted the twin gums.

His friend and mentor, Mr. Rex Battarbee, suggested that the whole legend was the creation of an enterprising Alice Springs taxi driver.

He was quoted as saying, "Actually, the trees made Albert famous and not Albert who made the trees famous."

I wonder if the trees have fully recovered and if they still call them 'Namatjira's Twin Gums'.

The sick ghost gums.

12

Sir Jasper Galahad

That night after dark, Jasper got himself mixed up in a fight. I was sitting outside enjoying a pipe in the cool of the evening. He was lying by my side.

Suddenly, from the distance came a scuffle and the high-pitched howling of a small dog in pain. Jasper took off like a stone from a catapult and disappeared behind a caravan. Then, all hell seemed to break loose—growling, snarling, snapping and the continued howling of the young dog.

Then, round the caravan streaked a large black and white dog of doubtful parentage closely followed by Jasper in full cry.

As they passed me, I managed to grab Jasper by the collar and slipped the chain on him. The howling continued and I went to investigate.

A woman whom I knew slightly was nursing and trying to console their small terrier which, I believe, was more frightened than hurt.

As I approached her husband turned on me in a fury and threatened to get his gun and shoot Jasper right then and there. I was taken aback.

His wife pleaded with him to keep calm as she knew that Jasper was not the culprit.

Seeing that their little pet had come to no serious harm, he calmed down and listened, while she explained how Butch, the black and white dog belonging to friends of theirs, had suddenly appeared, picked up the terrier by the scruff of its neck and shaken it like a rat. He was still doing this when Jasper arrived, but dropped the terrier to mix it with Jasper.

Jasper is not normally aggressive, but quite enjoys a good set-to when provoked. He had made the most of it and sent Butch off with his tail between his legs.

I felt quite proud of him when the good lady insisted that Jasper had saved their little dog's life.

When I returned to him he was licking his paw. There was blood all over the ground. I examined him and found a very deep gash in the large pad on his left foot. It was bleeding profusely. I bathed it in an antiseptic solution and tried to bandage it without much success.

Throughout the night I used yards and yards of bandage, lint and adhesive plaster. No matter which way I tied it or taped it, he had it off in half-an-hour.

Finally, I gave up in disgust and went to sleep to the accompaniment of his noisy licking. I assumed that he knew best.

There was no veterinary surgeon in private practice in Alice and I was directed to the Department of Animal Husbandry, where a veterinary service is available for pets as well as stock. I thought that the cut, being so deep, would need a couple of stitches but the efficient young man who examined him said it would be better if this could be avoided. It was still bleeding slightly.

He said it would heal quite quickly if only I could manage to keep it covered for two or three days. That was the problem!

He bandaged it much the same as I had done saying "He won't get that off in a hurry".

Less than an hour later I was back. The vet.'s bandaging was little better than mine. This time, he made a little bootee by shaping and sewing a piece of tough canvas he produced from a drawer. Imagine a private, city vet. taking so much trouble without charge!

I managed to keep this on and intact for two days until his teeth found the stitches in the bootee and before long it disintegrated. In spite of all the sand and dirt which collected round the cut, it then healed rapidly.

He even forgot to limp when he became interested in a lizard or, on our usual early morning walk on the racecourse, he ploughed into a flock of galahs which settled in hundreds on the track.

The end of March came and the locals told me the 'wet' was over. Everything was back to normal. All roads were open, the 'Ghan' was running regularly again with supplies from the south. The days were still very hot but the nights were becoming pleasantly cool—almost cold sometimes.

I still hadn't visited all the interesting places around, but there was one place that it had been my ambition to see for many years. Ayers Rock and the Olgas were a definite 'must' before I left Alice Springs behind.

13

Ayers Rock

The Rock is three hundred miles to the south-west of Alice Springs. Mt. Olga, or the Olgas as the group is called, is another twenty miles further west towards the border of Western Australia.

Knowing that the first hundred and twenty-five miles to Erldunda Station was a horror stretch, and the balance not even called a highway, I reckoned on at least two days' driving to reach the Rock.

I planned to spend two full days there and take another two days getting back to the Alice.

At ten o'clock on the Monday morning we left after telling the caravan park owner that I should be away about a week. Previous experience enabled me to negotiate that terrible road to Erldunda without incident. As we turned off to the west the road improved. It was rather corrugated but this could be partially avoided by driving with near-side wheels in the sand on the extreme left.

Overhanging bushes and small trees were the only real objection to this method and, of course, I had to be careful where rivulets had ploughed deep furrows across the road.

At a quarter-to-five I found a cosy spot twenty-two miles past Mt. Ebenezer. In spite of keeping the Kombi closed up, the interior had a fine layer of red dust over every surface and I had to wash up both before and after the evening meal.

Again the countryside was flat and almost featureless, comprising mostly stunted mulga and spinifex grass but, away to the left the long flat-topped shape of Mt. Conner could just be seen on the horizon.

The night was cool and the sky very clear, showing the stars as you never see them within a hundred miles of a city. Even the moths seemed to have taken a holiday.

We didn't leave that site until a quarter-to-nine and covered the remaining forty-six miles to Curtin Springs by ten o'clock, which was pretty good going.

Although I didn't really need it, I topped up the main tank here because there was no petrol available at the Rock and I liked to maintain a full supply out in this desolate country.

A few miles further on I stopped to speak to an old Aboriginal standing at the side of the road. He tried to sell me a woomera, but his English was very limited and I had the greatest difficulty in convincing him that I was not interested in his woomera but would consider a didjeridoo if he could rustle one up. We didn't do any business, but shook hands and parted with grins all round.

Then I nearly ran over a snake, or thought I did. On pulling up and jumping out to investigate I found it was not a snake but a line of large processional caterpillars crossing the road. They follow their leader bow-to-stern quite blindly and, it is said, if you kill the first one the others pile on top of each other's back like an acrobatic pyramid act. I hadn't the time or the inclination to test the truth of this, and left them in peace to continue their journey.

Another twenty miles or so and I was thrilled to get my first view of the fabulous monolith, the largest in the world and whose native name is Ul-U-Ru.

There it was standing up 1,143 feet above the otherwise flat and mulga scrub-covered plain. It was a purplish-brown colour in the morning sun and heat haze.

As we got nearer, detail became clearer, its folds and ridges carved by water action over the centuries, deep shadows showing the natural caves and overhanging ledges.

Its colour changed almost while I watched with the changing angle and intensity of the sunlight as it was varied by the light clouds which drifted across the sky.

I had heard and read so much about the beauty of the Rock that I was almost prepared to be disappointed. I was enthralled and impatient to commence my exploration.

Ayers Rock, the Olgas and much of the surrounding land is a national park and reserve, and all visitors are required to attend at the ranger's cottage on arrival.

Here I paid the necessary two-dollar fee for the privilege of camping there and was given a list of regulations covering the lighting of fires, disposal of rubbish, etc.

The ranger's wife gave me some useful information on when and where to take the best photographs. She told me of a spot on the other side of the Rock where the most impressive sunset pictures could be taken and the time that evening when it would be at its best. The spot she mentioned had been named Sunset Strip where a wide parking space had been cleared at the side of the road leading to the Olgas. There was ample space for tourist buses and cars to park while their occupants clicked their cameras during the few seconds when the lowering sun made the scene the most impressive.

She also told me position and time for sunrise shots.

It was getting on for midday as I drove slowly round the five-and-a-half mile circuit and back to where the road went westwards to the Olgas. I drove down this till I came to Sunset Strip, quite unmarked but obvious. I didn't fancy getting my pictures from here so I turned and came back about half-a-mile, walked fifty yards or so through the spinifex and salt-bush to a position on the opposite side of the road from the Strip. The view was good and the composition of my pictures should be far better.

I took a shot and marked the spot with a big cross which I scraped in the sand with my foot. I then went back to the Kombi and pushed three pieces of dead mulga wood into the sandy bank to identify the place where I had left the road. My rib-soled shoes gave me a clear indication of my tracks to the shooting position.

I resolved to come back later in the afternoon for another shot from exactly the same position before the last visit at sunset. I returned after a brief siesta.

Next I found the camping area, which was adequate if not luxurious. There were showers, toilets and a water tank. I needed nothing more.

I prepared my meal all ready to start cooking and returned to my exclusive position for the crucial sunset shots. My markers were quite effective and I had no difficulty in finding the same spot each time.

The optimum time for sunset that day was 6.15 p.m. I was standing ready at 6.10 when a coach pulled up immediately behind the Kombi. A flock of tourists burst out and swarmed on to the ground right in front of me completely spoiling my view. I was livid with anger and disgust when one of them spotted me and called to the others. My anger dispersed as they melted away to re-form on either side of me.

To make sure, I took a shot a few seconds before the last rays of the sun struck the Rock and gave it that red-hot, luminous appearance.

I was about to take the final master shot when a young woman leapt out of the bus where I presume she had been asleep and took up a position where all I could see in my view finder was a sun-blistered back. Someone called to her but she was too busy trying to focus her camera to take any notice and my master shot was ruined.

Thinking I might yet save the day, I dashed back to the Kombi, across the road and into the scrub on the other side and took one last desperate shot as the sun's rays passed their peak.

When I got back to the road, the bus was already loaded and started off as I reached the Kombi. I was feeling very annoyed that of all the land available, they should have chosen *my* position.

The colour of the Rock had now changed to a bluish-grey as the sun sank further below the horizon. It was such a contrast to the bright orange colour a few minutes before that I took another shot before returning to the camping area.

We both slept well and were up at 6.30 a.m. to catch the sunrise from a spot on a sandhill not more than two hundred yards from the camping area.

The twenty miles of road to the Olgas had recently been graded and was in excellent condition. The tourist season had hardly begun and we saw no one.

Unlike the Rock, the Olgas comprise a group of sandstone promontories in extraordinary formation. The domes have been weathered in a fantastically symmetrical fashion as if carved by some huge, super-human hand.

There are sixty-one in all and the highest of these, Mt. Olga itself, is 1,769 feet high.

Everything was still and the silence almost eerie.

The good road ceased at the foot of this formation and branched to left and right. A signpost pointing left said Olga Gorge six miles. The right-hand one indicated Valley of the Winds ten miles. We took the road to the left.

The gorge started off with a wide rock-strewn floor with a stream of clear water on the left. It rose and got narrower as the sheer sandstone cliffs converged to a narrow overgrown cleft at the top. We went as far as we could but could not get through the cleft because of the thickness of the undergrowth. Jasper spent most of his time in the water or leaping up the rocks in pursuit of anything that moved.

We doubled back to the signpost and drove the ten miles over a very third-class track to the Valley of the Winds. It got steadily worse as we went further into the valley. I then saw a small tourist bus pulled up a few yards ahead. This, I thought is the end of the road. If that bus can't go any further, neither will I make the attempt.

The six people in the party were having lunch. The driver was lying on his back with his cap over his eyes. As we got up to them I said "G'day" in my best Australian. They replied with "Hi", "How are yer" as well as "G'day".

I asked, "Have you been up the valley?"

The driver, now awake, replied "Sure!"

"Is it far to the top?" I queried.

"About half-an-hour".

"Worth going?"

"If you like that sort of thing," he grunted anxious to resume his nap.

One of the women volunteered, "We didn't go right to the end. It's too windy!"

The driver muttered, "When you get to the dead mice, that's it!" He lay down again and replaced the cap over his eyes with an unspoken "Now go away and leave me alone".

Thinking he was pulling my leg or, perhaps, using some Australianism with which I was unfamiliar I said "Thanks" and we carried on.

If he was trying to take the mickey out of me why hadn't at least one of the others sniggered? But not one of them had batted an eyelid when he had said "dead mice". I thought that it was perhaps a local name for some type of flora or even rocks. I made a mental note to look out for anything resembling defunct rodents.

107

It was quite a stiff walk up that valley. The towering dome on our right was nature carved with caves and ridges from some fantastic architectural plan.

I now began to understand why it was called The Valley of the Winds. It wasn't just a refreshing breeze, but a steady blow so consistent that it might have been activated by some giant electric fan. I didn't find it unpleasant, but it made the going harder.

The cleft at the head of the valley came into sight but it was still a long way off. I looked down and there, at my feet, was a dead mouse. A few yards away was another, then more until, as we went on, the ground was literally covered with them. Some were wet, some were dry. They must have been freshly dead for none was covered with ants or in any way showing signs of decomposition.

So he wasn't pulling my leg, after all. But this wasn't it! We continued for another twenty minutes until we reached the top of the valley.

The cliffs fell away on both sides to reveal a magnificent view of flat country backed by even more fantastic domes in the distance.

I sat for a few minutes enjoying the scene. I took a picture and started back. The dead mice covered an area of maybe ten yards. I was intrigued to know why and how they had died. Some could even have been drowned.

When we reached the Kombi again, Jasper was showing signs of fatigue. I was not surprised, considering the fact that he had covered three or four times the distance that I had.

This suited me because he would sleep peacefully in the van while I took a trip up the Rock. We had to pass the 'climbing point' on the way to the camping area.

Less than half-an-hour saw us at the base of the Rock again. It was deserted. I looked up and remembered seeing photographs of a party of tourists ascending. I could see the line of posts connected by a chain to assist climbers to negotiate a 'saddle' which formed a particularly steep portion.

I wasn't really bursting with energy after such a strenuous morning but, I thought, it doesn't look too severe. I'll just nip up to the top, have a look at the view and nip down again.

I got past the chain rail and realised that it was not so easy as I had imagined. I looked back and downwards. I could just see the top of the Kombi like a little 'Matchbox' toy. A few yards further and I couldn't see it any more, only the road like a thin straight line stretching to the Olgas.

When I had the chain rail I didn't need it, but at this point I could have used it because, in my opinion, the next 'saddle' was quite dangerous, falling away steeply on both sides. If I fell either way there was nothing to stop me—no bushes or anything to grab hold of—rolling with ever-increasing speed to the ground.

In the middle of this awkward section, a large eagle swept down to within a few feet of my head. It was so close that I could see every detail of its plumage. Its eyes were fixed upon me as it circled around.

I sat down and reached for my camera. It was too good an opportunity to miss but I did miss it because, by the time that I had opened up the case and got the view finder to my eye, the eagle had dropped to some point below me and was out of sight.

However, I was glad of the excuse for a rest as the going was not too easy. Apart from the gradient, the surface was scaly and small pieces would flake off as I pushed against them with my feet.

The way was now marked with painted white lines which took me up over a ridge then down into a trough, then up again to a higher ridge, then down again, and so on, as the track crossed the numerous waterworn depressions which cover the monolith.

The gradient was now generally much easier, but I was feeling the effects of a busy day coupled with the fact that I was not so young as I used to be. I nearly turned back but, having come so far, I just had to reach the summit.

At this point I saw the first human beings since my encounter with the tourist bus at the Valley of the Winds. Two young fellows were on their way down. They gave me a welcome drink from their water bottle and told me that the summit was only about ten minutes away.

When I reached it I found a post surrounded by a cairn of stones. Beside it was the wreck of the original post, and notice board lying on the ground with a metal box containing a book of signatures of all the hardy visitors who had made the climb. I added my name, took a picture and started the descent.

Coming down was as tiring as going up, but in a different way. It was all a matter of opposing the laws of gravity. To haul the body up by leg-power is one thing. To hold it back and prevent it from reaching the ground too fast is another.

When I finally staggered into the Kombi, my thighs and calves were aching abominably. I don't know how long it took to climb up, but from the summit to the ground took me thirty-five minutes.

Next morning we were up early and visited all the main interesting features of the Rock itself—the natural caves curved like the inside of a shell with Aboriginal paintings on the walls and ceilings, the springs and waterholes.

After lunch, we started on our journey back to the Alice. I would like to have stayed longer, to have found a full-blooded Aboriginal who spoke English and could have told me the legends of Ul-U-Ru without the semi-humorous, parrot-learned jargon of the white tourist guide.

I wouldn't have missed that visit to Ayers Rock for anything. To visit the Centre of Australia without seeing the wonders of the world's greatest monolith would be like going to Egypt and skipping the Valley of the Kings.

The journey back to Alice Springs was uneventful apart from meeting an old Afghan with two mission Aboriginals and a couple of camels. They demanded twenty cents to be photographed. I paid the twenty cents, but never saw the picture. Perhaps I forgot to remove the lens cap.

From the Rock, I had tried once to contact Alice Springs on the two-way radio without success. Reception was not very good, but I had several homesteads nattering to each other. Not one was using correct procedure and giving their call signs.

One opened up "Hello Harry, this is George. How'd you get on today. Over."

Presumably Harry answered, "Hi, George. No good. The rotten hack came in fourth. I did about fifty dollars. What about you? Over."

"Hard luck, Harry. I just about broke even. Got something good for Saturday. Ten to one and a cert. Coming over tomorrow? Over."

"Can't make it tomorrow. Next week perhaps. Over."

"Okay. Give us a call. Cheerio."

"Hooray!"

And that was that.

I happened to meet George in the flesh when he was in Alice just before I left. I asked him why he didn't use correct procedure as laid down in the Rules and Regulations of the P.M.G.'s Department. Radio Branch and, in particular, why he didn't give his call sign.

"Why the hell should I?" he argued. "Everybody knows who *I* am. Everybody knows my voice!"

Friday saw us back at the caravan park, where I planned to spend the weekend cleaning up and making final preparations for the long haul up the Stuart Highway to Darwin. We were greeted with an overcast sky.

Before I left, I wanted to get my radio transmitter checked by George Brown, the Director of the Royal Flying Doctor Service in Alice Springs. He was very helpful and tested it thoroughly both on his equipment and on the air. He said it was perfect and probably I had failed to hop in quick enough during my test from the Rock and had been swamped by nearer transmitters. I was relieved that it was in good order, and promised to call him on the way to Tennant Creek for a practical test.

On Sunday a tourist bus pulled into the caravan park and the passengers took quick advantage of a lull in the rain to erect their little double tents. The driver slung portable fluorescent lights from the branches of trees, set up their small petrol-electric generator and got a fire going for a barbecue tea.

Then the rain started again. The sizzling of the steaks was accompanied by the spitting hiss as the rain made a determined attempt to put out the fire.

It was a pitiful sight to see these poor campers wandering about with a loaded plate in one hand, 'irons' in the other and a plastic raincoat over their heads, trying to find somewhere dry to consume the meal which, no doubt, they had all been keenly looking forward to. Some went back into the bus, others into their tents and the remainder into the 'summer-house' which housed our community fridge.

But there was worse to come. As darkness fell the rain increased and kept up a steady downpour all night. Most of the tents were washed out, deep pools of water built up over the whole of the park.

It was six o'clock in the morning before the rain eased. By half-past, patches of blue sky appeared. Then the blessed sun came out in all its hot glory to dry out the blankets, bedding and clothes which had been exposed to the effects of the deluge.

Once again the Todd Tiver was flowing. The indicators showed five feet of water at the Causeway and had cut the east side of Alice off for all motor traffic.

Many east-siders had come over for shopping and now had to leave their cars and walk back across the high-level footpath to get their lunch.

It was quite an occasion. Crowds gathered to see the river actually *flowing* through the town. It may happen once a year, but seldom with the spectacle it presented this day.

It was quite late in the evening before the water had fallen enough to allow bold drivers to churn their way through the still fast-flowing torrent. Aboriginal youngsters were having a fine time pushing through cars which stalled in the middle.

Then came the news on the radio. The Finke River had cut the railway again. The south road was cut in several places and sections of the Stuart Highway were impassable.

They had assured me that the 'wet' was over!

The road to Ayers Rock was a temporary write-off, so I had timed my trip luckily.

I had planned to leave the Alice at crack of dawn the next day. I now had serious doubts that I should make it so I decided that, weather permitting, I would do my washing and have another go at removing the dust from the cupboards and shelves in the Kombi. Better spend the day in some useful occupation than sitting on the banks of some river waiting for the water to go down.

I did these and several other minor jobs before taking a trip to the police station to ascertain the condition of the Stuart Highway. The officer told me that it was still cut at one point between Alice and Tennant Creek but the water was falling and, if no further rain occurred, it was expected to be passable by tomorrow.

When I went to bed the sky was still clear but I awoke several times in the night expecting to hear the tapping of the first drops on the windows portending a further deluge.

But it kept fine and at seven a.m. I was ready to go when I noticed that I'd got a 'flat'—in the brand new tyre I had had fitted a week ago. I tried to change the wheel and stripped the thread on my jack.

Seeing my predicament, Reg came over with his jack but even this wouldn't raise the heavy Kombi high enough to get the wheel off.

I walked to the nearest public telephone to get assistance from the A.A.N.T. The phone was out of order so, by the time I had found a telephone working, got the help and driven into town to get the puncture fixed, it was eight-thirty. My friends, the tyre service people, found that a three-inch nail had gone straight into the tyre.

My 'crack of dawn' departure was postponed till ten o'clock.

Tennant Creek is three hundred and fifteen miles from Alice and I particularly wanted to make it that day.

I hadn't much hope but the bitumen was good, the day was fine and reasonably cool so I put my foot down.

Approaching the 'Olgas'.

Katherine Gorge.
A large goanna looking for a tree up which to escape. He was about 7 feet long.

Combo Water Hole, the inspiration for Banjo Paterson's 'Waltzing Matilda'.
The 'puddling' tank.

14

Up the Stuart Highway

Just outside Tea Tree Well, one hundred and twenty miles north of Alice, I stopped and erected my 35-foot telescopic antenna.

I called RJD, the call-sign of the Flying Doctor Base at Alice after waiting for a suitable opportunity to 'jump in' between telegrams. I was delighted to get a 'loud and clear' answer to my test call.

This operation took about half-an-hour and the flies were so bad that I preferred to postpone lunch and push on a little further.

Another thirteen miles and we were at Central Mt. Stuart, the geographical centre of Australia.

The road was good and the scenery uninspiring so that there was no encouragement to dawdle. The miles were dropping off the speedo like water from a dripping tap and the next seventy-two miles brought us to the famous Devil's Marbles.

These huge granite boulders were strewn about on both sides of the road and piled one on top of the other. Some were balanced precariously as if the slightest touch would send them crashing down to the complete destruction of anything they might land on.

According to aboriginal legend, these were the eggs laid by the mythical Rainbow Snake.

They were an impressive sight which I wished to photograph, but those which would have made the most striking pictures had been defaced by vandals. The pictures I took were less spectacular, but, at least, were free from such painted lunacy.

Hurrying back to the Kombi, I tripped and fell flat on my face. In saving the camera from damage, I fell heavily, twisting my arm and wrenching my shoulder. I assumed that the spirit of the Rainbow Snake disapproved of me taking photographs of her hard-baked eggs and hoped that she had treated the vandals with much greater severity.

The going continued good and we arrived in Tennant Creek at 5 p.m.— exactly seven hours after leaving the Alice. Allowing at least an hour for

113

stops, I was very surprised to find that we had *averaged* over 52 m.p.h. for the trip of over three hundred miles.

I was not impressed with the architecture or the layout of Tennant Creek. It had all the essential services of a mining township but, apart from that, there was little of interest.

Driving through I was hailed by a man supervising the work of a road gang (the main street certainly needed a lot of attention). I pulled up and recognised him as a very friendly type whom I had met at the Wintersun caravan park a week or two previously.

He told me that there was no caravan park yet open in Tennant Creek but that his wife was in charge of the first caravan park under construction and at present being used by the Main Roads Department Construction teams.

I found the park and was welcomed. Everything was laid on except electricity which I didn't need anyway. The amenities block was new and ample hot water was supplied by a solar system. That night I had my shower by candlelight.

We set off from Tennant Creek about 8.15 on the following morning without any planned destination. Katherine was the next place of any consequence. This was over four hundred miles away and I didn't fancy tackling it in one hop.

There could be some interesting features in between but I should make a note of these and take them in on the way back.

I was anxious to get to Darwin as quickly as possible because my mail from Alice was being re-directed. There ought to be some processed film there which might suffer if left too long in the steamy heat of the 'Top End'.

Sixteen miles north of Tennant Creek we came to the junction of the Stuart and Barkly Highways. As we passed the Flynn Memorial I looked along the Barkly Highway—two hundred and eighty miles of practically nothing to the Queensland border. That was the road we should be taking to Mt. Isa when we returned from Darwin.

The bitumen now started to deteriorate and I can only describe it as moth-eaten and treacherous. Deep potholes were encountered without warning and at any speed over 45 it was essential to keep my eyes glued to the surface of the road ahead.

We passed through Elliot and Newcastle Waters, Dunmarra and Daly Waters, Larrimah (the beginning of the railway line to Darwin) and Mataranka.

At 5.15 p.m. I was tired and hungry so decided to pull off the road and camp for the night. It had been a fairly good day's run—three hundred and seventy miles and only about forty miles short of Katherine.

For the first time for months I had my shower in a bucket.

We got going again at 8 a.m. Passing through Katherine I noted that this place was worth seeing much more of and I looked forward to spending a day or two here on the way back.

A strong head wind kept our speed down. The scenery became more and more interesting and the road more and more difficult—narrow, winding and in poor condition.

From Pine Creek to Adelaide River we struck a horror stretch of a new kind—waves!

These waves occur at what a motorist could be excused for imagining as a carefully calculated frequency as the violent up and down motion builds up to a climax so that, if the roof of the vehicle were removed, the driver and passengers would be ejected as a pilot from a supersonic jet in distress.

There is a fixed sequence for this type of entertainment.

Firstly comes a stretch of good bitumen for about half-a-mile just to give you confidence, then waves till you are on the point of exhaustion. This is followed by deep potholes so arranged that, if you steer to avoid one, you are bound to plumb another to its depths.

One hundred miles of this and you're thinking unkind thoughts about the Northern Territory Administration Main Roads Department.

Then, to add to the fun, come Caution signs and Curve indicators. Some are genuine, some are phoney and some are missing altogether. The game is to give you a series of genuine ones, then a couple of phoneys. These are to demonstrate just how bad a hazard can be if you haven't been warned.

There's never a dull moment. Maybe there's something in the scenery that you're not supposed to see. You get no chance to look.

When you're wise to all this (if you're still mobile) they play another game. This is called 'Road Works Ahead' consisting of signs indicating that men and machines are doing something about this lousy road. You keep a sharp look-out without reward.

I imagined that all these busy workmen had heard me coming and hastily 'went bush' complete with their graders, rollers and what-have-you.

We eventually arrived in Darwin about 3 p.m., gasping and sweating in the sticky heat.

15

Darwin

Darwin had had three inches of rain in the night and there were pools of muddy water everywhere. My first impression was not a good one. It seemed like a city which had outgrown itself.

Buildings of great architectural beauty stood side by side with tumble-down shacks, some still showing evidence of the Japanese bombing in 1942.

Whilst the majority of streets had a strip of bitumen down the centre, only those in the centre of town could boast kerb-to-kerb sealing. Even here narrow streets linking the three main thoroughfares would have made a bush track look like a speedway.

I went straight to the Post Office, a fine modern building. I was both disgusted and disconcerted to find that no mail had come through for me.

Next I went to the Government Tourist Bureau for all the relevant literature. Included in this was a list of caravan parks describing amenities and rates charged.

After an overpriced and under-serviced night in the Mendil Beach camping area, we spent the morning touring around, getting the hang of the geography and inspecting the other caravan parks. There is a free camping area at Eastpoint amongst the old concrete fortifications, but a sight of some of the tents, shacks and their occupants put this at the bottom of the list and only to be resorted to in desperation.

In my opinion, all these parks were too expensive for the doubtful amenities they offered and a trip further afield seemed called for.

We went back along the Stuart Highway eight miles till we came to the Berrimah turnoff. Here, the Overlanders Caravan Park was full so I took a right-angle turn into McMillan's Road. A few hundred yards off the main highway was the Bindaree Park.

This was fairly new and had excellent amenities including hot water, washing machines and electric shaver points. What was more, the charge was only 50 cents per night or three dollars a week, I booked in and we were happy there for the rest of our stay.

It was less than fifteen minutes drive into town, peaceful, quiet and relaxing.

We had lunch there and then returned to the city for a further exploration. Fannie Bay is a pretty spot and very popular for sailing but I was more interested in having a swim. It was not the enjoyment I had looked forward to. The water is too shallow and too warm. There was no surf.

I like to get a little bit of a shock when I plunge in but this was like getting into a warm bath. I found it enervating instead of being exhilarating—rather like the Red Sea.

Jasper seemed to enjoy it but only found one solitary seagull to chase. A local resident told me that there were no seagulls around Darwin and was quite staggered when he saw that Jasper had discovered this one. We never saw another.

It didn't take long to see the sights of Darwin so, as the weather had settled down, I thought it would be a good idea to visit some of the outlying places of interest.

It is a sixty-six mile run to the uranium mines at Rum Jungle. We arrived there at 10.20 a.m., just in time to join a conducted tour. A young Sydney couple was the only other interested party and we were taken round in a station wagon by an official who explained everything and even allowed us to take pictures and a sample of the ore which, he warned, should be kept clear of cameras or photographic equipment.

Knowing that I couldn't take Jasper into the mine, I had let him loose when we arrived for a sniff round and general investigation.

Of course, he had found water—a large lake adjoining the mine and had spent at least ten minutes swimming round and round.

I learned during the tour that this water was contaminated—not by radio-activity but by sulphuric acid. I was very worried until our guide assured me that no harm would come to him or anybody swimming in it, so long as they had a shower afterwards.

On the way back, we stopped at the Manton River crossing which was about six inches over the road. We found a shady glade for lunch and a cooling dip in the crystal-clear water where, I hoped, Jasper would de-contaminate himself. He must have been successful, because he didn't froth or generate chlorine gas when he subsequently went into the sea.

A few more similar trips out between showers and I had had as much as I could afford of Darwin.

I had been shocked at the high prices of essential commodities in the shops—even higher than at Alice Springs. My bank balance was leaking away and the prospect of getting a job before we got to Mt. Isa was remote.

I don't think I could have worked in Darwin even had I wanted to. I suppose I should have got used to the humidity and immune to sand-fly bites in time but, having seen enough of the 'Top End', I was only too anxious to start south again.

Again it rained all night and all day. The radio said that Darwin had had the heaviest May rainfall for eighty-nine years—six inches so far this

Fannie Bay, Darwin.

Uranium ore produced from opencut at Rum Jungle. Stockpile of zinc ore in background.

month. The forecast was for no let-up for thirty-six hours. The rain stopped for half-an-hour then started again, worse than ever.

I spent most of the time in the van reading, sleeping and listening to the radio. A news flash! A potential cyclone was developing about forty-five miles off this coast. All small ships were warned to look to their moorings! Rain for the next two days at least!

Both the Stuart and the Barkly Highways were cut, likewise the south road from Alice Springs. Ayers Rock was completely cut off still—even by air as the airfield was flooded. Tourist buses and the chalets were running short of food.

I thought of those people I had passed on their way to the Rock. They must be still stranded there.

I lay back on my bunk with feelings of frustration at being stuck in this expensive and remote little city, on my way to more interesting places. Jasper added to my irritation by taking off into the rain and returning an hour later in such a state that even the mosquitoes wouldn't go near him. He had managed to find some evil-smelling muck to roll in.

The next day—the day I had expected to leave—the rain ceased about ten in the morning. In spite of a heavily overcast sky no more rain fell.

We drove to Fannie Bay. Jasper was still smelling and I thought a swim might help to alleviate it. The sun came out and we returned to the caravan park after doing some shopping.

For want of something better to do, I diligently started sorting out the contents of the drawers and shelves. Lots of old shorts and shoes were jettisoned and by a redistribution of the contents I found that I could practically empty one of the suitcases from the roof-rack to take some of the clutter from inside.

I felt better now. Jasper had also jettisoned most of his smell in the sea. The radio said that the Stuart Highway should be open by the morning with care, but travellers should check with the Civil Defence authorities before proceeding.

The next morning was sunny but still with a few clouds about. The early morning news bulletin said nothing about the Stuart Highway so I drove into town for a call at the P.O. and the Civil Defence H.Q. They had no news about the road and assumed that it was passable. I decided to chance it.

16

We turn south again

I set off with relief at being on the move again. I had originally intended spending only three days in Darwin. I had been there for nine and exceeded my living allowance.

The Manton River had risen since we last saw it. It was now about ten inches over the road, but offered no serious obstacle. The Glenluckie Creek was quite a torrent but, being shallow, was quite easily negotiated.

The bad bitumen was now even worse. The potholes were deeper and more numerous than when we had come up this road. These were now the only signs of the recent heavy rains.

It was 4.15 when we arrived in Katherine. We only stopped for a few minutes then made for the Katherine Gorge, twenty miles to the east along a dirt road.

I expected to camp in the bush here, but was surprised to find a caravan park under construction. Clean toilets and showers were already in use. Bulldozers and graders were making a level site under the trees in a delightful setting.

From this point, boats could be hired complete with outboard motor and driver who also acted as guide to the beauties of this magnificent gorge. I booked for an early trip in the morning.

I gave Jasper his dinner after which he wasted no time in making his usual tour of inspection and local smells. I sat down to my meal with the door open to air the Kombi thoroughly before the mosquitoes got busy on *their* evening meal.

Suddenly, under the table I felt something cold on my thonged foot. I immediately thought of a snake sliding across my ankle. Don't move, I thought. I was petrified! I sat frozen for what seemed an age with my loaded fork half way to my mouth.

There was also no movement from the horror under the table. I slowly and carefully put the fork down and very, very gingerly stretched my neck so that I could look down without moving my body.

Still I couldn't see my foot. The rapidly approaching darkness and the added gloom under the table made it impossible.

By a further bone-wracking stretch I could just reach my torch, which I always keep handy on the top of the medicine chest. I aimed it and switched on.

Two eyes in a little green head looked up at me and I could see the pulsating of its throat. Had it really been a snake I don't know what I should have done, but as it was only a little green frog I relaxed and burst out laughing perhaps a little hysterically. With that it hopped up on to the bunk beside me, then right over the table on to the other bunk.

I had no wish to have a bed-fellow, at least not one as cold and clammy as this little chap, so I spent the next few minutes chasing it round the inside of the Kombi until I finally persuaded it to leave through the doorway. I closed the door, switched on the light and finished my meal, which was now almost cold.

I was having my second cup of tea and a smoke when I felt something crawling on my back. Normally, I would have brushed it away and thought no more about it but a little voice within me said, "Grab it and have a look at it in the light."

I did just that. It was a tick! It was about to get its head in, but I removed it without much difficulty. Ticks are mighty hard to kill and offer more resistance than a flea, but I managed to crush it with the aid of the handle of my knife.

By now, Jasper had returned and I hastily called him in for an inspection. Lo and behold, there was one about the same size and colour getting itself organised in his ear.

I disposed of it in the same manner and resolved that, from now on, he would receive a twice-daily inspection.

When we went to bed quite a few more campers had arrived and I anticipated that the boats would be well patronised in the morning.

I had booked on the eight o'clock trip and we were at the little jetty on time. The driver wasn't up, wasn't even awake. However, his only competitor, whose party was ready to go, woke him and he turned out smartly, unshaven and without breakfast.

He was in no hurry to go and showed me his collection of live snakes in plastic jars and bottles. He was quite young, wore a billy-goat beard and came from Sydney he told me. He had taken this job because he was fascinated by natural fauna.

He was very proud of his snakes, particularly the golden brown one he had caught a few days ago. He had no idea whether it were venomous or not and, I gather, didn't care.

He told how every evening at dusk he watched the flying foxes making their way up the gorge to the feeding grounds but, to date, he has never witnessed their return. He had often waited up all night in the vain hope that he would see them come back.

Jasper and I were his only clients and we chugged up the gorge in a

121

flat-bottomed boat which could, if necessary, accommodate six or more passengers. The rain continued for the first mile or so and then, true to his prediction, a patch of blue sky appeared, the rain ceased and the sun came out.

The clear, deep water between the sheer cliffs on either side was an impressive yet peaceful sight. Several times he pulled in under the cliff walls to examine a cleft, crevice or small cave. In some of these, bats were resting. In two others, we discovered dangerous-looking yellow and brown banded snakes, coiled and dormant in assumed security.

Our friend got quite excited about these and announced his intention of coming back later in the day to get them for his collection.

I would like to have seen him in action but refrained from suggesting that there is no time like the present. I had no wish to share the boat with a couple of reptiles which could have been highly venomous.

Coming back we landed on one or two small beaches where crocodile tracks were clearly visible in the sandy gravel. In this case I was not worried because I knew that, whilst many crocodiles live in the dark waters of Katherine Gorge, they are the fresh water variety and supposedly harmless to man.

Back at Katherine I took a quick look around the township and thought what a good base it would make for a wild-life photographic safari. I was told that there were plenty of wild buffalo around here.

My next objective was Mataranka where I hoped to call at the homestead and then bathe in the hot bore baths.

This seemed to be a day of snakes. Just short of Mataranka I spotted a very long black snake crossing the road ahead. He was taking his time and I pulled up about four yards away.

I leapt out with the camera but, as I moved forward for the shot, he accelerated rapidly and disappeared into the long grass before I could even get the viewfinder to my eye.

17

I pick up a hitch hiker

Just before the turn-off to the homestead I was hailed by a young man obviously hoping for a ride. I waved him away for two reasons. Firstly, I do not normally pick up stray people cadging a ride and, secondly, I refuse to be encumbered with a passenger when visiting a place where I may desire to remain for some hours.

I made the turn and drove the six miles to the homestead.

On the way back I decided to talk to that hitch-hiker and weigh him up—if he were still there. He had looked a decent type and my rule wasn't inflexible.

He was there and greeted me with a pleasant smile. I asked him where he was making for. He answered, in good English with a strong German accent, "Tennant Creek!"

Still not sure of him, I explained that I was not going to Tennant Creek. At this point I didn't think it necessary to tell him that I turned off only sixteen miles short of it.

He told me that it was his second day in Australia. He had come from Frankfurt and had worked his way through Yugoslavia, Greece, Turkey, Iran, Afghanistan, Pakistan, India, Ceylon, Thailand, Malaysia, Singapore, Indonesia and had flown from Timor to Darwin.

His name was Paul Hausmann and his plan, he said, was to work his way to Sydney, take a ship to Panama via Tahiti and then travel north to Canada.

I hesitated no more but said, "Hop in, I'll take you to Tennant Creek".

I didn't regret that decision. For the next hundred and six miles he kept me entertained with stories of his adventures.

Just south of Daly Waters, I spotted another snake crossing the road in front of us. As usual, I pulled up, grabbed the camera and made a wide arc on foot to get in front of it so that it would have to make an about-turn to get away before I could get a picture.

This specimen was between four and five feet long and quite fat—I should say up to four inches in diameter. It was a dirty yellow colour with irregular brown rings. Its head and neck were a shiny jet black, as if it had been dipped in gloss enamel.

It didn't seem concerned that I was slowly creeping nearer and nearer to its black head. I am not usually so bold, but my enthusiasm to get the picture ran away with me.

I focussed, pressed the release then slowly retreated without taking my eyes off that head, watching for the slightest indication that he might have a go at me. I had heard that this was the proper thing to do.

I needn't have worried. He seemed more interested in sunning himself than in what I was doing.

My problem now was to get him out of my path. I had got what I wanted and had no wish to run over him. Only by throwing rocks at his tail did we finally persuade him to glide unhurriedly into the grass and allow us to proceed.

We stopped at Dunmarra hoping to get a cold beer and some petrol, but this proved to be the 'pub with no beer'. The proprietor told us that there had been a wedding party the night before and they had cleaned him out.

When I asked for petrol he said he was out of that too, so I assumed that when the grog ran out, the revellers had started on the petrol.

I described the snake and asked him if he could identify it.

"Oh, that was a bandy-bandy," he replied. "I've no time for those bastards. Always take a shot gun to 'em."

I doubted if it were a bandy-bandy which I always thought were smaller than that. (It was identified later as a black-headed rock python.)

There was no point in dallying in Dunmarra so we pushed on for a few more miles before pulling off the road for the night. I set up the annexe for Rolf's benefit, cooked a meal and, after clearing up, we talked on till quite late.

The night sky was the most beautiful I had ever seen. The stars were especially brilliant. Two especially large ones fascinated us both. We looked at each other and wondered. These two were flashing—green, blue, red, yellow in no fixed order—almost like traffic lights seen at a great distance. Could they be U.F.O.'s? Finally, we agreed that they were stars and turned in.

We arrived at Tennant Creek next afternoon. Rolf intended to try his luck in the Peko mine. He had five months to work his way to Sydney where he expected to embark for Tahiti on Oct. 28th. Was he going home from Canada? I asked. No! Japan was the next country on his list.

I left Rolf at the employment office, did some shopping after cashing another travellers' cheque and doubled back the sixteen miles to the Barkly Highway.

I had hoped to cover the four hundred and eighteen miles to Mt. Isa by the following night so that the more miles I could put behind me today the better.

After ninety miles I had had enough and camped.

18

Mud lark

The Barkly was in excellent condition—all good bitumen in a strip just wide enough to pass another car without leaving the sealed surface. Passing the numerous beef trains is a different matter. These juggernauts have to be treated with great respect. They comprise a huge and powerful truck towing trailers loaded with live cattle. They can transport mobs of cattle hundreds of miles to the sales or abattoirs without loss of condition and have made the traditional drover almost obsolete.

I left the overnight campsite at 8 o'clock and it took only a few minutes to reach Frewena.

This little collection of buildings is a few hundred yards off the bitumen. A muddy track constituted the road. The combined pub, store and petrol station was the hub of many other muddy tracks leading from all directions.

On requesting petrol, I was told that I should have to wait about twenty minutes until the man arrived to 'start the engine'.

A couple of other vehicles had arrived for petrol. We waited and waited long after the twenty minutes and, from chance remarks overheard, I gathered that the engine starter was still sleeping it off after a bender the night before.

In desperation, it was suggested that we should have to get our petrol from a 44-gallon drum by the aid of a hand-pump. All the customers left the bar to help set it up. It was just 'petrol'. Nobody knew what make or grade.

I took five gallons aboard, paid for it and moved off. I drove along the track I thought I had come in by. I had gone about a hundred yards when the surface became softer and softer and I saw a large pool of water in front. Realising that I was on the wrong track I pulled up, slipped into reverse and tried to back up. The back wheels spun and sank up to the hubcaps in black mud. Nothing I could do would stop those back wheels spinning and sinking deeper. I jumped out into ankle-deep mud.

It had become so much cooler since leaving the Stuart Highway that I had put on fresh clothes that morning—clean shorts, clean shirt, clean socks and new sandals which I had bought in Alice Springs and not worn before.

Jasper leapt out after me straight into the oozy black mess.

I squelched my way back to the pub for assistance. Inside I announced my difficulty. One man immediately offered, "Don't worry, I'll get you out".

Outside, he got into a Holden of ancient vintage and drove out to the Kombi. He delved into the boot and extracted a length of tatty-looking rope. We coupled up and commenced operations. The rope went taut, and the Holden went down to the hubcaps.! We took the rope off and he did everything he knew, but couldn't shift that Holden.

So we both squelched back to the pub where a conference was convened over glasses of beer.

There was no four-wheel drive vehicle available, so it was decided that the one and only truck should back as near as possible to the vehicles whilst remaining on firm ground. A long rope would then be attached to each vehicle in turn and the extraction made in that way.

It took some time to find sufficient pieces of rope to be tied together to reach the distance but, when this was done, the Holden came out easily and was driven out of the way on to dry ground. The Kombi proved more of a problem. Not only was it heavier, but it had gone farther into the morass.

Having no towbar on the Kombi, we hitched the rope round the rear bumper bar and hoped for the best.

The first tug broke the rope. The thin edges of the bumper had cut the rope. I then found lots of rag in the toolbox and made a pad to prevent a recurrence.

After much revving of engines and creaks from the truck, the Kombi was pulled clear and on to dry ground.

We didn't even think of cleaning up before entering the bar where I 'shouted' for everybody. I tried to 'shout' again but they wouldn't allow it. I had bought them all a beer—now it was their turn. It wasn't every day that something happened to justify a celebration. Everyone bought a round, including the publican, and still they wouldn't let me buy them another.

I was regaled with highly coloured and graphic accounts of vehicles which had been bogged; how a grader had completely disappeared into a claypan never to be seen again; how a bulldozer had sunk to the top of its exhaust pipe and it had taken three months to recover it.

Everyone had some story to tell and I enjoyed them all—probably on account of the beer I had consumed.

I washed off as much of the mud as possible and got away at 11.30. This incident had completely upset my timetable but it was worth it to experience the camaraderie of these out-back Australians. This is the first time I had asked for help and it was given willingly and cheerfully.

126

Later that day I had another encounter with a snake. I didn't see this one in time to avoid all four wheels passing over it. Discounting the waves of its body, it was considerably longer than the width of the Kombi. At a rough guess I should say it was eight or nine feet long with a shiny, olive-green body.

In spite of the fact that all four wheels had passed over it, it disappeared like a flash into the scrubby side of the road.

The Barkly Highway is no scenic delight. The road is so straight and the country so flat you can see the road like a gradually thinning ribbon vanishing at the horizon.

We crossed the border into Queensland and ran into Camooweal about 3.30 p.m. I was told at Frewena not to blink as I went through otherwise I should miss it. It wasn't quite as bad as that, but I found no encouragement to stop.

At a quarter to four it was nearly time to call it a day but we pushed on for another twenty miles. I was looking for a firm, clear spot off the road where we could camp well clear of long grass. At this particular time snakes seemed to be very active. I have heard that it is not uncommon for a snake to crawl up under a vehicle and find a cranny somewhere to hide in. I had met a man who had actually been bitten while changing a wheel on the bitumen. He was convinced that it had been concealed under the car and was disturbed by the jack.

19

Queensland again

It was good to be back in the Sunshine State again, but there was a marked deterioration in the highway as we crossed the border.

On the Northern Territory side, the edges of the bitumen were straight and neat. There was an indicator post every five miles so that you knew where you were. There were also adequate warnings of 'soft edges'. On the Queensland side, the edges became ragged. White posts at irregular intervals gave no indication of how many miles you were from anywhere.

However, the main area of bitumen was good and we made a leisurely and uneventful run into Mt. Isa, where the scenery was rugged and much more interesting.

The red and white bandied stack of the mine was visible long before we entered the town, as it was then. It was declared a city during our stay there.

We arrived at 10.45 by my watch and the clocks in the Kombi. I thought they had all gone haywire when I saw that the Post Office clock said 11.15. Then I remembered that, somewhere along the highway we had crossed the line between Central and Eastern Time.

I drove round to get my bearings and noted with satisfaction that the main capital city self-service stores were represented, but when I went into one I was shocked to find that the prices were even higher than Darwin.

The charges for a camping site were staggering—$1.50 per night. Experience had proved that caravan parks near the centre of activity were usually expensive and not necessarily good.

I heard of one just fifteen minutes quiet drive back along the highway to the turn-off to Lake Moondarra, or the 'Dam' as the locals call it.

We crossed the Leichhardt River by a causeway over which a few inches of water was flowing. We drove up a fairly steep slope to the left and found ourselves in the park—right on the high bank of the river. A rugged hill in the background formed a picturesque setting. The toilet blocks were new and well equipped with ample hot water and two washing machines. The charge was 70 cents a night. This would do for us!

Here we met Lyn and Arthur who were to contribute so much to the very happy time we had at Mt. Isa.

Arthur was a 'Pom', a plumber by trade. Lyn was a New Zealander, able and willing to tackle any job. They started from Perth and had been on the road for six years working their way from place to place. They owned a Landrover and quite a palatial caravan in which we, that is Jasper and I, spent many happy hours listening to stories of their adventures.

To them, life and everything about it was interesting. Flora, fauna, geology, conchology, photography, engineering, Aboriginal lore and every other subject that I got on to, between them they could contribute in some practical way. On the very few subjects where I was more knowledgeable, they would listen and absorb, ask intelligent questions and argue logically. I couldn't have wished for better friends to relieve the loneliness which, without Jasper, would sometimes have been unbearable.

Funds were getting dangerously low and a call at the Employment Office was not encouraging. For tradesmen there was plenty of work, but there seemed to be a glut of painters.

A tour of the mine was a must. My first visit was in the afternoon. It was extremely well organised, starting with a brief talk by an executive on the function of the world's largest producer of copper and silver-lead. This was followed by the screening of a colour film showing the underground workings which we should not see on this tour.

We were then issued with protective helmets, a dust coat and eye protectors.

A bus was drawn up outside and we were taken all round the extensive surface workings of the mine, with numerous stops when we were shown at close quarters every phase in the treatment of the ore when it reached the surface.

On the way back, I said to our guide, "Any chance of getting a look underground?"

"Sure!" he answered, "but underground tours are for small parties of men only. Can't have women down below. All the men would come out on strike if we dared try it."

It was arranged that I should attend at the underground gate house at 8 a.m. the following morning.

Next morning I duly presented myself at the mine where I was met and conducted to a room for the issue of suitable clothing for the tour. I began to understand why it would be impossible for women to participate in such a tour.

Firstly came the special dungarees, then woollen socks, heavy boots, gloves, a massive leather belt, safety helmet and eye protectors.

By the time I had changed, four more men turned up for the tour.

We proceeded to the lamp room where we were each fitted with a

129

helmet light and a heavy battery box which was attached to the leather belt.

The party of six, including our guide, were now all assembled and equipped, so we entered the cage for the descent to Level 2—1,400 feet below the surface.

It was a smooth trip in spite of the speed with which it dropped. Level 2 is the most extensive of the drives and covers one and three-quarter miles of workings.

Down here, there are not only stores and crib-rooms (where the men can relax and eat) but also spacious workshops for the maintenance of the heavy mechanical equipment used for cutting out and transporting the ore. These and most of the tunnels were, of course, electrically lit, but when we got nearer to the actual working faces we realised the importance of our individual head lamps.

Underfoot was very rough, rocky and often under an inch or so of water, so the going was not too easy. In addition, we had to negotiate narrow and steep shafts, climb ladders, clamber over newly blasted ore and filling and often had to dodge ore trains in the main tunnels.

Generally speaking, the air was clean and cool. There are really no actual working faces, as I had imagined, where men used picks and gads and brute force to cut their way in and extract the ore. All the latest mining methods and machines are used to save time and human energy and maintain a higher standard of safety than was possible with the old methods.

I imagine that every move underground is first made on the surface with drawing-board and computer to eliminate guess-work and ensure safety.

One system being used is known as 'MICAF', which means Mt. Isa Cut and Fill. This, I understand, describes the method of cutting into the roof until it becomes too high to work, then filling in to build up the floor and raise it to support the heavy machinery for further drilling and blasting.

A drive is commenced and blasting holes are drilled in an arc around the top and sides at five to seven-foot intervals. Explosive charges are placed in these holes and are only fired at special times when all miners are either off duty completely or tucked safely away in the crib-room on smoko. This depends on the size of the charges being used.

Normally, three and a half tons of explosive are used at a time to blast out 20,000 tons of ore, but double that magnitude is not uncommon.

The ore is then collected by diesel-driven loaders and delivered to the skips which carry it away and automatically tip it down shafts leading to the crushers at Level 20. Here it is reduced to a workable size before being lifted to the surface for treatment. Thus, all the ore goes down before it comes up!

We witnessed the drilling for the charges by a variety of semi-automatic devices. The drills are driven by air whilst the activating pressure is hydraulic. Theoretically, all the men have to do is to guide them, but it was obvious that even this was extremely hard and heavy work.

A certain amount of local blasting is done, and we witnessed this. A bag or two of ammonium chloride and diesel oil suitably fused are slapped on to the face. When the fuse is lit a power whistle is operated and everyone within earshot takes cover.

The explosion itself is just a dull thud which you feel rather than hear, but the warning whistle, which keeps going until all the debris has settled, is nerve-wracking.

Next, after having to wait quite a long time for the cage to take us down, we descended to Level 20 to see the crushers in operation. At this level, 3,400 feet below the surface, the heat was pronounced and we were all perspiring freely.

We had been underground for over three hours and I was not sorry to board the K57 cage for the ascent to daylight again.

The heavy boots, the weight of the battery box and so much walking and clambering had made me very tired, but it was a fascinating experience.

Arthur was working on a new state school project and told me that the man with the painting contract was two months behind schedule. He had only one man working on the job and was in trouble with the Works Department. He knew that more men would have to be taken on so suggested that I went along to try my luck.

20

Back to work again

The man on the job contacted his boss and got the authority to take me on. He was a good tradesman but working under difficulties. He was short of ladders, trestles and planks.

My first job was assisting him in painting the facia board round the whole of the toilet block. We had only two trestles, which we borrowed from the plumbers who were completing the roof, and one long plank. The board was ten feet above ground level and we both had to stand on the same plank. He was tall and I am short, so we had to compromise in setting the height of the plank.

The height was enough for me when I was working on the end of the plank but as I moved towards the middle, the plank sagged under my weight and put the facia board almost out of reach of my brush.

This wouldn't have been too bad but when my mate also moved towards the middle, the plank not only sagged even more but the motion of us both painting caused the springy timber to take on an up-and-down movement, making it extremely difficult to paint in a straight line when 'cutting in' white paint against a black gutter. Only by putting my brush movement out of phase with his was I able to keep some modicum of control over the area I was painting.

All the work I did was under similar difficulties.

However, I managed to get in a couple of weeks at a very healthy rate of pay and then I heard some disconcerting rumours about the contractor's financial position.

It seemed that all local credit had been stopped and I was advised to get my money quickly and 'give it away'.

After a bit of a struggle I got my money and started looking round for something else. In spite of the flourishing state of Mt. Isa, work was scarce. I was told that it was nearing the end of the financial year and many projects in which I might have found lucrative employment were being held up until the new year commenced.

I now had a little money in hand and was not unduly concerned but I thought it might be a good idea to take a trip to Cloncurry, a sizeable town eighty miles west.

It is, of course, much older than Mt. Isa and was the world's first flying doctor base. The first emergency call from the outback was answered from here in 1927. Cloncurry also featured prominently in the foundation of the famous Qantas Air Line. I thought there might be a better chance of getting some work there.

There is a really good bitumen road all the way from Mt. Isa, and it didn't take us long to cover the eighty miles. It was about 11 a.m. I thought we had struck a ghost town.

Not a soul was to be seen. I drove down the main street and saw one car parked outside a pub.

Then I saw a solitary woman come out of a smallgoods store.

I went in to buy some dried milk and said to the owner, "Where's everybody? Is it siesta time or something?"

"Oh no!" he replied. "It's always like this!"

It was hot, dusty and almost deserted and I could see no point in prolonging my visit, so we doubled back forty miles to the turn-off for Mary Kathleen, where open-cut mining and the production of uranium oxide was commenced in 1957 after extensive uranium deposits had been discovered in 1954.

I knew this to be in 'moth balls' since the completion of existing orders, but I thought it might be worth a look round.

The mine workings were closed off, but the little township which was built for the mine workers was accessible. It is a pretty little place with neat little homes and gardens, stores, banks, Post Office, pub, cinema and everything the employees should need to live contented lives without the forty mile journey to Mt. Isa or Cloncurry. There were few signs of life now that the mine was not producing and I imagine that those few people I saw were 'caretaking'.

Although everything was closed up it was less derelict-looking than Cloncurry. I got the impression of suspended animation—just waiting for the time when export orders for uranium snapped their fingers to bring it out of its trance.

133

21

A geology session

That night in Lyn and Arthur's caravan we got around to the subject of rocks. I showed them my collection of rough opal and a few stones I had cut and polished. These comprised some opals I had experimented on and which had inspired my deep love for them. Also there were agates and jaspers, smoky quartz and chalcedony, plus a few odd stones which were beautiful, though valueless to a gem dealer.

Both Lyn and Arthur were fascinated and suggested that I might like to go with Lyn the following afternoon to a site which they had heard of to see if we could find any magnetite. This is no gemstone, but nevertheless it is most interesting as a specimen of iron in crystalline form.

We agreed to leave the Kombi behind and go in the Landrover as they had no idea how bad the track and creek crossings might be.

The next morning I called at the Employment Office. The lady was again charming, but told me that nothing had come up for me.

After lunch, Lyn, Jasper and I piled into the Landrover and made for a locality north-west of the mine. Lyn had fairly precise instructions and a faint track served to guide us over creek beds, through clumps of trees and around rocky outcrops.

Whatever I had previously thought about women drivers, Lyn was the one to convince me that I had misjudged them. The way she handled that Landrover over that rough terrain was a demonstration of skill and nerve. Her judgement was superb and she never hesitated or fumbled. My complete confidence in her enabled me to concentrate on remembering the route taken and note several interesting features worth investigating later.

We covered many miles through the rocky hills, counting off the creeks as we crossed them, through gates and along fences until we came to the masses of quartz outcrop where the magnetite was supposed to lie on the surface.

I knew what to look for—heavy black octahedrons which could be picked up with magnets, with which we were both equipped.

Neither of us had any idea of the size of these crystals. They could have been the dimensions of an egg or even a grain of sand for all we knew.

Lyn and Arthur had been told that they varied in size and occurred near the milky quartz, so we sat on the ground and began to rummage in the dirt.

Lyn dropped her magnet and on picking it up saw several black specks adhering to it. A close examination revealed that they were magnetite crystals.

We now started to dig a few inches beneath the surface and uncovered quite a lot of much larger ones, many as much as a quarter-of-an-inch from apex to apex.

Not all of them were perfect. The good specimens took the form of two four-sided pyramids stuck squarely base to base to make an eight-sided symmetrical crystal.

Also outcropping in this area were many hunks of mica schist and chipping this with my geologist's hammer revealed the source of these crystals.

We were thrilled to find them here in abundance—buried in the schist. The largest one we found was over an inch long.

We collected half a bucketful and called it a day.

Even though they were of no monetary value, as geological specimens they would be greatly appreciated by my rockhound friends to add to their collections. I was more interested in them as evidence of the colossal mineral wealth of Australia, and of Queensland in particular.

We collected Arthur from his work and returned to the caravan park, where it was suggested that, at the weekend, we should all go out to the Painted Rocks, another place not well known to the average tourist.

Lyn and Arthur had been there before. We turned off the Cloncurry road on to a bush track which got rougher and rougher until we reached a spot where the average visitor has to leave his vehicle and proceed on foot for the remaining three miles.

Arthur ploughed straight on over the narrow, boulder-strewn track on the side of the hill, tree branches banging and scraping the driving cab as we lurched out way forward, down into gullies and up the other side. For me, this was quite a hair-raising experience but to Arthur and the Landrover it was all in a day's work.

When we arrived at this delightful spot I was a little disappointed to find that its name was exaggerated. There was only one Aboriginal painting of a crude figure, that was all.

The waterhole beneath the sheer cliff was clear and cool and offered some magnificent reflections of the colourful trees and rocks surrounding it.

Jasper, of course, went straight in and enjoyed himself while we took pictures. But this wasn't the climax of the trip. Lyn led the way over rocks and through thick scrub until we came out on a most uninteresting-looking flat piece of ground.

This, they announced, was where they had found Aboriginal spear-heads. My interest was immediately aroused. The ground was littered with quartzite. A closer look and a grub around unearthed many pieces of rock which had quite obviously been deliberately chipped.

How I wished I had had time to make a study of Aboriginal implements, so that I should have a better idea of what we were finding.

No complete spearheads came to light that day but we collected many portions and other pieces which could have been tools for shaping boomerangs and weapons, or even special ceremonial knives for cutting the flesh at initiation rituals.

Of course, this was all guesswork and conjecture, and we imagined the natives sitting under the small trees chipping away laboriously and patiently. A spearhead which has taken hours of shaping is almost finished. Then a slight miscalculation and it breaks in two. The broken pieces are cast aside and a new one commenced.

Most of the chippings were under trees, the broken pieces some way away as if tossed there in disgust.

We also found ochre, which forms as a kernel in round pebbles. Some of these had cracked open in the sun and revealed the soft, chalky-looking kernels of red, white, blue and yellow. Arthur said that he understood that this is the pigment used for Aboriginal rock paintings, mixed with the juice from a chewed root.

It seemed reasonable to me, but I collected as many representative specimens as I could carry, both of the chips and the pigment, for verification when I got back to civilisation and had access to an authority on Aboriginal lore and culture.

I always made a point of never taking more than I needed of finds such as these, for two reasons: greedy tourists can quickly denude an area of valuable material and, had I accepted all the rock samples I had been offered by various enthusiasts, I should have needed a trailer to accommodate them all.

On the way back, Lyn suddenly called out to Arthur to stop. She had seen something beside the track. We piled out wondering what she had seen. She walked back a few yards and stooped to admire a wildflower.

The delicate beauty of this specimen was very striking when Lyn pointed it out to me. Arthur was just as enthusiastic. They both examined it carefully but made no attempt to pick it. I was impressed that they were content to leave it in peace.

My next call at the Post Office was more productive then it had been for many weeks. The letter which interested me particularly was from Mike, who had been back in Brisbane since before Christmas.

This was addressed to me in Alice Springs and sent by air mail. It had been re-directed to Darwin and then to Mt. Isa. It had taken five weeks! A camel train would have delivered it quicker!

With this letter, Mike enclosed a letter he had received from George. This described how George had been back to Andamooka and, not satisfied that we had done justice to the site of our divining, had decided to have another go. Three feet deeper than we had gone he had struck good colour and subsequent cuts on the same line were showing great promise. Was it coincidence, or is there something in this divining business after all?

22

Hot tars and scars

I had been down to the Employment Office again without result and, after doing some shopping, parked near the Post Office for my daily call.

Outside was a Falcon utility belonging to an electrical firm, which had been clients of mine some ten years ago in Brisbane. I figured that its occupant would hardly be on a holiday tour as the back contained wooden crates. If he was on an installation job I might possibly get some work.

I hung about until two men came from the Post Office and got in. I approached them and enquired if the sales manager I had known quite well was still with them.

They told me that he was not only still with the firm but that he was now a director and responsible for the contract they were here to complete.

I told them my name and explained my previous connection with the firm and asked if there were any possibility of some work.

They introduced themselves as Joe and Wally. Joe was here for a few days to establish local credit and supply arrangements for materials and Wally would remain to supervise and execute certain technical work.

They were about to install some electrical equipment of their own manufacture and design at the airport. There would be no call for employing anyone of my qualifications. They only needed one labourer as a general assistant to Wally.

I told them my story and that I needed some job, however humble, to earn tucker and get enough to continue my itinerary.

The pay allocation was on Brisbane standards and made no allowance for the high cost of living in Mt. Isa, but Joe promised to put the question of the special bonus to the board when he returned. In the meantime, if I liked to accept the offer, the job was mine.

I made a quick calculation and, as my personal and running expenses were not high, I agreed to see them the following Monday at the airport. At least I could stop this worrying leak in my working capital, and the job might be good fun with a technical interest thrown in.

I didn't quite know what to expect when I turned up at the airport on the Monday morning, but I soon found out.

A two-thousand gallon fuel tank stood outside the building which was the centre of our operations. I was told that this had to be painted— with hot tar!

A fire had to be made to melt the pitch, but before I could do this I had to take the utility down the highway and search for dead timber —to load the 'ute' with sufficient to feed the fire till the painting was completed.

It took me all the morning to collect the timber, organise a fireplace with anything I could find—old bricks, pieces of iron and rocks.

The pitch had to be extracted from a drum, broken into pieces small enough to go into an oversize 'billy' and the fire kept lively, but not excessive otherwise the pitch would catch fire.

In the afternoon I started 'painting'. The fire was built as close to the tank as possible but, even so, it required some skill to whip the can of boiling pitch off the fire, carry it to the tank and apply it with a brush before it cooled enough to cause the brush to stick to the tank.

Whilst the sun was hot, there was a cool breeze which, without warning, became a momentary gust. I still have the scars as a memento of this.

Imagine a large can of hot, bubbling tar held in one hand, a large brush in the other. The brush is dipped into the molten tar. The full, dripping brush is extracted but before it can be applied to the surface of the tank, a sudden gust of wind whips it off the brush and distributes it in varying sized splashes on bare legs, arms and face.

The first time was the worst as I wasn't prepared for it, but I received many burns before that fuel tank got the last of its black overcoat.

While I had been tarring the fuel tank, a mechanical digger had been excavating a hole about eight feet deep to accommodate it. When I arrived at the site the following morning, I found that a great pile of sand had already been delivered. My next job was to shovel this sand into the hole to form a bed for the tank to lie in.

In the afternoon, a mobile crane came and dumped the tank snugly into the bed of sand, leaving me to hump and distribute a few more tons of sand around it to keep it in position prior to putting reinforced concrete on the top.

Wally was a good 'gaffer' and we got along famously. He had travelled all over the world by car and kept me entertained with stories of his trips. He talked and I listened as we worked together installing the feed pipes into the building.

During that four weeks of work I did many jobs under Wally's guidance —mixing concrete, pouring it, bricklaying, plumbing, welding—jobs which I never imagined I should do except as an amateur around my own house. It was hard work, but good experience and I enjoyed every minute of it.

I was feeling fitter than I had felt for many years before I started this trip. Although tired, I no longer ached in every joint at the end of the day. My hands became tough and blisterless.

The tank was almost covered with sand and it now remained for the concrete top to be laid after it had been filled with the fuel to hold it down.

Wally was anxiously watching the weather. We had had a few light showers and a sudden deluge was by no means impossible. Should this happen before the tank was filled, the hole might become flooded and the tank, being buoyant, would float out of its sandy bed, leaving the sand behind, but taking our boxing and re-inforcing rods with it.

The tank couldn't be filled until all the pipes leading from it had been fitted and tested.

Wally worked like a nigger to do this while I hurried to complete the boxing and reinforcing.

The weather was kind and everything went according to plan but we were both very relieved when the tanker arrived with the 2,000 gallons of diesel fuel.

The concrete for the slab was ready-mixed and came in bulk. This meant another sweat to get the whole lot spread and packed before it started to set. It was a big slab and it required the combined energy of both of us going flat out to finish it off.

At the weekends, Wally and I and Jack, an inspector from the Department of Civil Aviation, would go out looking for rocks and fossils. We found many places off the usual tourist beat—places which even the locals were unfamiliar with.

I appreciated this new friendship because Lyn and Arthur had pulled out for a new location and a new job—at Mareeba on the Atherton Tableland near Cairns. Their departure had been fairly sudden but, as he had finished his commitments at the new school, the news that work was waiting at Mareeba was convenient and they had left with barely a week's notice.

They were ready to leave. The truck body of the Landrover was loaded to absolute capacity and everything lashed down. The caravan was hooked on and we were saying our goodbyes.

Suddenly Lyn realised that I had not taken my share of the magnetite we had collected. She asked Arthur where the bucket was containing those specimens.

It was one of the first things he had packed on the back of the Landrover. Without hesitation, he started to untie the ropes which secured the load.

It was typical of these good people that I had to be very firm in restraining them from at least an hour's extra work just for the sake of a few crystals. I had to point out that I could find my way to the location, and was going there anyway to take Wally and Jack.

23

Fossils

Jack said he had heard of a place where we could find fossils of sea creatures just by splitting the stone which lay on the ground.

It was known as Beetle Creek and he had obtained directions, but had heard that it was a pretty rough road.

We assembled at the airport at 9 a.m. on Sunday morning. Jack had no transport and rode with Wally in the 'ute'. We turned south off the bitumen on to a dirt road just west of the mine. This road steadily deteriorated until it was almost undetectable for rocks and boulders.

Thanks to good directions and Jack's excellent navigation, we managed to find all the landmarks specified and, after twenty miles of the roughest going I had yet encountered, we arrived at Beetle Creek.

It was, of course, a dry creek with a bank on one side rising to about forty feet. Outcropping from the earth were masses of a white shaley rock and lying around were many smaller pieces which had weathered off the main outcrops.

We each had a hammer and a cold chisel and were soon splitting some of these pieces and separating layer from layer.

In many cases, the faces where the rock split revealed perfect fossils of pre-historic sea creatures which had bodies longitudinally furrowed forming lobes in groups of three. There were other creatures represented too, but these were in the majority.

I learned subsequently that the scientific name for these is *trilobites* and they are of the Cambrian period, somewhere in the vicinity of five hundred million years old!

This was my first experience of fossil collecting and I brought back half a sugarbag full of rock slabs. I knew of many people who would be glad of a specimen of Cambrian trilobite.

On the way back, Wally again led. We had been going about twenty minutes when he pulled up suddenly. He made frantic signals to me by pointing to a spot a few yards off the track.

Sensing that he had seen something interesting, I grabbed the camera, closed my window so that Jasper couldn't follow and got out quietly.

Wally and Jack both climbed out slowly and proceeded in a wide arc to encircle the spot to which Wally had pointed. I could now see that it was a large goanna, a beautiful specimen which must have been nearly seven feet long from nose to tip of tail.

Wally knew that I was anxious to get a close-up shot of one of these. Normally, they move very fast to the nearest tree and are up and out of range before you can photograph them.

This one was now encircled and there was no tree to climb up. We closed in and I was able to take a couple of pictures before we opened the circle and allowed him to waddle off to peace again.

Jasper was disgusted that he hadn't been allowed to give chase and expressed his displeasure by howling at the top of his voice.

Had I been sure that he couldn't have caught up with it, I might have let him go but, when he is aroused, he goes like a cheetah. I have been told that a goanna of this size can inflict a very ugly bite if cornered and forced to fight.

I have no doubt that Jasper would have won any contest of this nature, and have rescued many a blue-tongued lizard from his playful ways. These lizards are called 'stumpy-tailed' or 'bog-eyed' according to the locality and are quite delightful and harmless little fellows. They are very ponderous in their movements. Their only defence is a vicious, spitting snarl which is really pure bluff. Like the rest of their kind, they do no harm but live on insects and thereby, no doubt, maintain the balance of nature.

The large goannas, I believe, help to keep down the snake population. But the snakes in their turn control the frog and rodent colonies. I maintain a policy of live and let live. My rifle was still unfired and, if I had to kill, it would only be in desperation in order to eat.

Searching for 'trilobite' fossils at Beetle Creek.

141

24

Bogged in the bush

Jack seemed to have some useful contacts. He came up with another idea. Were we interested in going out after some 'Maltese crosses'?

I had heard of these, but had never been anywhere near any known deposits. They are actually crystals of staurolite occurring as twins. A well-formed ninety degree twin makes a perfect cross and they can be used as attractive charms to hang on a necklace or the tiny ones as earrings.

It was a fairly long trip—forty miles along the Cloncurry road and, instead of turning left to Mary Kathleen we had to go right, through a property known as Rosebud Station.

It was now well into winter and the mornings quite cold—cold enough for me to wear a wind-cheater.

This time, Jack shared the front seat with Jasper and we led the way. Wally was behind in the Falcon 'ute'. We reached the Mary Kathleen turn-off and stopped to wait for Wally who was not in sight.

We waited and waited and were about to go back to look for him knowing that some sort of trouble must have delayed him as this was a good road and without junctions.

Before we could turn, he appeared driving very slowly with his head out of the window. As he got closer we could see that the windscreen had been shattered and crazed so that what remained was quite opaque.

He explained that it had just happened. No vehicle had passed him. No stones had been thrown up. Suddenly—wham! and no forward vision. He had not stopped to knock it out as we were waiting, but had struggled on so that we could all help.

He drove the Falcon off the road and we all got busy with hammers. In spite of placing plastic bags, newspaper and canvas over the seats and floor, it took the three of us an hour to remove all the glass from the screen, upholstery and the floor.

We turned into Rosebud Station and Jack navigated from his pencilled instructions. I thought the Beetle Creek trip was rough, but this was really putting the vehicles through their paces. The track itself was just an ordinary horror but the creek crossings were murder. The wheels had to traverse and grip a mixture of fine gravel and stones through a range of sizes up to boulders two feet long by a foot wide—some half buried, others loose on the surface.

This, combined with steep gradients up and down through the creek beds, made the going very difficult. Even the light Falcon rolled about alarmingly.

We grubbed around for two hours but found no Maltese crosses or anything remotely resembling one. Time was getting on and we set off on the return trip feeling disappointed that not one of us had found a 'cross'.

Jack was now riding with Wally and we had covered about five miles of the return journey when we came to a creek which had given me a little anxiety on the way out.

The gradient down had been about one in six followed by a very steep climb up the other side. The Kombi had rolled about quite drunkenly down the loose slope, but the steep jump-up the other side had been fairly solid and had presented no problems.

I now had to negotiate this the other way round.

The Falcon had gone down the bank very carefully then accelerated violently to climb the loose slope. Stones and gravel flew everywhere and, with wheels spinning, it just made the top to level ground.

There was no way in the world that I could rush it like that. I drove quietly down on to the creek bed and backed up under the bank to get the longest run at it that I could.

In spite of several attempts, I could not get more than half way up the slope. Finally, after approaching it from several different angles, I succeeded in getting to within about six yards of the top, then bedded down solidly.

We tried a tow but the rope wasn't long enough to let the Falcon get its back wheels on to firm ground, so we had to give that up.

We tried everything we knew. We jacked the Kombi and put limbs of trees under the wheels. Still they spun, hurling boulders and branches out at the back.

Wally decided to drive on to Rosebud Station to get help while Jack and I continued our efforts to get the Kombi free.

An hour went by and still we persevered but only succeeded in progressing about a foot. Then a Holden car appeared going back the way we should be going and we watched to see how it would fare going up that slope. There would be room for him to pass so long as he didn't skid.

He roared up, got opposite the Kombi and stuck. The driver and his wife got out for a consultation. We decided that we might get him out by brute force as he was travelling light. The wife took the wheel while the three of us lifted, pushed and dragged the Holden mobile again. They offered to help us, but there was little they could do that we hadn't tried already.

It transpired that they had also been looking for 'Maltese crosses' but had been luckier. The correct site had been less than a quarter-of-a-mile further on from where we had stopped and searched so fruitlessly.

Grateful for our help and to compensate for our disappointment, they gave us nine 'crosses' from their collection—three each.

We saw them on their way and soon after Wally returned, followed by a four-wheel drive vehicle.

The driver of this was a cheery young mining engineer from Mary Kathleen who, to use his own expression, was "cooling his heels and waiting for something to happen" when the phone call came through from Rosebud Station.

Within ten minutes the Kombi was on firm ground again and away we went in convoy. He said he would stay with us till we were safely back on the bitumen in case of further trouble as it was now getting dark and the track no picnic for night driving.

We left him at the Rosebud gate and he refused to accept anything for his trouble, saying that it was a welcome relief from Sunday afternoon boredom.

In due course, the job at the airport finished. My friend Wally left for Brisbane and Jack departed on another inspection job a few hours later. I had a little money in hand and, having already sent off my income tax return, could be fairly confident of receiving the refund cheque at my next forwarding address which, I had decided, would be Longreach.

There was nothing more to keep me in Mt. Isa and I was most anxious to push on to what I believed would be the toughest, but most interesting part of the trip.

A few days now would see me back in opal country—the band extending right down through Western Queensland and over the border into New South Wales.

25

Opal country again

It was noon before we got away after a few minor delays. We passed through Cloncurry at a quarter-to-two without stopping. The bitumen finished here and the dirt road following it was remarkably good. However, I could see that it would be very difficult after even a little rain. The day was fine and pleasantly warm without being hot. Once again, scenic features were few and far between.

It was one hundred and fourteen miles to my next objective, Kynuna, the first red spot on the geographical map of the Queensland opal mines.

According to the speedometer, I was about four miles from Kynuna and watching closely for signs of an opal-bearing landscape when I noticed what I thought was a flat willy-willy some way ahead. It looked like smoke being moved in a peculiar fashion by wind.

It changed its shape very quickly. It now looked like a huge grey veil waving in the breeze.

As we got closer, I got the impression of some gigantic, invisible being executing a scarf dance. The movement and change of form was a delight to see.

Getting closer still, the colour of this 'veil' changed from grey to a delicate green as it caught the rays of the sun, which was rapidly going down.

It now occupied a large part of my forward vision and I realised that this ballet-like phenomenon was caused by thousands of bright green budgerigars flying in close formation, all turning and wheeling in perfect synchronism.

I was so enthralled that I forgot the camera until it was too late. They swooped and all settled as one in the vegetation on either side of the road.

As I passed, they all took off again and I was surrounded until the whole flock vanished behind me.

It was 5.30 when a small cluster of buildings came into view. It was little more than a name on the map, but Kynuna boasted a post office, a store and a police station besides a cattle yard. I drove straight through and camped for the night just a few yards on the other side in a paddock off the road.

Next morning I called on the local police officer to enquire about the opal mine. He told me that nothing but a four-wheel drive vehicle could possibly reach it. Also, it was quite derelict and washed in after the recent heavy rains.

I crossed it off my list and pushed on towards Winton.

Soon we came to the Combo Waterhole where we stopped for some refreshment. This was said to be the inspiration for Banjo Paterson's famous song and Australia's unofficial national anthem—'Waltzing Matilda'.

The billabong was dry and I saw no jumbuks, but the coolibah trees were there. There is a story that the ghost of a swagman can occasionally be seen there at night because Banjo Paterson's story was based on fact. A swagman had actually drowned in the billabong in trying to escape from the troopers. Whether he took a jumbuk with him in his tuckerbag is not known.

Paterson wrote the lyrics of the song during his stay at the nearby Dagworth Station.

The day's objective was Longreach, but I was anxious to have a look at Winton on the way. We arrived there at lunchtime. The main street had a wide carpet of luxurious green grass right down its centre. This made me feel cool, even though I wasn't. The buildings had a well-cared-for look. Even the people seemed to smile at us as we passed. Perhaps they were just amused at Jasper's lordly posture, which he always adopts when we enter a built-up area after long stretches of nothingness.

Following my usual practice, I made my first call at the police station, told them who I was and what I was there for.

The sergeant was interested in my plans and invited me into his office to inspect a very large map of the district.

As far as opal mines were concerned, he suggested I should contact Bruce Simpson, the sadler. Bruce, he said, not only knew the country but he was also a lapidary. I should also see the Evert brothers, Vince and Peter. Vince had a gem and souvenir shop and Peter the pharmacy.

He not only told me of these people, but took the trouble to write down their names for me and particulars of where to find them.

My original idea of only spending a couple of hours in Winton expanded so I enquired about camping. I was told that there was a free camping site out by the showgrounds, but a young couple had recently opened Winton's only caravan park. I decided to give it a go.

On the way there, I had to pass Bruce Simpson's place so I stopped.

Bruce gave me a friendly welcome, lots of information and showed me some specimens of boulder opal, but as it was now getting late in the afternoon I promised to call again and went on to the Waltzing Matilda Caravan Park.

I hadn't had a shower since I left Mt. Isa so it headed the priority list of needs.

The 'hot' water was very hot. The 'cold' water was very warm. My first impression on turning on the tap was that there must be a dead rat or something in the water supply. I then remembered having read that hot bore springs were often heavily mineralised. I knew that all Winton's water came from bores. I tasted the water. It was sweet and wholesome. Once I got used to the smell, I enjoyed that shower and hardly noticed it after the first few minutes. It made excellent tea and, once exposed to the air, the smell disappeared rapidly.

From subsequent enquiries of the Council Engineer, I learned that Winton water is, indeed, a spa water full of health-giving natural minerals, including fluoride.

The smell was caused by minute bubbles of sulphuretted hydrogen which quickly disappear into the air when the water reaches the surface.

Sandra and Ron Mackenzie had opened the caravan park as a business venture and, like all new businesses, it was a struggle to get it off the ground. I greatly admired their courage and hoped that it would soon be recognised as one of the best caravan parks in Queensland.

Ron was engaged from Monday to Friday on the new beef road project near Boulia while Sandra looked after the caravan park.

Her constant companion was a hefty black and white dog, a cross between a cattle dog and a bull terrier. He was devoted to Ron and Sandra, particularly Sandra, for whom I'm sure, he would have given his life if necessary. This was good considering that Ron was absent from home for the best part of the week.

I have yet to find a dog that I can't make friends with, but whilst he accepted me as of no evil intent towards his beloved mistress, he and Jasper were sworn enemies from the word Go.

They had five fights in all. The first was of no consequence. The second was more bloody. Jasper managed to get his teeth through the lower lid of one of Digger's eyes. In the next set-to Digger retaliated by doing exactly the same thing to Jasper. In the fourth fight, they finished up square, as each got the other's opposite eye.

Sandra and I did all we could to stop these bloody contests and arranged a rota system for each dog to be loose.

When we arrived, I was the only guest and it gave me the opportunity of a long talk with Sandra and, later that day, with Ron when he came back for the weekend. They told me a lot about the locality and I was delighted to learn that they were both keenly interested in opal.

I was particularly interested in a place called Opalton—another red spot on my Mines Department map. It is about seventy-five miles south of Winton.

Ron knew it well and was actually taking somebody down there the following day and invited me to accompany them.

The road was remarkably good at first but as we got further south it deteriorated into a black-soil track.

A black-soil road can be really good, almost like bitumen when it is dry but terrible when wet. The sticky black mud adheres to the tyres and builds up until it reaches the mudguards. Unless you stop and dig it out it will lock the wheels as efficiently as the best brakes.

On this occasion it was dry and hard, but we were still hampered by the effects of the last downpour.

Goods for the distant homesteads are delivered by mail truck. The drivers of these trucks are a very hardy race and will carry anything for delivery to places en route—mail, merchandise, machinery or even human freight if the need arises. If it is at all possible they keep to their weekly or fortnightly schedules. The prospect of rain doesn't deter them. If the track becomes impassable they just stop and wait until it is passable.

Naturally, they don't wait longer than is absolutely necessary, but push on as soon as the truck will move.

At least forty miles of our route showed evidence of this and I was able to get a mental picture of one resolute driver who got going as soon as his wheels would turn and grip.

A pair of deep ruts scored the now concrete-hard surface. In some places these ruts were over a foot deep by the width of a double back wheel. I could almost see him slithering about from one side of the track to the other, throwing up mud as he struggled to keep the heavy truck on course.

We had to keep stopping to open gates and close them behind us. There were all sorts of gates—wooden gates, iron gates, dog gates, heavily wired and some which weren't gates at all but just sections of fencing where the posts were floating. The complete section had to be dragged aside and then replaced.

Parts of the track had the deep, hardened imprints of hundreds of cattle hooves, which imparted a shuddering vibration to the vehicle at the speed we were forced to go.

The track wound through low red hills containing many bizarre wallaroo caves weathered in the sandstone. The tops of these hills were bare, but around the base were wattle, gidyea, dogwood and mulga trees.

Eventually, the black soil gave way to the sandy gravel again and we turned off to the right to what is left of the once thriving opal mining township of Opalton.

The presence of the red-trunked minaritchi trees would have told the old prospectors to start digging here because there is a saying that "where the minaritchi grows, there you will find opal".

The most prominent surviving feature was a 400-gallon ship's iron water tank which stood at the approximate centre of activity. Stumps in the ground once supported the timber post office and, presumably, a pub. Some hundred yards away was all that was left of the bakehouse—one wall built of rough-hewn stones.

We drove through this jumble of relics and on to the diggings, with its characteristic heaps of mullock and washed-in shafts.

We 'noodled' some of the dumps and found a few colourful chips. The opal found here is similar to that found at Andamooka and Coober Pedy.

My own most interesting find was several pieces of opal matrix of no value except as specimens. These were hunks of ordinary-looking sandstone which, when wetted or immersed in water, showed a mass of tiny points of brilliant colour—specks of precious opal in the pockets between the grains of rock which make the sandstone.

Some six hundred men worked here in 1869, but the water supply was very poor and had to be carted fourteen miles. This shortage of water and the drop in the market value of opal caused the field to be abandoned many years ago.

The only work done at Opalton while I was there was by weekend enthusiasts like Ron and Bruce and a few rock-hunting tourists who spend a few hours 'noodling'.

For anyone with a slightly wider interest there is a wealth of historical evidence of past activity. The collector can find much of more value than chips of opal from the dumps.

Beer, lemonade and castor-oil bottles of a design long since abandoned by the manufacturers are highly-prized finds by those who spare them a second glance.

They are no longer litter. They identify the old camps and, if you take the trouble and have sufficient imagination, you can build up a picture of how these old-timers lived and worked. There are no old motor tyres to suggest their mode of transport, but bits of dried up leather harness and maybe an old saddle half-buried in the sandy gravel.

Four tree branches stuck in the ground show where someone had built himself a camp bed. Ashes and the blackened remains of long-cold kindling and the stones which supported the camp oven had remained undisturbed since the original miners had given up in despair and returned to civilisation, or had died and been buried on the spot by their mates.

At 4 p.m. we started back. I could not maintain Ron's speed over that rough track so I suggested that he went on and left me to return more slowly.

Being alone, the many gates delayed me and it got dark when I still had twenty-five miles to go.

Bush tracks in the dark are no joke and to add to my discomfort, I encountered many kangaroos which sat on the ground in my path apparently hypnotised by the headlights. They would remain immobile until I was only a few yards from them when a blast from the horn broke the spell and they hopped off into the darkness.

26

I set myself up as a Lapidary

My new friends had all shown me beautiful pieces of opal matrix which, unlike the matrix from Andamooka, requires no chemical treatment. Being in the dark brown ironstone, the pockets and seams of precious opal show up without any artificial darkening.

I was very impressed with its brilliance and range of colour, but felt that the surface could have been more highly polished. If I can't do better than that, I thought, I'm no lapidary!

This thought became an obsession and I longed to have a go at some of my specimens. I was too wise to criticise and suggest to these good people that they had fallen down on their polishing. The only thing to do was to show them by example how good polishing could improve an already beautiful stone.

I removed my brand new lapidary equipment from the roof-rack and set it up.

I selected a likely-looking piece of brown ironstone with thin parallel seams of brilliant opal running through it. I shaped it carefully on the grindstone. It would make a lovely pear-shaped pendant an inch long by three-quarters wide.

I was pleased with the shape. I worked on it until it was perfectly symmetrical with all curves smooth and the proportions right.

All this I had done holding the stone in my fingers. I now had to 'dop' it for the final stages in which I used four silicon-carbide coated discs of progressively finer grades. The ultimate stage is a disc of wood covered with chrome leather, which you have to impregnate with cerium oxide to give a mirror-like surface to the stone.

'Dopping' is sticking the stone to the end of a piece of wooden dowelling by means of shellac and sealing wax.

It is necessary to keep the work wet all the time to reduce the heat generated by the friction. I was quite skilled in these processes and had no difficulty in handling the stone through the four disc stages. The coating of water on the stone gives a false impression of the smoothness obtained, so before going on to the leather buff I dried the stone to get a true assessment. I was very disappointed.

The fourth disc should give a smoothness which is only just short of a polish. The thin veins of opal stood out well but the surrounding matrix was dull and lifeless. Ah well, the leather buff should bring it up, so away I went after coating the leather liberally with the oxide paste.

At first, I let the stone just kiss the buff to get the feel of it, not having used this buff before. Then I started to press at first lightly then more heavily as I rotated the stone on the 'dop' stick.

Suddenly there was a sharp crack, followed by a rattle as five separate pieces of stone hit the side of the splash guard and dropped to the board.

My beautiful pear-shaped pendant had disintegrated!

I put it down to the fact that opal and ironstone each have a different coefficient of expansion, and the heat set up by the polishing action was more than the mixture could stand.

I began to think. Perhaps there was more in treating this beautiful opal matrix than I had bargained for. Maybe, I was not so clever as I thought I was.

While I was pondering over what to do next, Sandra came over to see how I was getting on and to tell me that Digger was in the house and that I could let Jasper loose. He was chained up and sleeping peacefully so I didn't disturb him.

I was showing her the results of my latest attempts when a ball of black fury streaked round from the front of the house and leapt snarling upon Jasper who was at a big disadvantage.

Sandra cried out in despair as she realised that she had not checked the front door of the house. The two dogs rolled over and locked themselves in combat.

Each had a grip on the other's head and neither would let go. I managed to grab each dog by the collar but could not separate them. Sandra held Jasper by the tail so I relinquished his collar and tried to choke Digger into letting go because I could see that he had a firm grip on Jasper again below the eye. This was no good, so I tried foolishly to force his jaws apart with my bare hands.

Of course, the best thing to do is to turn a hose on the adversaries but if there's no hose available, what is one to do? The situation was now pretty desperate. A crowd had gathered and advice was coming from all directions.

Suddenly, I was horrified to see a fellow camper appear with a large rock which must have weighed several pounds. Before I could protest or attempt to stop him, he brought it down with a sickening crash on Digger's skull. I expected to see Digger fall down dead with his head smashed in.

Instead, he just let go, then tried to come back to resume his grip but now I had a firm hold on his collar. Sandra transferred her grip on

Jasper's tail to his collar and dragged him clear. By a mighty effort, I was able to pull the still snarling and straining Digger to the end of his chain.

Both dogs were covered in blood. Digger had wounds on his chest, neck and ear. Blood was flowing from Jasper's eyelid for the second time. One of his front teeth was hanging over his lip.

Both dogs lay panting. Sandra brought a bowl of warm water and antiseptic. I got some cotton wool from my medicine chest and cleaned up both dogs.

There seemed to be no serious damage but I was a little worried about Jasper's eye. The lid was badly torn but, as far as I could see, the eyeball had again escaped. I removed the hanging tooth and saw that it was a clean extraction.

Still the blood dripped to the ground and I examined Jasper carefully to see where it was coming from. Then I looked at my hands. I had felt nothing but the forefinger of my right hand had got mixed up with somebody's teeth. The flesh had been torn from the knuckle revealing the bone and was hanging down like a flap.

Sandra tied it up and insisted that I go over to the hospital less than a quarter-of-a-mile away for more skilled attention.

I took her advice and received three stitches and a tetanus injection. The doctor said I might lose the flap and have a funny looking finger as a souvenir of the occasion. He gave me some antibiotic capsules and told me to have an early night.

Jasper was limping and his cheek was swollen, so I took him along to the Stock Inspector who also acted as 'pet vet'. He gave him a thorough 'once over', annointed his eye with ointment and could find no cause for the limp. All I could do was to watch for clues.

He invited him to come back in a couple of days for another dose of ointment in his eye.

Lapidary was out for the moment, so I had to be content with studying the stones I had finished. I showed them to Bruce and asked him where I was going wrong.

He told me that, in his opinion, jeweller's rouge was better than cerium oxide for polishing opal matrix. He put some in a tobacco tin for me.

I now did much better but it was a hard, tedious grind improving on the polish I had at first despised. I was now completely deflated and felt justified in freely admitting it to my new friends.

This led to an introduction to Charlie Phillot and the Lyndon B. Johnson opal mine at Carisbrooke.

27

Another old-timer

Charlie Phillot owns Carisbrooke, a 50,000 acre sheep and cattle station about fifty miles south-west of Winton.

He was in Brisbane when I first tried to make contact, but he called at the caravan park to see me on his return and invited me to visit him.

I checked on my route with the local mail-truck driver and found it quite straightforward. The road was gravel but remarkably good. It was a very pleasant drive around the escarpments formed by the weathering of the sandstone to create the typical flat-topped opal bearing landscape.

Carisbrooke Homestead lay at the foot of the escarpment on the edge of a wide valley. The property itself took in many thousands of acres of the tableland including Aboriginal tribal and corroboree grounds.

Charlie Phillot had worked out a scenic drive for selected tourists to study these places and enjoy the beauty of the panoramic views from the top of the escarpment—in all a round trip of over sixty miles.

He took me round in the company of a grand old-timer named Tom Pether, who had originally found the opal mine which was named the Lyndon B. Johnson mine after the President of the United States of America, who had once made a forced landing very near its location during the war.

We visited the mine, which was a shallow open-cut still being worked by old Tom, occasionally alone or more often with Charlie himself.

Here I planned to do some filming and took some notes in preparation for working out a rough shooting script to be put into operation the following day.

Whilst old Tom was remarkably fit for a man only a few years short of ninety, he had recently been in hospital and his legs were no longer capable of the daily trek of five miles out to the mine and the arduous digging and shovelling in the heat. Nevertheless, he still enjoyed a few hours work when Charlie had time to take him out and bring him back.

I looked forward to seeing and hearing more of old Tom Pether before I returned to Winton.

Charlie Phillot was the youngest grazier I had met so far, but one of great knowledge, foresight and enterprise. If all graziers were like him, there would be considerably less grumbling about the state of the industry and the crippling effects of drought.

He had invested money in a scientific survey, as a result of which he had put into operation an irrigation system known as 'Keyline'. He showed me the dam, the channels and the control arrangements. He explained the theory and even I, ignorant about most phases of primary industry, could see the sense, the logic and the practicability of this system for keeping his paddocks green and ensuring adequate feed for his stock even under extreme drought conditions.

The plan, when worked out scientifically by a specialist engineer, was a simple one and Charlie had done the bulk of the work himself with a bulldozer.

That night, over coffee, he showed me a series of aerial photographs of the property. It was fascinating poring over these and tracing out the route we had taken that afternoon.

The following morning we loaded up Charlie's vehicle with the cine camera, tripod and the various trappings necessary for filming.

Charlie himself had engineered these roads aided only by the bulldozer. Some of the gradients were very steep and the surface loose, but it offered no problems to a Landrover or a lighter conventional vehicle.

Old Tom was the star performer in this little segment of my film. For a man of his age, he did remarkably well in taking direction and produced all the action I asked of him.

It took about one-and-a-half hours to get the shots I wanted, after which we loaded up and made for the waterhole. This was only accessible through a narrow cleft in the rock, where earth movement had split a chasm about twenty-five feet deep.

A sheer cliff overhung the pool. On the face of this cliff were Aboriginal paintings of fascinating assortment which I photographed for future reference. The deep, still pool gave delightful reflections of the colourful flora which surrounded it.

Old Tom seemed to know every tree and rock that we passed, and reminisced freely as we drove along. This was his country. He loved these hills and valleys and wished for nothing more than to stay and finish his eventful life here.

We returned in time for lunch, after which Charlie had to resume the mustering of his sheep for the shearing which was going on. I must have been a nuisance to him but such willing and unstinted co-operation which he had given me was typical of the friendliness and hospitality of these north-west Queenslanders.

Had he wished, old Tom could have lived at the homestead, but he preferred to 'camp' in some outbuildings which, I imagine, had been

Carisbrooke Station from the top of the opal-bearing escarpment.

The Pub and Post Office, Lightning Ridge.

shearers' quarters at some time. He lived rough. He was happier that way. He looked after himself, cooking his own meals over a wood fire in an old oil drum.

Even though his health sometimes confined him to his camp, he was never inactive. He took a keen interest in life, read his newspapers (not always up-to-date), and listened to the radio.

His chief hobby was painting. His favourite subject was women—big-bosomed, narrow-waisted women with frizzy hair—a combination of the Victorian era with the early twenties. The skirts were short to show the shapely legs and tiny feet.

He told me that he had concentrated on mastering the art of depicting women. Judging by the number in his gallery, he had succeeded. They were nearly all facing west if you looked at them as you would a map, and I wondered if there could be any psychological significance in this.

He was a bachelor and, I should imagine, a gay one in his younger days. For a man of his age he still had a strong, handsome face.

He was not only an artist in his own way but also a poet, composer and writer. At that very moment, one of his stories had been submitted for publication and he was awaiting the outcome.

Later, he entertained me with several songs of his own composition. The musical phrases were rather repetitive but the lyrics would have stood up well against those of Banjo Paterson.

He was not only an opal miner but also a lapidary. He demonstrated his methods to me. They were crude according to modern practice but, I was told, he had done some beautiful work in his lifetime. He sat on a box with one leg on either side of a corner.

An old, very ordinary hand grindstone was his only machinery and was screwed to a corner of the box he was sitting on. He cranked the grindstone with one hand while he manipulated the rock with the other. Tobacco tin lids formed the finishing discs which he bolted to the grindstone after sticking on a piece of abrasive paper.

Maybe some of his earlier work now adorns the necks or ears of lovely ladies with big bosoms and thin waists somewhere in the world. It would be a fitting tribute to the talents and aspirations of old Tom Pether.

That night, Charlie showed me some of his opal. The colours were amongst the loveliest and most brilliant I have ever seen. I reciprocated by showing him some of the colour slides I had already taken on the trip. We had a very pleasant evening.

It rained while we were asleep. The weather people forecast more rain and, as I had no wish to negotiate those black-soil sections in the wet, I started back to Winton soon after eight o'clock.

Back in Winton, I was told of a possible painting job. It was only a week's work and consisted of coating an old corrugated iron roof of a residence in the town with red roofing paint.

The contractor told me I could start as soon as the paint arrived. It had to come by train from Townsville and was expected tomorrow.

156

The stitches in my finger were due to come out this day and I went along to the hospital about noon. 'Out Patients' was at 8.30 a.m. and was finished for the day but the sister obligingly did the job and expressed great satisfaction at the way it had healed. I should not lose the flap and have a comic finger for the rest of my life.

Next day, I checked with the painter. The paint was there so I agreed to report in the morning.

I didn't think it would be an easy job. It wasn't!

One cannot stand up to paint a roof. One cannot sit down on the roof in these conditions. The iron gets too hot to touch with the bare hands and the heat will quickly penetrate the seat of a pair of shorts. I thought that an old sack or mat might solve this problem but, as I had to be moving all the time, this was not practicable. Too much time was lost in re-arranging the upholstery and preventing it taking off in the wind.

Therefore, all I could do was to stand up and bend over from the waist to wield my brush. In spite of this, the heat from the old red painted iron penetrated my sand shoes. Why anyone should want to use heat-absorbing red paint on a roof in a hot climate is beyond my comprehension.

I had used roofing paint many times before but never had I done a job so patchy and glossless.

Each evening my back ached with the constant stooping. My feet throbbed from the heat and having to stand on those corrugations.

I was very dissatisfied with the job. My employer remarked that it was patchy but, as he didn't blame me, I gathered that he realised that I had done my best.

That week's pay helped a bit but didn't solve my financial problems. I was now resigned to breaking into my capital to finish the trip, although I would work at anything if I got the chance.

Time was getting on. My scheduled two-hour stop in Winton had stretched to six weeks. Except for the bloody dog fights, I had enjoyed every minute of it.

I was about to embark on the trickiest and perhaps the most hazardous part of the trip—the part which the motoring organisation had advised me to miss because of little information about water, food and petrol supplies and the possibility of the tracks, if any, being impassable.

28

Boulder Opal

By the time I had filled up with petrol, water and provisions and made my round of goodbyes, it was after midday when I turned out of the Waltzing Matilda Caravan Park and made for Longreach.

My original planned itinerary had included Opalton and Vergemont. Local information had confirmed the other advice I had received about the Vergemont area to Stonehenge. The road was very rough and rocky all the way. Why cut my tyres to pieces when there was so little to see. I had already been to Opalton and it would have meant an additional hundred miles of even worse conditions.

To go via Longreach to Stonehenge was about the same distance and the road far better. In addition, I needed to find a branch of my bank to get some more money. Longreach had one!

We covered the one hundred and fourteen miles in three hours but I just missed the bank. That meant that we had to stay the night, but I wasn't really sorry. It gave me the chance to have a good look round and a hair-cut. I also had a severe headache caused by striking a series of waves in the road at speed. I had hit my head on the roof three times in rapid succession.

I should have learnt my lesson after the experience of waves on the Stuart Highway, but I was not expecting such violent undulations on a reasonably good gravel road.

I had to wait till the bank opened at ten o'clock. In the meantime, I checked on the road to Stonehenge and Jundah. The police officer told me the road was 'rugged', but I shouldn't have any trouble if I watched my step and took it easy.

For a gravel road, the first fifty miles was quite good, then it started to get 'ruggeder and ruggeder' over the next forty miles. No wonder they call it Stonehenge! I now began to appreciate what they had said about cutting the tyres to pieces.

The country was hilly without being mountainous. There was little which could be described as features in the landscape, yet it was not monotonous. The recent rains had brought a profusion of colourful wild flowers to the borders of the road and the whole effect was relaxing rather than exciting.

We arrived at Jundah just after five and camped on the banks of the Thompson River.

Another fifty-seven miles in the morning brought us to Windorah. I was now making for Eromanga via Kyabra. This area is rich in boulder opal and the map around this area looked like an attack of measles, so thick were the red spots.

I had been advised not to attempt the direct route to Kyabra but to detour via Thylungra.

We got to Thylungra and followed a track which I believed led to Kyabra. I may or may not have been right but if I passed the homestead which put the name on the map, I saw nothing of it. I kept a close look-out and kept going until I saw another cluster of buildings beyond a gate.

I passed through and was surprised to find I was in Eromanga.

In the morning, I managed to catch the local police officer before he went off somewhere in his Landrover. I knew there were many, many opal mines in the area and, when I told him of my mission, he suggested that I couldn't do better than visit the Little Wonder mine about 35 miles to the west.

It was at present being worked by one or two men, and he gave me directions which I carefully recorded in the notebook I carry for that purpose.

I don't write down everything my informant says in longhand. I have developed a sort of shorthand code for map drawing. The directions usually go something like this:

"Go down here (pointing). See that clump of bushes with a bit of a hill behind it? There's a track off to the right about a hundred yards past that. Don't take it! Go straight on for about two miles till you come to a wooden gate with a red oil drum on it. Go through that and you'll find three tracks. One turns sharp to the left. Take the middle one: about five miles on you come to a creek. Turn off the main track 'cos you won't get across, there's a fallen tree across it. You'll see wheel tracks turning off. Follow these and you should be able to get across the creek bed about half a mile lower down. Look for the wheel tracks. Follow these and you'll join up with the main track again. Keep going for about four miles. Then there's an iron gate. Go through that and take the track on the right and follow the fence. The left hand track doesn't go anywhere. About ten miles on you'll come to a tank on the left. There are several tracks leading to this. Don't take the main track. That leads to a homestead fifteen miles to the right. Take the one on the left of it. There should be a sign-post there. You can't go wrong. There's another creek crossing about two miles on. Then there's another. The first one's easy but watch your step on the second one. It's very steep and rough. The next fifteen miles is quite straightforward —only two wooden gates and a dog gate—no forks" . . . and so on until the typical and final climax to all directions: "You can't miss it!"

These were not the directions I received for getting to the Little Wonder, but I quote them to give some idea of the difficulties of a stranger in finding his way without adequate signposting.

My route to the mine was comparatively easy to trace. The only trouble was that the police officer forgot to mention one gate. I had one too many and didn't know what to do with it. Luckily, no forks were involved before I came to a clearly identifiable landmark, so I found the Little Wonder without unnecessary delay.

The country around was not what I would call typical opal country as I knew it. It was rugged and hilly with plenty of trees and bushes. In fact, I found it attractive.

A low hill showed the scars of an open-cut. On the flat, bare ground immediately in front of the hill a caravan was parked., I wondered how long it had been there and how it had been hauled over some of those creek crossings.

I pulled up and got out to have a reconnaissance on foot. Jasper followed as I walked towards a big bulldozer and a ditch digger. The bulldozer had evidently just finished work for the day. I could see the heat shimmering from over the engine.

We walked past and round the hill. A little further on was a tent and a vehicle. Three men and a girl appeared to have just finished a meal and were huddled round a billyful of rock which they were examining.

I said 'G'day,' introduced myself and explained my reasons for being there.

They were Kay, Tommy and Johnny trying their luck amongst the tailings of the bulldozer and doing a certain amount of shallow digging.

The fourth member of the party was Frank Fazzari, a young miner with his own claim nearby.

After a brief chat, I left them and returned to the Kombi. A Landrover was now parked beside the caravan and the door was open. An elderly, distinguished-looking man was busy at some chores outside.

I strolled over and we introduced ourselves. He was Edwin Adamson, the well-known but now retired professional photographer from Melbourne. He and his wife were out here fossicking for fun and recreation.

That evening Ed and Doris Adamson invited me over to their caravan for coffee. Frank Fazzari also joined us and I had a very pleasant and instructive evening.

I learned much about the Little Wonder and the opal it produced. They told me that Jack, a Dutchman, was working the open-cut and was half owner of the lease. I should meet him tomorrow. Frank had his own claim which he was working alone. This was about half-a-mile away.

160

The opencut at the 'Little Wonder'.

Frank's mine under the cliff.

He was very interested in my filming project and invited me to visit his camp the following day.

Ed and Doris were keenly interested in opal in a non-professional way and were obviously liked and trusted by those whose livelihood depended on it. They had accumulated a very extensive and useful knowledge of the gem.

I heard the bulldozer start up before I was even out of my bunk. After breakfast, Ed took me over and introduced me to Jack whom I liked on sight. He was big, jovial and enthusiastic. His task that morning was to dig up boulders with the big bulldozer. Having unearthed a few he would stop the dozer, get down and crack the boulders with a sledge-hammer. It is in these boulders that the opal occurs. Cracks, crevices and apertures in these rocks have been filled with the silica solution which, in the course of millions of years, has become opalised.

Every boulder has to be broken to find out whether or not it contains opal.

Some contain only potch, some nothing at all but, if you are lucky, the broken rock will reveal a display of magnificent colour through almost the entire spectrum.

Boulder opal has one disadvantage: It is seldom found in layers thicker than about a quarter of an inch. However, it has one big advantage and that is, being contained in the very dark ironstone, it can be cut and polished leaving a backing of the ironstone matrix to enhance its colour and, at the same time, make the finished gem physically stronger.

Ed and I spent the morning helping Jack to smash the boulders and select the useful pieces.

Jack gave me a specimen of which I'm very proud. Whilst it is of little monetary value from the jewellery angle, it shows a range of brilliant colour and I shall always prize it as an example of beautiful Queensland boulder opal.

Later that day, I decided to try my 2-way radio again. I was in the Charleville Flying Doctor area but could not tune to that frequency so I tried Mt. Isa.

This was being very optimistic as Mt. Isa is nearly 500 miles away. I could hear some homesteads talking to them but could not hear base replying.

I switched to the Alice Springs frequency. They came in strongly. It should have been at the end of their telegram traffic period, so I waited for a lull and called them never dreaming that they would hear me.

"Hello VJD, Hello VJD. This is Sugar How Charlie calling and testing. Over."

I was surprised and very embarrassed to hear in reply:

"Hello, Sugar How Charlie. This is VJD. Loud and clear but please don't butt in during traffic. Over."

I had forgotten that, being in Queensland, we were on eastern time. Alice Springs is on central time and the telegram traffic was just beginning instead of ending.

162

My chagrin was largely dissipated when I realised that Alice Springs was over six hundred miles away in a straight line. I was astonished that my transmitter had such a range.

Time was going too fast and I was running short of water and provisions.

Not wishing to sponge on any of these good people here although they offered to see me through, I still had to get back to Eromanga. I had already been away twice as long as I had anticipated and, having notified the policeman of my plans according to 'advice to travellers in the outback' I thought it only fair to put in an appearance before they organised a search party.

I needn't have worried. There was no reception committee or sighs of relief when I pulled in.

I left a message with the policeman's wife to say that I had returned from the Little Wonder and was making my way to Quilpie.

The road was rather bumpy and uninteresting, except for the wild flowers which again were growing in masses on both sides of the road. It is surprising how a little rain can so quickly turn the bare, rocky ground from apparent desert into a glorious conglomeration of colour.

As a town, Quilpie gave me rather a negative impression.

I suppose I had been spoiled by Winton, but I was far from delighted to learn that I had to wait there till the coming Saturday for airmail to arrive. It was then only Wednesday.

I had run short of film and had telegraphed Brisbane to air-freight the balance of my stock which was being held for me under refrigeration.

I took the opportunity of my enforced stay in Quilpie to 'make and mend'. I got out my 'housewife' and made an onslaught on the numerous rips in shirts and shorts made by barbed wire and other projections which had impeded my efforts to open and close the many gates I had passed through.

My little fan had given up the ghost so I stripped it down and had to fashion a new brush from a fragment of springy brass I found in my toolbox. A number of other maintenance jobs kept me busy until, by ten o'clock on the Saturday morning, I was all packed up and ready to move on.

29

Compass and guesswork

While I was waiting for the plane to arrive, I called at the police station to find out the best way of getting to Duck Creek, another famous opal field somewhere in the wilds about seventy-odd miles to the south-east.

All my maps showed a very minor track leading off the Thargomindah road at a place called Toompine.

I was told that the map was correct and that there was a track from Toompine leading to Duck Creek, which is located on a property known as Tirga Station, not very far from Toompine.

I saw the plane come in and waited for the freight to come to the agent's office by truck. My film stock was on it.

The road to Toompine was in fairly good condition and we covered the forty-five miles by lunchtime.

Toompine was just a pub among the trees as far as I could see. I ordered a beer and asked the publican about the road to Duck Creek. "What road?" he asked.

I showed him the map. "Oh that," he replied. "There hasn't been a road through there since Cobb & Co. days."

"Is there any way through?" I asked.

"Well, yes, I think you'd get through all right," and he proceeded to give me directions about following fences, crossing creeks and dodging tree stumps.

Two shearers were drinking in a room adjoining the bar and seemed very interested in the directions he was giving me as I was making my hieroglyphic code map in the notebook.

"The last creek's a bit tricky, though," he concluded, "but you should make it all right."

At this, the shearers could contain themselves no longer. One of them muttered, "Like hell he will!"

"It's not that bad," argued the publican.

"When were you there last?" asked the other shearer.

164

"About three months ago," the publican replied. "It wasn't too bad then."

"Maybe not," agreed the first shearer, "but we're working out there and, unless he's got a bulldozer with him, he'll never get up that bank. It's like the side of a house!"

They continued to argue until I butted in, "What's the alternative?"

"Go back the way you came from Quilpie but turn off to the right till you come to the Charleville Road. Keep going till you come to Cowley. That's about fifty miles from here. You'll see a bunch of signposts there. You can't go wrong."

This meant a trip of about eighty miles. Tirga Station was only twenty-two miles away as the crow flies.

One of the shearers said, "Try it if you like, mate. I'm pretty certain you'd never get over that creek but we'll be there to get you out of trouble."

I thought it over and decided that the long way round might be the quickest in the end.

I offered to buy them a beer but they declined and went on their way. I had one with the publican and then got going myself.

There was no difficulty in finding the Charleville road. At Cowley, there were the signposts as they said—a bunch of them—five, all nailed to the same post and pointing to the right. The top one said Tirga, another said Beechal, and a third Big Creek. I can't remember the other two.

These signposts were not the product of the Main Roads Department but were crudely but legibly lettered on bits of board which could have come from broken crates or off-cuts from a building job.

Nevertheless, they were clear and definite and I felt that, as they said, I couldn't go wrong.

This track followed fences for a large part of the way and, in places, had been washed away by water rushing down the fence line so I often had to make a detour through the bush.

There was never any doubt about the track until I came to the first fork. Here was another signpost. The two places I have forgotten about were to the left. Two signs to the right pointed to Beechal and Big Creek. The fifth to Tirga, and the only one I was interested in, was missing!

I stopped and searched for the missing board. I scoured the bush all round but there wasn't a trace. I examined the post carefully for evidence of nails or nail-holes to give me a clue. There was nothing! I was convinced that there never had been a Tirga post here.

I got out my maps and a compass. A compass bearing suggested that Beechal might be in the right direction, so there was no alternative but to take it.

I kept going till it was nearly dark without seeing anybody or any sign of life except for birds and an occasional kangaroo.

We camped beneath the trees at the side of the track. It was cool without any breeze to stir the tree branches. The silence was absolute and very impressive. Before taking to my bunk, I stood outside for quite a while just soaking up the peace of it all, looking at the stars and feeling perfectly relaxed.

I went to sleep immediately, then woke up suddenly wondering why. Then I heard the faint sound of an approaching motor vehicle. Jasper growled and I sleepily tumbled out of my bunk and looked at my watch. It was 1 a.m.

Now, I could see its headlights flickering through the trees. It pulled up alongside and I was too sleepy even to think of getting my rifle. I saw that it was a sedan containing the driver and two figures in the back.

Jasper growled again and we both got out. The driver opened his door and walked round the vehicle towards me.

"Sorry to disturb yer, mate," he said, "but am I right for Big Creek?"

There was no sign of movement from his two companions in the back.

"I was just going to ask you if I was right for Tirga," I replied.

"I dunno, mate." He sounded very despondent. "I only know that I've got two drunks in the back and I've got to get 'em to Big Creek. They hired me in Quilpie and said they'd tell me the way and now they're both out cold."

I felt sorry for this taxi driver but, no doubt, he would be suitably rewarded in the morning.

I told him that, to the best of my knowledge, this track led to both Big Creek and Beechal, but how far they were and which came first, I hadn't a clue.

He went on his way and Jasper and I returned to our slumbers.

The sun woke me up and, during breakfast, a car came past going towards the Charleville road. The driver was an elderly man and, unlike most people one meets in such circumstances, he would not stop for a yarn. This being Sunday morning, he was on his way to church. I wondered where the church could possibly be. It was not yet seven and had he not been in such a hurry I should have asked him. It must have been a long, long way.

He was able to assure me that I was on the way to Tirga but couldn't stop to tell me how far it was.

After breakfast, I decided that Jasper and I both needed a little exercise so we went walking.

We had gone less than half a mile from the Kombi when I saw a gate across the track. Beyond it I could see the homestead. It could have been thirty miles away for all I knew last night.

Within half-an-hour we were exploring the deserted opal field of Duck Creek. In a way, it was very similar to Opalton with its evidence of past activity.

There was no action to film but I took some panoramic shots of the field, stopping at a roofless, corrugated-iron hut still containing the frame of a bed, shelves and a fireplace.

I sat on that side of the bed which was still supported and tried to

A typical Western Queensland bush track.

The derelict hut at Duck Creek.

imagine the last occupant when the roof was on and the bed frame supported on both sides. I wondered if those shelves had contained books, beer bottles or bags full of opal.

A few blackened rocks and some ashes were all that remained of the fireplace at the far end. I don't believe there had ever been a fireplace— just a place for a fire and a hole in the roof to let the smoke out. Whoever had built that shack wouldn't have been too finicky. Anyway, the smoke keeps the flies out.

The remains of that hut were depressing rather than romantic and I wasn't sorry to move away to the mullock heaps for an hour's 'noodling'. I found a few bits but nothing to excite me.

So much for Duck Creek. My next objective was Yowah.

30

Yowah—where the Nuts come from

To get to Yowah I had first to follow the Yowah Creek to Dundoo Station. There was a signpost to guide me but the track was amongst the worst I had encountered anywhere on the trip. There were extreme wash-aways and difficult creek crossings. The way had now deteriorated to a barely recognisable bush path between the trees.

As it was late in the afternoon before we got going, I didn't expect to get much further than Dundoo Station. It was only a matter of twenty-two miles but our speed was reduced to about 5 m.p.h.

The sun was now very low and it would be quite dark in half-an-hour so we camped by the side of Yowah Creek which, at this point, had plenty of water in it and was flowing strongly.

Next morning, once again we had hardly got going before the home-stead appeared. We must have been within 'Coo-ee' distance without knowing it.

I pulled up outside to get directions. The lady of the house was 'taking school' as she put it, but very obligingly told me how to get to the Yowah opal fields—five miles to the main road. According to my maps, there was nothing even resembling a main road within twenty miles of Dundoo.

Apparently, it was a new road from Toompine to Eulo. Several mistakes later I found myself on the right one.

I was soon approaching the fields. There were shacks and rough signs offering 'opals for sale'.

The road followed the bore drain. The banks of this were covered with lush, green grass. The water was clear and sparkling in the sun.

Outside a shack on the right was parked another Kombi with a tent alongside. I saw the back view of a woman taking advantage of the hot bore water to do some washing in an old bath tub.

I pulled up alongside and said "G'day!"

Thus began a friendship which I hope will last a very long time. She looked up and smiled a greeting. I introduced myself and Jasper who, by

169

this time, had decided that Mrs. Gwen Wood was a dog lover and would be well worth making up to.

She took me over to their Kombi to meet her husband, Clive, who was having a siesta in the heat of the afternoon.

Gwen and Clive were on holiday from Brisbane and I couldn't have met a more charming couple to put me in the Yowah picture, show me round and prove such interesting company during those few days we spent there.

We had many trips to the nearby diggings together—'noodling', filming, joking and generally having fun. In the cool of each evening, Jasper and I went over to their camp for coffee brewed over their open fire. Jasper spent this time alternately sleeping and chasing nocturnal creepy-crawlies such as spiders and centipedes while we discussed rocks, U.F.Os and numerous other subjects.

Gwen and Clive were enthusiastic rockhounds and spent most of their holiday periods in remote, interesting places just fossicking. Gwen was also a writer and kept me enthralled with amusing and graphic descriptions of some of these expeditions.

Once again, I outstayed my provisions and, as I wanted to spend some time here, devoted one morning to a trip into Eulo. It is a small but quite attractive township. It had one store and an hotel called the Eulo Queen, which was well worth a visit if only to view the beautiful collection of rough and finished opal on display.

I planned a longer stay later, posted mail for some of the Yowah people and collected my foodstuffs. The storekeeper asked me if I was returning to Yowah. If so, would I deliver a parcel to Alcoy Station on the way back?

Naturally, I said I would be delighted. It was no trouble as I had to pass it anyway.

When I arrived there, I was given another typical Queensland welcome and invited in for a 'cuppa' by Mrs. George Haig. Her younger son, Duggie, asked me if I'd like to see his collection of oddities which he had found whilst roaming around the paddocks on his father's property.

I was fascinated by this very young man's interest and knowledge of the articles he had found. There were 'black man's stones' used by the Aboriginals for grinding roots and seeds to make a kind of flour. There were old buggy lamps, huge fossil shells and a collection of old bottles which must have been worth a great deal of money. He had been offered $200 for one old round-bottomed glass bottle by an American tourist, but Duggie wouldn't sell. He seemed to know all his bottles, what they had been used for and how old they were.

That night over coffee, we listened to a miner in a nearby camp 'cracking nuts'. This man was quite a character. He spent all day down his shaft digging out 'nuts' and most of the night up on top cracking them.

These famous 'Yowah nuts' are small boulders of ironstone which occur in a stratum of pink sandstone at varying depths. When cracked open with

170

a tomahawk they reveal a kernel which may or may not contain precious opal. The general opinion on the field seems to be that one in four hundred will contain opal. Some will only contain a white powder; some just a fluid like water; others are quite hollow and have no kernel. Of those that contain opal, this can vary from valueless potch to brilliant colour worth a fortune.

Our friend was naturally seeking the latter and whenever he cracked one which looked hopeful by his own meagre light, he would come running over to show us and see it better by the pressure lamp which Gwen and Clive were using.

It seemed like mighty hard work to me and he deserved to find something worth while. He may have done, but if he did he was wise in not shouting too loudly about it.

It was quite a party over coffee that night. Our 'nut-cracker' friend (I could never remember his foreign-sounding name and referred to him in my journal as 'Casse Noisette'), came running over as usual, but this time the cracked 'nut' he brought definitely showed a promise of good colour in the light from the pressure lamp.

It started to rain and the party broke up. I hadn't thought to bring my torch as the starlight gave sufficient illumination to see my way along to the Woods' camp.

Now it was overcast and pitch dark. I thought I was going in the right direction but I realised my mistake when I fell headlong into the bore drain. I didn't mind getting wet. The water was, of course, warm and I always had some sort of a wash before going to bed.

I had now completed my scheduled tour of the western Queensland opal fields. Whilst the going had been harder and more hazardous I had gained so much experience in those sandy wastes of South Australia and the short trips from Mt. Isa that the state of the tracks didn't worry me unduly.

I had met so many real people, as opposed to the one-track minded, beer-swilling, money-grubbing, stomach-ulcerated business men who make up so large a percentage of our urban population. What miserable lives they lead compared with this free, healthy, interesting and instructive way of life.

Such were my thoughts as I slipped into a deep, peaceful sleep to the accompaniment of the gentle pattering of the rain on the only exposed parts of the Kombi's roof.

At Cunnamulla, forty-three bitumen miles away, there was a 200-foot spool of processed film and two letters which had chased me from Andamooka.

One was from old Franko which caused me much amusement and a lump in my throat. He was glad that I had met his old friend, Vic. Williamson and, I quote, "It must be 50 years since I saw him first. I was up there in 1919 the year of the Spanish Flue. I went out there on my bike from William Creek". (William Creek is 90 miles from Coober

Pedy and, even today, it is just a rough track!) He went on, "I got the Flue but I wasn't very bad or I would have left my bones there. Yes, you left your hat here but it was too late when I noticed it. You were too far away for me to catch up to you, so the only thing I could do was to hang it up in my Camp just above where you were sitting and wait till you come back. It just reminded me of Paddies Kettle at the bottom of the sea. He said it wasn't lost as he knew where it was, but you have one on poor Paddy. You can get yours, but he can't."

He concluded, "I nearly got flooded out a few inches the Well is full and everything in the Garden is lovely".

What a wonderful old man!

The other letter was from England. It had been re-directed by my friend Gordon, the Andamooka postmaster who had scribbled on the back "Old Albertoni is keeping your hat wrapped in newspaper and hanging from the rafters. Anyone spending at least a week here always comes back".

I feel that I *shall* go back and hope that it will be still in the lifetime of Francis Albertoni.

I was glad to get back to Eulo and the friendly hospitality of Joan and Barney Norris who run that delightful hotel, the Eulo Queen.

I was now able to spend more time admiring their collection of opals and other interesting things.

But now, we must go south. We got under way after lunch. The road was fairly good and quite straightforward. The country on either side was flat and sparsely covered with trees. A wild pig shot across the road in front of us and Jasper howled with desire to get out and give chase. I nearly let him but, whilst I would back him against any dog of his size and weight, I believe these wild pigs can be ugly customers if cornered.

So far, all the emus we had seen had been at a great distance and he had only been slightly inquisitive, with his ears cocked as he watched them out of sight.

We caught up with a group of three big fellows who just loped alongside without paying us much attention.

I pulled up, opened the door and let him go. I knew he would never catch those fleet-footed, flightless birds. They took off into the bush with Jasper in full cry. I've never seen him run so fast. They all disappeared!

I lit my pipe and waited. It was some time before I saw a little brown speck approaching through the trees. It took him much longer to appear than to disappear. I got out his water bowl and filled it.

It was a very breathless dog which drank half of that bowlful without stopping. He had had enough of emus for one day!

3 1

Over the New South Wales border

At 4.30 p.m. we arrived at the little border township of Hungerford. We should sleep in New South Wales tonight!

Another twenty miles and we camped by the side of the track. It promised to be a cool night.

My next objective was the famous opal area of White Cliffs. I was most keen to see this place as I had heard many rumours about it. Some said that it had been worked out and almost deserted. Others, including a fairly recent radio news item, had said that a new strike had been made and that a minor rush was on.

According to this broadcast, a fabulous harlequin opal had been unearthed. It was so big and beautiful that it was priceless. A casual fossicker from Melbourne had found it, but he had been so scared of it being stolen that he had rushed it straight into a safe deposit without showing it to anybody except the reporter who had sent the item in.

I had now learned to take all these 'news' reports with a pinch of salt, and it would be interesting to get some first-hand information on the spot.

I hoped to get to White Cliffs next day and the next place on the map was Wanaaring. I thought that outback Queensland signposting was bad but in New South Wales I felt that whoever was responsible was a practical joker. I imagined him hiding behind his signposts having a good giggle at the frustrated traveller having had to go down one arm of a fork before he can even see what is on the post, standing in front of it cursing because it is either a complete blank or else pointing backwards telling him where he has come from, which he already knows and couldn't care less about.

It is very creditable that they re-paint their signposts every twenty years or so, but why must they obliterate every post within the radius of some forty square miles during the course of this operation without leaving any clue as to what had been removed and would be replaced?

Still, this sort of thing takes your mind off the monotony of the scenery.

173

Which way?—but there's a signpost on the right.

Mt. Isa from the Miles Memorial Lookout.

I took the wrong arm at one of these comic forks and eventually got to Wanaaring after following what I thought to be the greater used of the two. I was told that I had taken the 'short cut' along a dry creek bed. I was half-an-hour covering the distance I should have done in ten minutes if I had come the 'long way round'.

I even had difficulty in finding my way out of the place, in spite of directions from the only two living souls I had found to ask. Neither seemed to know for sure. Their directions were conflicting. In the end, I used my maps and compass and, more by luck than skill, I managed to hit the right track.

I only knew it was the right track because I passed a car whose occupant told me he had come from Wilcannia. If it hadn't been for that, I should have had strong doubts.

My journal described it as 'foul'. It had every hazard one can think of. It was a mixture of black soil, gravel, red and white sand. It had rocks, gates, grids, corrugations and bad creeks—the whole works! It would have made a good practice road for a would-be outback traveller.

It was here that we encountered our first big brown snake. As usual, he was crossing the road and I was able to get a picture before he slithered off into the long grass.

Then I came to a signpost—actually pointing the right way and telling me where I wanted to go—White Cliffs!

It was then about 6.30, time for a meal and bed. The only building of any pretension was the pub. There were other buildings and a Post Office, but we drove straight through and on to the diggings where we camped for the night.

32

White Cliffs

The landscape had taken a turn for the worse. I felt that there was a familiarity about it and, as I studied my maps, I realised why. We were now only one hundred and twenty miles from the South Australian border and less than three hundred and fifty miles from Andamooka as the crow flies. Had there been a straight bitumen road, I could have nipped over and retrieved my hat in a couple of days. But this was semi-desert country, dry and inhospitable.

White Cliffs was not a thriving, bustling place like Andamooka. The township itself was rather run-down looking, but certainly not dead.

There were shacks and dugouts, a few vehicles moving about but no evidence of a 'rush'. Water was quite plentiful and obtained from an arrangement very convenient for a truck containing 44-gallon drums to be filled. The pipe was an overhead one with a valve too high for me to reach without standing on something, but I managed and topped up my bottles.

The pub was a substantial building of fairly recent origin. The one and only petrol bowser was outside. I had the tank filled and, as I moved off, discovered that I had a nearly flat back tyre.

I jacked the Kombi up, took the wheel off and put one of my spares on. I put the wheel nuts on without using the brace, lowered the Kombi to the ground, pulled the jack aside and picked up the brace, intending to tighten the bolts.

Before I could do this I was hailed:

"Hello, Sugar How Charlie. What's the target for tonight?"

I looked up to see the grinning face of the driver of a Holden station wagon which had pulled up at the bowser.

I got up and walked over. He had seen my call-sign, which I had painted on the back of the Kombi to make myself easily identifiable to anyone I may have talked to on the radio.

He had assumed that I had named my vehicle after the official number of an aircraft I had been connected with during the war.

To me, it was quite understandable that he should have thought this in the light of the names given to many vehicles on an extended trip, and I was sorry to disillusion him.

As an ex-R.A.F. bomber pilot, I think he was just a little disappointed to find that I had been in Fighter Command rather than Bomber Command.

In spite of this, we talked the same language and within a few minutes, he and his wife were in the pub with me conversing over a beer.

Ken and Marion Clayton had only been in Australia for eighteen months and, like so many other enterprising migrants, were seeing it by doing a 'working tour'.

Ken was a handy-man and carried a full range of tools and a portable electric power plant. There were few jobs around a homestead that he couldn't do, from re-hanging a door to building an outhouse and wiring it for electricity. He was making a fair living and had jobs booked up well ahead on his itinerary.

It appears that I had camped quite near their caravan the night before, and he had intended contacting me.

After a few more beers, we agreed to meet again for a further talk after we had fulfilled our day's programme. Mine was to tour round the diggings and see what was going on.

I looked at the tyre. It seemed a bit soft, so I got out the foot pump and worked on it till the flat where it touched the ground seemed to balance the other flats. Somewhere along the line I had lost my tyre gauge. I put the tools away.

I drove through the diggings. At some time in the past when this field was the most productive in Australia, there must have been great activity within a mile of the township. Shafts were so close together that there was little room between them to pile the mullock. The track was very tricky to negotiate as it wound round the mullock heaps and washed-in holes.

Going round a curve on a fairly steep incline I felt the Kombi behaving most strangely. This was coupled with an irregular knocking noise.

I heard a ringing 'clank' and knew that I had shed a hubcap. I pulled up to investigate. To my horror, I found the wheel that I had changed was nearly off. I had lost three bolts and the other two were almost out. A few more yards and the wheel would have parted company.

Out came the jack and up went the Kombi. The two surviving bolts were so badly chewed up that I couldn't tighten them.

I walked down the track scanning the ground carefully but pessimistically as I did so. Trying to find three comparatively small bolts over two hundred yards amongst all that rough rock seemed a hopeless task.

Luckily, I had the wheel tracks to follow and I found one about ten yards back. The other two turned up lying neatly side by side right on the lip of an old mine shaft which almost cut into the track itself. The hubcap was further back still.

These three bolts were not badly damaged and I succeeded in replacing the wheel sufficiently tightly to get moving and return to my campsite where I got to work on the damaged threads with a file. This was a tedious job but an hour's work saw them screwed right home once again.

I made a resolution never to allow myself to be interrupted again while changing a wheel.

I was having a light lunch when the Claytons returned to their caravan, which was parked within fifty yards of the Kombi.

Ken came over and asked me if I would like to have dinner with them at seven that evening.

I asked jocularly "White tie and tails?" to which he countered "Please yourself but I used my white tie for a handle on the garbage can".

"Good!" I replied. "Then I'll wear jeans and a sweat shirt."

So dressed, I presented myself at the door of their caravan promptly at seven. When the door was opened and I stepped inside I got a great surprise. Soft lights illuminated the dining section and the sight of the table made me feel that I should not have been out of place in a dinner jacket.

A snowy white cloth covered the table which was set out with gleaming glassware and cutlery. Tall glasses contained linen serviettes and two pink candles in crystal candlesticks gave a soft, warm glow to the tasteful decor.

Ken poured beer into the lager glasses while Marion served the oyster soup. This was followed by Spaghetti Bolognaise with toast. For dessert, we had tinned pears, chocolate pudding and cream. To round off this delightful meal we had coffee and Drambuie. To add a final stroke to this touch of civilisation, Ken produced a box of good cigars.

Their witty conversation supplied the sweet music and I couldn't remember when I had enjoyed a dinner party more. I felt that I had been transported back for a few brief hours into a life almost forgotten.

It was a good feeling and I understood perfectly when they explained that they had been waiting for an opportunity, or rather an excuse, for entertaining in a more gracious manner than they lived in normally during their nomadic existence.

I am convinced that all three of us felt the benefit of that short trip back to civilised living.

We talked into the small hours, and I was quickly brought back to reality when I all but fell into a disused shaft on my way back to the Kombi in the contrasting pitch darkness.

I was well overdue for service on the Kombi and decided that I must leave White Cliffs for the moment and push on to Broken Hill, where I might manage to get some work for a week or two to try to stop up the hole in the financial bucket.

I could complete any unfinished business in White Cliffs on the way through to Lightning Ridge.

We camped the next night at Spring Creek which was a picnic area on the banks of a dry creek. It had no amenities, toilets or means of getting a shower, although there was a water tank and rubbish bins.

It was not easy to get a radio time check here because reception was good from stations in four different states. Broken Hill, although officially in New South Wales takes South Australian Central Time whereas the rest of New South Wales, Victoria and Queensland are on Eastern Time, so it was difficult to know just what time it was to within half-an-hour.

The wind got up in the night and by morning it was a howling, icy gale. I was glad to get moving.

We now came to quite long stretches of bitumen and the silence left over by the lack of rattling sounded strange.

We pulled into Broken Hill at half-past twelve and made straight for the Council-owned caravan park. I was delighted that the charge was only 50 cents per night, and the new amenities block positively luxurious.

Having booked in, I went to the V.W. service station for lubrication and check-up and, whilst this was being done, called at the Employment Office. I was treated with courtesy but they couldn't give me much hope of any job. There was no casual work available whatsoever and skilled or semi-skilled jobs could not be obtained without full union membership. Even had I been armed with a handful of union tickets, I should still have been unlucky as preference was always given to local residents of long standing.

I accepted this with reservations and called at a paint shop. Here they obligingly gave me a list of all the painting contractors in Broken Hill.

The first one I called on welcomed me with open arms. Yes, I could start tomorrow. He needed brush hands urgently. His face fell when I explained that I was not a union member. He then informed me that he *dare not* put me on. He would be forced out of business if he gave me even a single day's work.

It was the same story everywhere I tried, so I determined to quit the 'Silver City' as soon as I could. Unfortunately, I had given it as a forwarding address and was expecting more film. I *had* to stay here until it arrived or risk it getting lost.

Had I not been near the point of financial embarrassment, I might have enjoyed my visit to Broken Hill. The shops were well stocked and the prices reasonable. The people were friendly, even though hide-bound by unionism.

For some weeks now, I had abandoned shorts and short-sleeved shirts after six o'clock in the evening in favour of corduroy slacks, a long-sleeved corduroy shirt and even a windcheater. Not only the nights were cold. I often found it necessary to spend the whole day similarly attired when that icy wind was blowing.

33

Heading east again

On the Monday morning, I was determined to leave Broken Hill. Surely the films would have arrived. It was over three weeks since I had sent the parcels off and, apart from re-direction they had always been returned within seven days, even to places as remote as Andamooka.

I checked out of the caravan park, stocked up with food and water and called at the Post Office. There was still no mail! The next plane in was on Tuesday night and, even if the film was on it, I couldn't collect it until Wednesday morning. I wasn't prepared to spend another two days in the 'Silver City', so I reluctantly filled in a mail re-direction form.

It was well after ten o'clock before we pulled out. As we did so, it started to rain heavily with a gale-force wind. The first ten miles was most unpleasant and a fitting conclusion to an uninspiring visit to a place which seems uncertain where it belongs. Whilst officially in New South Wales, its loyalties appear to lie in South Australia.

The rain stopped, but the wind was stronger than ever. A few miles further on we ran into a wall of dust at least two hundred feet high. As we got into it, visibility dropped to absolute zero and I was forced to stop. It was ten minutes before we could go on again. The dust was actually running down the windscreen like water.

It gradually thinned out, the grey gloom changed to brown then orange, then yellow until the sun broke through again.

For the next hour, we could have been travelling in the Northern Territory at the height of summer. The heat was searing and I cursed the corduroy shirt and slacks which had been such a comfort when we started off this morning.

There now appeared evidence of recent heavy rain. Creeks were flowing swiftly across the roads, sometimes as much as a foot deep.

Many times I had to stop, pull my slacks up above my knees and check the depth of the water before I dared venture across.

This is necessary because, although you may think that in such a

180

slight dip the water could not be very deep, a torrent such as some of these were would quickly find a weak spot in the surface and, within minutes, could cut a channel of treacherous depth and width.

At other places, the road just vanished in a long sheet of water. I gathered that these places were notorious for I always managed to spot the well-worn tracks where other vehicles, presumably local, had made a detour into the bush to get around these temporary lakes.

That hundred and eighty miles to White Cliffs would have taken first prize for variety. We had experienced intense cold, torrential rain, searing heat and blanketting dust.

It was half-past four when I pulled up at the Post Office. The post mistress showed me some fine specimens of White Cliffs opal and told me that, on the previous day, White Cliffs had received thirty-one points of rain in eight minutes.

No wonder some of the roads had suffered!

Both Jasper and I were asleep by eight o'clock.

The morning was bright and sunny so immediately after breakfast we sallied forth again to tour the diggings and do the filming I had intended doing when I nearly lost a wheel.

During my enforced stay in Quilpie I had devised a means of holding the cine camera rigidly in such a position that I could drive and film at the same time.

Naturally, I had to drive very slowly but, by running the camera at sixteen frames a second instead of twenty-four, I figured that the projected film would look as if a normal speed had been maintained. I had already used this device at Yowah, but with how much success I had no means of telling.

Dodging the abandoned shafts at White Cliffs might be quite a thrilling sequence. Even without the wheel trouble, I doubt if I could have taken anything worthwhile before, as the dust had been so annoying that my eyes were sore and possibly the camera would have suffered too.

This morning the rain had laid the dust, conditions were ideal and I made the most of the opportunity.

Retired from farming and now keen opal miners, Mr. and Mrs. John Hall had a very comfortable routine. They got up early and went to their claim where they worked down the shaft until about noon. Then they returned to their neat dug-out for lunch, after which they relaxed or did household chores in the cool of the dug-out.

This dug-out home was roomy and well furnished and, I should imagine, remained at a constant temperature in summer and winter to within a few degrees.

Mrs. Hall was a keen lapidary and once I had made their acquaintance I spent a long time examining her neat array of equipment and some of the lovely work she had done on the products of their own mine.

I asked them if they knew anything of the fabulous harlequin which had been found recently. They both laughed and told me that they had

181

seen it. It was quite a nice piece—something to justify a day's work, but certainly not a harlequin nor even a stone of sufficient value to make a buyer's eyes boggle.

The reporter who had sent the item in had some property and a business to dispose of in White Cliffs and would have welcomed a 'rush'.

In the course of conversation, I told them that Lightning Ridge was the next and final stop-over of my tour. Two men from their home town whom they knew very well were, at present, trying their luck at the Ridge.

They suggested that I look up Alan Beasley and Ted Hoover when I got there. They didn't know exactly where they could be located, but they had been staying at the Tram-O-Tel. The names were good enough for me. I didn't think it would be difficult to find them. My experience has been that the Postmaster knows everybody and, on the opal fields, is always willing to help.

I was very glad of this introduction as, so far, I had no contacts at Lightning Ridge.

By three o'clock I was on the road to Wilcannia again. Sudden, exceptionally strong wind gusts forced me to keep both hands on the wheel to keep the Kombi on a straight course, but sixteen miles from Wilcannia the strain became excessive and I realised that all was not well.

I stopped to investigate and found an almost flat nearside front tyre. By the time that I had changed the wheel and got moving again it was just on five o'clock by all my timepieces when I arrived at the same service station where the previous puncture had been repaired. I calculated that I should have half-an-hour to do some leisurely shopping before the stores closed at 5.30.

But the local clocks all said 5.27, so I only had time to buy some sausages before they all shut down for the night. Where the time changes from central to eastern I had no idea. The folks living on this 'time-line' must have fun. Still, unlike city people, they are not slaves to the clock, so half-an-hour one way or the other shouldn't bother them.

We had left White Cliffs on Tuesday afternoon. At 3 p.m. on Wednesday we arrived at Walgett.

As it was only another forty-eight miles to Lightning Ridge, I decided to push on if road conditions were good enough and complete the journey to the last of our major stop-overs.

Although it was a dirt road of mostly black soil, conditions were fairly good and we arrived at four o'clock, in plenty of time for me to get my bearings and find somewhere to camp.

34

Lightning Ridge

My idea of the 'Ridge' had been obtained from books, tourist brochures and hastily-produced information sheets supplied by the motorists' organisation.

They said there was a pub. There was a store where certain provisions could be obtained. Bread could be purchased if ordered two days in advance.

The only photographs I had seen showed the main street as an area cleared of bush and lined with one or two decrepit-looking edifices.

But power poles were dotted along the streets to show that there was a reticulated electricity supply. Many television antennas were visible and a few modern homes were established or in the process of being built.

There was a miners' co-operative self-service store and another general store and cafe besides a novelty shop selling stationery, photographic supplies and other things.

Lightning Ridge had certainly progressed since the photographs I had seen were taken.

The countryside was quite heavily wooded and water was no longer a problem.

How different was Lightning Ridge from all the other opal fields I had visited. This was civilised!

The road to the left contained the police station, a little church and the 'Tram-O-Tel', a sort of motel consisting of old Sydney tramway cars converted into cabins to accommodate visitors.

All the time I had been looking round the town the memory of that sign, Bore Baths One Mile, had been with me so, without further ado, we set off to find out all about it.

In no time, the baths appeared on our left. I turned off and pulled up at the entrance to the fenced off area. A rather rough building housed the showers, toilets and dressing rooms which were situated behind the main pool.

The temperature was dropping rapidly as the sun got lower. A mist rose from the circular pool and I realised that this was no ordinary swimming pool where you could dive in, swim around and splash about, but a spa and a hot one at that.

I let Jasper loose to roam around by himself while I went into the building to change into my trunks and have a much-needed shower. Hot and warm water was laid on and when I came out was quite ready to 'take the waters'.

The main pool was about forty or fifty feet in diameter with concrete paving all round, steps leading into the water and a rail just about water level.

At that time it was deserted so I gingerly tried the water with my foot. It was about the temperature I would take a hot bath.

I gradually lowered myself into it until I could immerse myself completely. It was a queer sensation. I couldn't make up my mind whether I was enjoying it or not and wondered what the physical effect would have been had I dived in. I was very glad I had not been tempted.

When my system became accustomed to the high temperature, I tested the depth. It must have been six feet and the same all over. I pushed off from the side and floated on my back.

A few minutes of this and I made for the steps again. As I climbed out I felt distinctly light-headed, as if I had had too many beers on an empty stomach.

I staggered around drunkenly then sat down to dry myself off on the well-cut grass surrounding the concrete paving. I must have sat for ten minutes before I felt normal again.

While I was recovering and having a smoke, cars, trucks and 'utes' began to arrive. Some of the miners had finished for the day and had come to clean up for the evening's recreation.

After their showers, they took a dip—but only a dip—because, according to the complaints I heard, the water was much hotter than usual.

At least a dozen vehicles were now parked around the site. Next to the Kombi was a utility the owner of which was talking to Jasper, who had completed his tour of inspection and had resumed his seat patiently to await my return.

As I approached, he grinned at me and said, "Nice dog you've got there. What do you call him?"

I told him and easily slipped into a pleasant conversation about the heat of the pool, the weather and the opal fields.

He said he had been here for many weeks and was working a claim with his partner at the Six Mile.

I mentioned that we had come direct from White Cliffs and he showed great interest when I told him I had met someone there who had suggested I contact two men on this field. I asked him, "Do you, by any chance, know where I can find Alan Beasley and Ted Hoover?"

He laughed, held out his hand and said, "I'm Alan Beasley. Ted Hoover has just finished washing his smalls. Here he comes now!"

184

Alan's bush camp.

Information for the tourist.

THE HISTORY
OF LIGHTNING RIDGE

Formerly known as Wallangulla, Lightning Ridge is famous for its Black Opal. Opal was probably found as early as 1886 but a boundary rider, Mr. Jack Murray, was the first to sink a shaft, in 1901. The following year, Mr. Charlie Nettleton, a gold prospector from Bathurst, recognised the potential of the opals and commenced digging. Nettleton and a mate (probably Murray) later sold a parcel of eight pounds weight of opal for £15 to Messrs. Tweedie & Wollaston of Adelaide.

In 1905, there were 200 men on the field and £4,000 worth of opal was won, being sold at between £6-£9 per ounce.

By 1906, 1,500 people were working the field. The original workings being on Dobbys. The 3 Mile was opened in 1907 by Nettleton, followed by Canfells, Potch Point, Bald Hill, Newtown, Telephone Line and Pony Fence and others.

WORLD FAMOUS OPALS

found at Lightning Ridge include the 'Pandora', 'Butterfly', 'Flame Queen', 'Pride of Australia' and 'Empress'. The 'Light of the World' was won at the Grawin Opal field and weighed 252 carat when cut and polished. By 1966, top quality gem opal was bringing $200.00 and more per carat and it was estimated that only one tenth of the opal-bearing deposits had been worked.

At the same time, gemstones valued up to $2,000.00 were still being found by mining and by 'puddling' the old mullock dumps on the surface.

This structure was erected by the Walgett Shire Council at the request of the Minister for Local Government, Hon. P. H. Morton, M.L.A. following an Official Visit by Mr. Morton in February, 1966.

This was a great occasion. We seemed to take to each other immediately. Alan was of rather heavy build and about my own age. Ted was taller and of the tough, wiry type. They both loved Jasper on sight and he treated them as old friends.

But time was getting on. They had to get back to their claim and I had to find a camping site and get us a much needed meal.

They told me how to find them and I promised to look them up next day.

At the baths there was a No Camping sign but I assumed that it referred only to the enclosure as there was plenty of evidence to suggest that I wasn't the first to get the idea of camping in a pleasant wedge shaded by trees, between the fences.

Jasper strongly approved of this site and, not being allowed to 'take the waters', found himself a muddy pool on the adjoining property where he wallowed and frolicked and got himself filthy but, as he was so obviously happy, I didn't mind having to wash him down each time he returned. I kept a bucket of water handy specially for the purpose. It was wonderful not having to worry too much about conserving water.

Even so, having learned to exist on a minimum and to appreciate what a precious commodity fresh water really is, I should never again waste it or tolerate a dripping tap.

As I lay on my bunk that night after writing up my journal, I became conscious of the fact that, after travelling nearly sixteen thousand miles, I was now only about four hundred from where I had started. I hadn't yet decided whether I should return to Brisbane or make my future headquarters in Sydney. Distance-wise there was nothing in it.

In the meantime, here I was at Lightning Ridge, the largest and most famous of all opal fields and I felt that I should need at least a month to become sufficiently well acquainted to form an opinion of any merit.

Next morning, I followed Alan's instructions. I turned left at the pub. At the end of the bitumen on this arm of the 'tee' which formed the Ridge's main street was the Tram-O-Tel. Straight on was the road to the Three Mile. I had to turn right on to the Angledool road till I came to the earth dam. Now right again through a gate after which I had to take my pick of any of the tracks which bore left. They all led to Shearer's Six Mile which was my objective. From there on a single, narrow track led to Rouse's and eventually to the Nine Mile.

This all sounded very simple but, bearing in mind that there are no signs whatsoever, a newcomer could be excused for failing to see a specified landmark through the trees when all his attention is taken up in trying to avoid deep ruts, branches of trees and treacherous stumps where trees had been felled and were now almost completely concealed by long grass.

I missed the track to Shearer's and found myself at the Nine Mile.

Amongst the diggings here I received further instructions which resulted in having to double back two and a half miles till I came to

186

Rouse's, which could only be identified by surface workings on either side of the track.

Here I stopped to chat with a man who was scratching at the dirt in a trench about a foot deep. He told me how to find Shearer's just a little further back and showed me a 'nobby' he had just picked up from the dirt.

It was a rough-looking pebble about an inch long by three-quarters wide and the hand-pick which he was using to loosen the dirt had chipped the tip of this pebble to reveal black opal with a brilliant flash of red.

He was very excited about it and was desperately anxious to get working on it with a grindstone to take off the dirty-looking exterior.

The sight of it made me excited too. If it lived up to its promise from the chipped end and was like that all through, it could be worth a fortune.

On the other hand, that could be the only spot of colour in a mass of potch.

He told me this was his first promising find in three weeks of diligent scratching. I admired his tenacity and hoped that this 'nobby' came good. While we continued chatting, I had a cigarette, and watched his technique which he explained to me.

Rouse's was at the bottom of the slope leading to the higher ground where most of the diggings were. Here the 'level' came very near the surface and 'nobbies' could be found in the gravel where they had been washed out of the opal-bearing clay and sandstone.

I made up my mind to come back to Rouse's when I had some time to spare and have a go for myself.

I drove through the mullock heaps to a clearing some distance from the main centre of activity. Here was a tent and a caravan with a high television antenna.

This was Alan's and Ted's camp. They lived separately and by great contrast. This contrast was a strange one because Alan, a one-time business man with a modern home in a large country town lived in the typical bushy's tent slung on rough-hewn timber poles between two trees with a heavy fly lashed to the branches. Alan lived rough and cooked over an open fire, boiling his billy and cooking his simple meals in a blackened old saucepan.

Ted, on the other hand, was the open-air type experienced in bushcraft and, if necessary, could live off the land. But *he* lived in the fly-screened caravan, watched TV in the evenings when he could get a picture, boiled his water in an electric jug and cooked most of his meals in a modern electric fry-pan. The power came from a heavy duty diesel generator set which supplied electricity at 240 volts 50 cycles A.C.

They were the best of friends and the staunchest of mates. Maybe this was because they lived like this. They shared the water and the sacks of potatoes and onions. They shared the chores of getting the water and doing the shopping. They shared the work, but relaxed separately. Perhaps that is the secret of successful mateship.

They had shared the cost of the equipment because they were partners in the venture of mining for opal. They had two things in common: a keen desire to win some good quality opal and a complete lack of previous experience. The latter they partly overcame by a very careful preliminary study of the gem—how it is found, where to expect it and the best way of going about the job of extracting it from the reluctant earth.

Ted had designed the electric hoist, the smoothest, most efficient and simplest to operate of any I had seen. It was based on an old car back axle complete with differential and brake drums geared down and powered by a one horse-power electric motor. One lever controlled 'haul', 'stop' and 'lower'. It was silent in operation.

They had not been cheese-paring over the choice of power plant. It was more than adequate to feed the hoist, four or five light points down the shaft, an electric jack-hammer and an air-blower to ventilate the underground workings.

When we turned up, Alan was in the process of boiling the billy for morning tea. They were having a break after being down below together making a drive. Ted had been tunnelling with the jack-hammer whilst Alan had been behind him shovelling the debris out of the way to the bottom of the shaft for hoisting to the surface later.

After having shared the morning tea, I was invited to go down for a look round which suggestion I welcomed, because the mining of black opal is quite different from the technique used at Andamooka, Coober Pedy, White Cliffs or for the boulder opal in Queensland.

Whilst opal can and does occasionally occur in seams in the sandstone, at Lightning Ridge the most sought-after finds are the small or, if you are lucky, large 'nobbies' or pebbles which are found in single isolation or clusters somewhere in the clay between the strata of sandstone or even in the sandstone itself.

There seems to be no golden rule exactly where these 'nobbies' will be found. Some miners say one thing, others have quite different ideas. It's all a matter of luck, no matter how experienced you are.

One thing is certain. Unless conditions are right for its formation you will never find opal. Conversely, perfect conditions are no guarantee that you *will* find precious opal.

You might drive for a month through dirt and rock which *should* yield without even finding any potch. On the other hand, fortunes have been made in conditions where, according to theory, there was little or no chance of finding anything worth while.

Ted and Alan had not sunk the shaft in which they were working. The original claim had been abandoned and whilst they knew that some 'nobbies' had been found fairly recently, nobody knew how much, if any, the original claimant had extracted.

The whole area is so promising that it has often paid handsomely to re-open old shafts and either go deeper to find a second or even third level or else make wheel-spoke drives at the original level.

This is what they were doing.

188

On their claim was another abandoned shaft with a drive towards the second shaft. It was their plan to make a continuous tunnel between the two shafts. This was good reasoning because in making the drive, they might strike colour and, what was more important at that time, once the two drives met a good circulation of air would result. When I arrived they reckoned that they had only about four feet to go.

So far they had found no 'nobbies' but only patches of 'angel stone' which is a very hard, white clay containing thin veins of potch. They had been told that it was a good indication of better things to come.

Their shaft was forty feet deep and a chain ladder made it easy to get up and down.

When I descended I 'bottomed' on a huge pile of loose dirt which had been cut from the drive and was now awaiting being lifted to the surface and disposed of.

The generator was running and three bulbs—one in the drive and the other two suspended from the roof of the main cavern at the bottom of the shaft—made it easy for me to see what was going on. The air-blower on the surface was, in effect, a vacuum cleaner working in reverse and, coupled to a long length of wide plastic pipe, made the air tolerable though still rather warm.

I watched the operation of 'pulling dirt'.

Admittedly, mechanisation makes it quicker and easier for the man on top, but the chap below still has to fill the buckets or converted oil drums as they were in this case.

I volunteered to go below and give Alan a spell.

Ted emptied the full drum and kept it aside while I went down. Alan was wringing wet with perspiration and was glad of the break for a smoke and to cool off.

I quickly learnt the drill. The empty drum was placed centrally at the bottom of the shaft. If you shovelled like mad, it was just possible to fill it before the other drum came down.

You don't stand at the bottom of the shaft gazing blissfully upwards to see how the downward plunging bucket is progressing. You stand well aside. You can hear it descending and, after a while, you can gauge its position by the intensity of the drumming sound it makes. You also watch for the shadow it casts on the side of the shaft as it nears the bottom.

As soon as the bottom of the bucket appears, you leap forward and grab it, haul it aside so that, instead of hitting the full bucket, it lands beside it.

The cable is now slack so you smartly unhook the empty drum and hook on the full one. The cable, being a steel one, has probably got a kink in it so you hold it out straight as you signal to haul away.

Probably the most satisfactory signal is three jerks on the cable. A whistle or a yell is not always audible to the man on top, because he is exposed to the wind and extraneous noises.

He gets the message and starts winding. You hold the cable straight until the weight is taken, then you grab the full bucket to stop it swinging

189

and guide it to the centre of the shaft. When it is clear, your next move is to kick or shove but never drag the empty bucket to the position the full one had occupied.

If you are smart and can shovel quickly enough, the bucket will be half full before the other one has reached the top. If you are still smart and not flaked out, you will throw the last shovelful in as the now-empty bucket starts rumbling down again, so you throw down the shovel and prepare to repeat the operation.

No wonder Alan was wet with perspiration!

It took me several loads before I got the hang of it. By that time, I too was wet. The perspiration on my hands and the clay made a perfect lubricant to prevent me holding the shovel so I had to have a break.

Alan took over again and, by working ten bucket shifts, we managed to clear the floor of the working ready for the next lot which the jack-hammer would disturb.

By four o'clock we had all had enough and Ted came clattering down the ladder so that we could all have a reconnaissance.

We yarned and smoked for another half-an-hour, examined the strata and each gave our own ideas of what the prospects were.

I decided that we should camp the night with them. We each cooked our own meal but shared a billy of tea round Alan's fire before turning in. It was very pleasant and peaceful.

Next morning I was awakened by a chorus of birds. So varied were the species represented that it was almost a cacophony. I had to do some shopping so set off to town early and promised to return the following day to try my hand with the jack-hammer.

I called at the Post Office and picked up some welcome mail, then did my shopping before returning to the bore baths where I found that my previous site was occupied by a tent. There was plenty of room so I picked another site and had lunch.

The weather was warm and blowy, so I took the opportunity of doing a full wash—sheets, pillow-cases, towels and such clothes as needed it.

After dinner, in the cool of the evening, I again had a refreshing shower and 'took the waters'. This time it was nowhere near as hot as it had been the first time. It was still very warm but so pleasant that I stayed in too long, swimming around and relaxing by floating on my back.

When I came out, I felt even drunker than I had before. When this effect wore off I felt very fit but sleepy, so I turned in early and had a perfect night.

On the way to the Six Mile, my sunvisor, which I had obtained for a dollar from Neil Watson at Alice Springs, started to vibrate violently.

When I got there, I found that the aluminium centre strut which I had made at the Alice had suffered a compound fracture and could not be repaired. Consequently, I had to make a new one using the pieces of the old one as a pattern.

Conditions were not good for an alfresco engineering job. Sweating in the sun encouraged hundreds of the little bush flies to settle on every part of me where they were most unwelcome—round my eyes, on my nose, up my nose, on and in my ears, round my lips and into my mouth if I dared open it.

The result was that it was late in the afternoon before I could retire to the cool air at the bottom of the shaft.

Alan and Ted had at last broken into the other drive and cool, fresh air was circulating freely.

I had a go with the jack-hammer. It was certainly quicker and easier than with a pick, but hard work just the same. Jack-hammers are good for cutting into rock to dig shafts and make drives but they'll never replace the light pick for finding opal.

It wasn't long before it was time to call it a day, so we all adjourned to the surface where I amused my companions by demonstrating my divining technique.

I used the wires and, quite naturally, they were very sceptical, but I obtained a very strong indication on a direct axis with the drive they were making. Another fifteen feet of tunnelling and they would be at the spot.

I was not very serious as I had never been convinced, but I put in a marker just the same.

I badly needed a shower after all that sweating in the sun, so decided to go back to the bore baths for the night.

The heat was on again. Not only was it a hot night, but the water was hotter than ever. A couple of minutes was all I could stand of total immersion, but this quick dip gave me no effects of drunkenness and I felt quite good after it.

Nevertheless, I had trouble to come. With the closing in of darkness, the flies went to bed but the moths and other minute pests came in swarms as soon as I put the light on.

I hastily closed up and disposed of those which had caught me 'on the hop'. I settled down to write up my journal and became completely engrossed until it suddenly occurred to me that the light was not so good as it should be.

I looked up and was amazed to see that it was rapidly becoming obscured by a solid cluster of tiny moths.

Spraying them had little effect. I assumed that either the door was not properly shut or else a screen had sprung a leak. A quick check showed that neither of these things had happened. I was mystified because, although these moths were very small, they were far too large to penetrate the fine mesh of the screens.

I watched carefully to detect where they were broaching my hitherto impregnable defences. They were thick on the outside of the screens and seemed to be moving towards the bottom. A closer inspection showed a gap of less than one-eighth of an inch under the frames. Both side windows were the same and, as I watched, I saw them flattening themselves and working their way sideways through the narrow gap.

I was fascinated and wondered what terrific urge made them take so much trouble. They were coming through the breaches at the rate of approximately three per second and heading straight for the fluorescent light.

I had to close these gaps somehow so I rolled toilet paper into thin tubes and forced it in with the handle of a teaspoon.

This proved effective and I sneered as I watched their frustration as they circled in frenzy on the outside of the screens. I disposed of those inside, cleaned the fluorescent tube and settled down once again to write in peace.

But it was not to be! Battalions of minute ones now started to penetrate the mesh of the screens. However, I knew all about these fellows. Even putting the light out hadn't stopped them tormenting me all night once they were at large inside. But I found a solution to this.

By shutting all the windows to stop any further entries and only switching on the red-shaded light over Jasper's bunk, they all made for this and gathered in a thick layer on the inside of the plastic shade. When all were present and correct, a blast from the sprayer at short range anchored them securely to the shade where, presumably, they died from drowning rather than the lethal effects of the liquid chemical.

Having disposed of the second attack wave, I instituted a total blackout and re-opened the windows. As I did so, it started to rain. It was only a shower but was quite heavy while it lasted and the temperature dropped several degrees.

I switched on the fluorescent light again to see if I should be subjected to another attack by reinforcements. Again I watched carefully but nothing entered. The rain and drop in temperature had evidently caused them to abandon their onslaught.

I had written about twenty words when the orchestra struck up with a faint roll of drums. The 'Tympanic Symphony' had commenced—Rumble, rumble! Boom! boom! Crash! Boom! Crash! Crash! Boom! Rumble!—and so on as medium and large moths hit the unevenly tensioned and different sized fly screens causing a not unpleasant variation of tone, volume and tempo.

I was quite soothed and the symphony lasted until I put the light out and the last notes faded with one final, defiant "Boom!"

It was a bright, fresh morning and I had planned to drive out to the Nine Mile in the hope of locating one of the oldest inhabitants of Lightning Ridge. This was Foley Kite, the oldest survivor of four brothers who were part of Lightning Ridge tradition. The eldest brother, Billy, had figured prominently in the Ridge's early history and Foley himself, I had heard, was quite a character.

I had some difficulty in locating his camp which was buried deeply in the bush away from the hurly-burly of the active Nine Mile diggings.

I drove around the narrow tracks in the direction I had been told and came at last to several mullock heaps of time-worn, weathered appearance.

Near a shanty, a man was working a windlass midst a fresh pile of mullock. He was too young to be the old man I was seeking but I approached with the usual "G'day!" and enquired about Foley Kite. Could he help me?

He was a pleasant, friendly type and introduced himself as Shirley Kite, the old man's nephew. Yes, this was his camp but he was unwell and in bed and he, his nephew, was here to give him a hand.

I introduced myself and told him my business. He was very interested and assured me that his uncle would be glad to see me and have a yarn when he was feeling better.

We talked for some time, then he invited me to visit him and his father on Sunday at their camp not far away at the Nine Mile.

I welcomed this, as they were all obviously experienced miners of the old school and should provide lots of interesting stories of the field.

On the way back, I had to pass Rouse's and took time off to do a little 'noodling' in the 'shallows', where I had been shown that promising 'nobby'.

I picked a trench which had been started and abandoned, then got to work with my geologist's hammer. After twenty minutes' scratching I turned up some grey potch which, although quite valueless, proved the possibilities of doing better.

After three-quarters of an hour, I found a small piece of almost black potch with a tiny flash of blue.

I felt the excitement building up inside me and knew that I must call a halt otherwise I might spend the rest of the day here and, if I found any more, get 'hooked' and forget that I had not come in search of a fortune in opal.

I had lunch there before continuing on to the Six Mile where Alan and Ted were about to go down again for a short afternoon spell. They intended finishing at four, so that they could clean up to visit friends that evening.

I was courteously invited to join them, but declined in favour of staying there and holding the fort for them while they were away.

I had called at the P.O. and picked up two spools of film which had at last been re-directed from Broken Hill. I was glad of an evening with my white gloves and spy-glass.

One spool was quite satisfactory, but the other I considered a sixty per cent write off. Most of the shots were too contrasty and I feared they would be impossible to copy satisfactorily.

I was asleep when Alan and Ted returned. Jasper growled at the sound of Ted's utility so I put my head out of the door, reported everything okay and promptly went to sleep again.

I woke early. The morning was crisp and fresh and I felt really good. Alan told me he had picked up a letter at the P.O. last evening and would have to return to his hometown for a few days, as he was the plaintiff in a court case. It had come up unexpectedly and the hearing was on Tuesday next.

He proposed to leave early on the following morning for the five hundred mile drive. Today was Saturday.

Realising that Ted would be alone, I suggested that I might fill in for Alan while he was away to keep the work going.

I pointed out to them that I wanted to do it for the experience, because only by doing a job can you really appreciate what is involved in the physical and mental energy needed.

I wanted to become an unpaid partner for a few days, knowing quite well that, in the event of making a lucky strike, my efforts would not go entirely unrewarded.

So it was agreed, but today I wanted to do some filming. I set up the camera and took some shots of 'pulling dirt' with the electric hoist.

A quarter-of-a-mile away was the most completely mechanised opal mine I had ever seen and Ted offered to take me along and introduce me to the owner who would, no doubt, show me round.

I had wanted to take a close look at this rig and see it actually working. It had been quiet each time I had passed—which had been during that period when all activity was underground and the hoist was not working.

It was busy this morning so we walked over and watched this ingenious piece of mechanism in operation.

Worked electrically from a mobile power plant such as we were using, it used one bucket of large capacity which not only lifted the dirt but also the men, to save them climbing a ladder.

This bucket travelled up and down on guides, which carried it not only to the surface but about ten feet above, where it travelled over a loop to deposit its contents into a waiting truck. Having shot its load, it then returned automatically to the bottom of the shaft for another load to be tipped in from wheel-barrows.

This was a mine where the mullock was not just dumped in heaps around the head of the shaft but carted away to the 'puddling tank' for further treatment before being discarded.

We waited for the bucket to come up with another load, but it stopped at the surface and a man stepped out. He was going off to lunch and told us that the boss was down below.

Ted stepped into the bucket and pressed the button telling me to come down when the bucket returned. In a few seconds it came up. I stepped in, pressed the button and down I went as smoothly as any office-block elevator.

It stopped automatically and I stepped out into a wide cavern brilliantly illuminated with fluorescent strips.

This, indeed, was a mine with a difference. The floor was hard and smooth. There was plenty of headroom and the high, spacious cavern was clean and airy.

Apart from the electric jack-hammers, the mechanisation of labour finished at the bottom of the shaft. The wheel-barrows still had to be filled with a shovel and man-handled along the drives to the foot of the shaft where they were tipped into the automatic bucket.

194

No matter how highly mechanised, opal mining is still no arm-chair, push-button affair. The human element plus experience is still the vital factor.

No machine is so sensitive that it can detect a possible fortune amongst the clay and rock and potch. The machine has taken over the actual drudgery without reducing the physical energy required to locate and extract the opal from its ages-old prison.

The hard work now takes place at the most interesting phase and the whole process is speeded up. The gamble, the excitement, the thrill and the heart-break are still there and always will be until some wonderful scientific detecting device is invented. Heaven forbid!

We found the owner down one of the drives squatting on an old piece of sacking, scratching at the wall in the end of the drive with a light pick.

Take away the fluorescent lighting and substitute a candle supported by a wire 'spider' pushed into the wall and the scene could easily have been the same as it might have been fifty years ago.

He stopped work as Ted introduced me and we all squatted down for a smoke.

He was very friendly and gave me much information about this mine and how he had developed it over the last few months. He and the three men he employed worked a day and a night shift. Normally the gouging was done by night.

In the morning, the drives were cleared of all loose debris which was carted to the bucket and automatically delivered to the waiting truck.

When the truck was full, it was immediately driven to the 'wet puddling tank' where the contents were treated and the empty truck driven back for another load.

I said I would like to film this and again was invited to 'help myself' whenever I liked. He would tell his men to give all the co-operation I wanted.

It was almost lunchtime and he was going off until about nine o'clock that night, but the clearing and puddling would be going on all the afternoon.

This seemed a good opportunity to get the shots I wanted so after an early lunch, I filmed the hoist in operation. When the truck was full, I followed it to the 'puddling tank' which I had visited by accident three days before.

This 'puddling tank' is really an earth dam, fed by the bore drain and surrounded by 'puddling' machines of all shapes and sizes.

They varied from converted tractors to very old cars whose engines had been persuaded to run again. The principle of these was essentially the same in each case, but individual inventiveness and the ingenuity to use available parts and material gave each one a character and a noise of its very own.

Our friend had adapted a tractor for the purpose and had fitted to the rear end a large rotating drum about four feet in diameter by about the same depth. The sides of this drum were of steel mesh.

The walls of the dam were wide enough on top to allow trucks to drive on to them to unload their mullock, a shovelful at a time into the drums of the 'puddling' machines which were placed on the side of the dam wall remote from the water.

Small petrol-driven pumps sucked the water from the dam and injected it at a fair pressure on to the mixture of clay and rock which constituted the mullock and was being steadily shovelled into the drums as they rotated.

The jet and agitation softened and washed off the clay and soon the drumful of mullock was reduced to wet rock and pieces of stone of various sizes.

When the clay had disappeared, the machine was stopped and a trap door opened in the drum to allow these stones to be ejected on to a flat tray. Here they were examined and sorted over for pieces of opal which had been missed at the diggings.

Enough opal is found by 'puddling' to make this method well worth while and, from this one truck load, three nice pieces were salvaged.

I filmed this process from all angles and was so absorbed that I failed to notice what Jasper was up to.

The 'puddling' machines are placed on the outside of the dam walls so that the sludge which comes out of the drums through the steel mesh can run down the outside of the walls and not run back into the clean dam water.

This pinkish-looking sludge has formed a wide lake varying in depth from a few inches to several feet. This was something quite new to Jasper and proved irresistible. He had gone in expecting a good swim.

When I spotted him, he was standing in it with the clayey mud up to his tummy and evidently wondering why his progress was so slow.

I called him sharply and made him go into the dam to clean off. Then he lay in the sun by the Kombi to get dry.

When I thought he had settled down for a sleep I resumed my filming and set up the camera on top of the truck's cab to get shots looking down into the revolving drum.

I completed these successfully and had just finished getting some close-ups of a piece of opal which was showing on the plate when I noticed that Jasper had disappeared again.

I immediately looked at the lake of sludge and could just see his head above the mud. He had gone further this time and was in difficulties. He was near the spot where it was several feet deep.

I was really worried and prepared to go in after him. He turned his head as I called and, with great difficulty, managed to turn his body round.

He was struggling and panting but succeeded in making a little progress. I called encouragement and watched closely as, inch by inch, he dragged himself to a less treacherous position.

I felt so sorry for him as he finally crawled on to dry land but couldn't resist the temptation to turn the cine camera on him, a bedraggled, pink mass of miserable canine.

196

He was nearly all in and I realised that it had been a close thing. That sludge was worse than quicksand.

He recovered in about five minutes so, for the second time that day, he had to be washed in the dam. I think it was a lesson to him because the next and last time we visited the 'puddling tank', he kept close to me and made no attempt even to chase a lizard in the direction of that sludge.

Sunday afternoon came and I made my way to the Nine Mile to keep my appointment with Shirley Kite and his father.

Their home was a typical old-timer's camp, constructed from the usual conglomeration of rock, rough timber, corrugated iron, packing cases and canvas. Such dwellings would never be tolerated in the environs of a city, but they had long provided all the amenities which these tough old men needed and given them shelter from the sun, wind and rain.

They never had to call in a plumber, electrician or carpenter and did all their own maintenance with a few nails and a hammer.

They were free from the necessity or the desire to 'keep up with the Joneses' and, as a consequence, were natural, hospitable and friendly.

Old Foley Kite was still unwell so, instead of going to visit him, we sat and chatted for a couple of hours.

Both Shirley and his father were very knowledgeable. They showed me specimens and discussed the field. They told me stories of some the present and past characters and, in all, made my visit a very pleasant and instructive one.

When I got back to the camp at the Six Mile there was no sign of Ted, but a strange car was parked outside his caravan. The generator was going so I guessed he was down below. I went to the top of the shaft and looked down. I could see that the lights were on and could hear voices so I yelled down to announce my return.

A faint voice floated up "Come on down!", so down I went. The visitor was an experienced miner who had worked this claim for a time and was explaining to Ted the exact position in which he had found a cluster of 'nobbies' of good colour before they had petered out and he had abandoned the claim in favour of a more promising one which he was at present working.

Ted introduced him as Arch McLintock. He was a short, nuggety man of about forty-five with a very strong Aussie accent and a ready laugh. I liked him on sight and felt that the reason for his visit was purely a goodwill one with the idea of helping the less experienced, rather than that of 'snooping' which seemed to be a popular pastime amongst some of the locals from other diggings.

There seemed to be a marked camaraderie here at the Six Mile. Willing help was never far away when anything went wrong. If you broke a pick handle, there was always somebody around who had a spare one to offer. If they couldn't help in a practical way, advice both serious and facetious was always forthcoming.

In one place at the side of the main chamber, the roof had been

197

undercut and Arch suggested that if a drive was made in here towards another abandoned hole where he now knew 'nobbies' had been found, there could be other pockets of opal.

Assuming that his information was correct, and there was no reason to believe that it might be otherwise, this seemed a promising line to follow.

Ted climbed up the pile of rubble which had again accumulated. He took with him a bulb on the end of a flex and secured it to the roof with a nail. Then he called for a pick and started to cut further under the roof. As he cut into the sugary-looking clay, it fell like a miniature avalanche down the sloping pile of rubble.

One piece hit Ted's boot, bounced off and landed at my feet. I idly picked it up and squeezed it, expecting it either to flatten or disintegrate between my finger and thumb.

It resisted my efforts. I was about to throw it down when I came back to earth and remembered that many a good opal has been tossed aside undetected in a lump of clay.

I got out my penknife and scraped it. By now, I had had enough experience to feel and sense that there was opal here. I called to the others as I carried it over to another light. Ted took a pair of snippers from his pocket and took off a corner. It was black and shiny—undoubtedly a 'nobby'!

It could be potch or it could be a gem.

We wasted no time in clambering up into the sunlight where Ted washed it and took another snip. Again the shiny black was revealed but it was entirely devoid of colour. Nevertheless, we all felt excited.

Arch was right. There were more 'nobbies' there!

It was getting late in the day. Arch had to go, but he promised to look us up again tomorrow to see if we had any real luck.

Ted and I reluctantly agreed to restrain our impatience until tomorrow and get ourselves some food. After the meal, we sat and yarned and speculated until it was quite dark and the nocturnal bugs forced us to retire.

It was quite obvious that, in our present state of excitement, we should, temporarily at least, cease to drive towards the spot which I had 'divined' as productive.

This was going to be a test of patience because we couldn't go far undercutting that roof. We had to have headroom and sufficient space to remove the debris. In addition to this, we still had a ton or two of dirt to clear from the bottom of the shaft before we could even think of driving in further—in any direction.

It was all very frustrating, but we rose early and got stuck into it. Ted worked the hoist and distributed the mullock while I filled the buckets at the bottom of the hole. It was hot and hard work for both of us but we cleared it by lunchtime.

It was quite enough for me for one day so, after lunch, Jasper and I made for the Nine Mile to see how old Foley Kite was. When we got there, Shirley was 'pulling dirt' alone, a thing the old man himself was quite used to doing.

It was not my idea of fun. First you lower the bucket, then you climb down the shaft and fill it. You then climb up again and wind the full bucket up. This now has to be emptied away from the top of the shaft and lowered to the bottom again. Down you go again to re-fill the bucket and so on. What slow drudgery!

Yet many of these old-timers did it for years, dug deep holes and made many drives—every one a long-odds gamble. What guts, what stamina they must have had!

The spirit is not entirely dead as I found when I met young Frank Fazzari at the Little Wonder. *He* had no chain ladders but had to go up and down a rope!

Shirley stopped work when he saw us and said that his uncle was much better, but not yet fully fit.

His camp was very similar to his brother's. We went in and found the old man sitting on his bed. He was wearing slacks and his pyjama jacket. He was looking very pale but, whatever was the cause of his recent indisposition, it had not affected his impatience to be up and doing again.

He greeted me warmly and, over the inevitable billy of tea, the three of us talked opal for the best part of an hour. His stories of the past were fascinating, and I could have gone on listening but I felt that it would have been inconsiderate to have stayed longer. I promised to call again at the weekend when I hoped he would be quite fit again.

When I got back, Ted had the jack-hammer going and had started the new drive. Another big pile of rubble had collected at the bottom of the shaft. It wouldn't be long before the interesting digging had to stop while we got rid of it.

We decided on a system. We would spend the mornings when we were fresh in 'pulling dirt'. We reckoned that, by starting early, we could clear it by lunchtime. After lunch, we would have a brief but necessary siesta before spending the remainder of the day driving and gouging as we went along.

Ted had made the drive wide enough for two to work at gouging under the roof at the same time—one on each side.

For the little of the day remaining we both gouged and found two more potch 'nobbies'.

At five o'clock we knocked off and were in the middle of our meal when Alan returned unexpectedly. His case had been adjourned for two weeks and he had come straight back.

He was very tired after his five hundred mile drive but, even so, it was difficult to persuade him to wait till morning to go down and see for himself what we had done.

I woke at six o'clock as Ted started the generator to cook his breakfast in the electric frypan.

By the time I had washed, shaved, had breakfast, cleared away, made

199

my bed, swept out and accompanied Jasper in our regular 'constitutional' into the bush and back, Ted and Alan had both disappeared down below.

I decided to give them an hour before reminding them that all that dirt had to be shifted by lunchtime, and was about to go down when a cheery-looking woman appeared walking up the track from the direction of the mechanised mine.

When she arrived I said, "G'day! Are you looking for Ted or Alan?"

"Not really", she replied. "Has Arch been here this morning?—Arch McLintock. I'm Ruby McLintock."

"Not as far as I know," I assured her, "but we're expecting him."

"He left me at the Lanskis' place for a chat with Leila while he went off to look over another old shaft. He said he'd pick me up here."

"Well, Mrs. McLintock," I said, "he must be on his way. Have a seat in the shade." I offered her a folding chair under the fly of Alan's tent.

I introduced myself and said that I'd let Ted and Alan know that she was here.

"No, don't bring them up just to see me. I'll just wait for Arch but, Lord knows how long he'll be. He forgets everything when he gets a new idea."

This was the first miner's wife I had met at the Ridge, and I was keen to hear more about family life in this environment.

They had two children who attended the local school and seemed to have settled in very happily during the five years they had been here.

Arch had been moderately successful, finding enough opal to keep them comfortable without being too affluent. They had built a decent house and had only very recently moved in.

Arch loved opal for itself, rather than the money it brought in and took as much pleasure in other people's finds as in his own.

Opal was his life and, to demonstrate this, she told me a true anecdote. There is no sewerage in Lightning Ridge and domestic toilet arrangements usually consisted of a deep hole in the ground covered by a 'sentry box'. All waste organic matter was deposited in the hole and lightly covered with a layer of the dirt which had originally been removed—rather like making a mulch heap.

In course of time, the hole fills up so another hole is dug and the sentry box moved to the new position.

Before they had moved in Arch had constructed his 'little house' and dug his hole. Being an experienced miner this had been no problem except that, once he had got down ten feet, he felt that he had to go down to the 'level' because, he argued, if he didn't, it would always be on his mind that he might be covering up a fortune!

It would be many years before they had to move that sentry box.

Arch arrived, just as Ted and Alan came up for a breather. On went the billy and we all sat round yarning, so that little work was done that morning.

I had enjoyed working with Ted but I was really rather relieved that

Alan had returned. I still had lots to do and people to see before I left Lightning Ridge.

Whilst I had had my regular showers in the garbage container, I was beginning to feel the need for a hot shower and a spell in the waters. There was washing and shopping to do so a trip to town was indicated. I did my shopping and called at the P.O. I washed my clothes and had my dip, then set off to find *the* oldest inhabitant.

He lived on the edge of the Three Mile and it took me a long time to find his camp which was similar to the others except that he had used more rock in its original construction.

Fred Bodel was 'at home' and greeted me courteously. He was eighty-nine and another example of unimpaired mental faculties, although physically he had obviously, and wisely, slowed down.

The old man told me many colourful stories of Lightning Ridge in the old days, of crooks and 'con' men he had known, but the highlight of his experiences was when he was visited in his camp quite recently by the Governor-General himself and his lady (Lord and Lady Casey). He showed me a framed photograph of this event, with him standing beside Lady Casey. He was very proud of that picture.

It had taken a long time to find Fred Bodel's camp but only a few minutes to get back to town so I took the opportunity of calling on Artie Bruce, whom I found hard at work in his lapidary workshop.

Artie was reputed to be the best opal cutter at the Ridge.

He was friendly and helpful. He showed me his equipment and many fine examples of his work.

I was glad he kept working as we talked. I was able to study his technique. I was pretty smug about my own ability and skill at shaping and polishing, but to see a master at work was an education and I quickly realised that shaping and polishing was a minor part of professional lapidary.

Only many years of practical experience can give that knowledge of how to get the maximum beauty from a rough stone.

Although Artie was at the top of his class, he was not too proud to discuss methods and techniques with an amateur like me. He agreed with some of my theories and corrected me on others. One of the things I respected and admired him for was the fact that, of the few questions I asked him which he couldn't answer, he admitted his ignorance instead of scrubbing round it with an evasive reply. To me, this is the true mark of a master of his craft. None of us, no matter how highly skilled, knows all the answers, but it takes a strong character to admit it.

Had I possessed a rough stone of fabulous worth, I would have trusted it to Artie without the slightest hesitation.

My funds were now on the 'dangerously ill' list and I knew that I couldn't afford to stay more than a few days longer. I had already been here over a month and there was much I hadn't seen and, no doubt, many interesting people I hadn't met.

Had I stayed for six months I don't think I could honestly say "I know Lightning Ridge", but I feel competent to assess it as Australia's biggest and most prosperous opal field. It has many big advantages over the others: it is the most accessible, it has abundant water, it is well wooded and it produces the most valuable opal in the world today. A reticulated electricity supply encourages development and, I believe, there are plans for a bitumen sealed road from Walgett.

Big business with its soulless and ruthless greed has already tried to muscle in, and my sympathies lie fully with the local Miners' Association who are fighting it.

To try to put opal mining on the same footing as copper, nickel, gold, iron and other minerals is, in my opinion, madness and I can only hope that sanity and legislation will be strong enough to curb such nonsense.

I stayed at the bore that night and the following morning I went out to see how Ted and Alan were getting on.

They had made good progress and more 'nobbies' had come to light. Several of these showed traces of 'sun flash' colour of blue and gold, but the brilliant greens and reds of true colour were still lacking. They were enthusiastic and hopeful as the pile of grey and black potch pebbles gradually mounted.

Unlike the potch from other fields there *is* a market for this. It is used for making 'doublets', which are pieces of precious opal too thin to be used for practical applications in jewellery but, backed with black potch, can make lovely gem stones.

I spent the afternoon down below helping to clear the dirt as it was gouged out and doing a little gouging on my own account.

It was Friday and I planned to pull out on Sunday morning.

Ted had a slide projector which he set up using the side of Alan's tent as a screen. He showed many of his slides and I reciprocated with some of mine. We kept going until the moths became so bad that they obscured the pictures. It was a very pleasant final evening but one for me.

My plans for my last day were not very involved. I had to do a little shopping, wash out a few things and make some minor checks on the Kombi. I also wanted to say goodbye to the Kites.

I got up late. Ted and Alan were already at work. After breakfast I did my chores and then went with Jasper on our usual 'constitutional' down the bush track.

He usually zig-zagged in and out of the undergrowth on either side according to where the lizards were the most abundant.

We were about two hundred yards from camp when he appeared in front of me. He had begun his dash into the grass on the other side when he suddenly stopped dead and froze about two yards in off the track. His head was thrust forward and his tail straight out behind him.

"What is it?" I called, expecting him to bark as he always does when he comes face to face with a lizard at bay. He didn't move. He didn't utter a sound but remained like a statue. I walked up behind him and peered into the grass in front of him. I could just see a portion of the thick scaly body of a snake, both ends disappearing into the grass so that I couldn't tell which end was which.

As I watched it moved very slowly away from us, or so it seemed but, for all I knew, it might have been backing up ready to strike.

It was the colour of a highly-venomous brown snake and the three-inch diameter body suggested a big one. I bent down slowly and grabbed Jasper's collar. I pulled him back to the track and, after carefully noting the spot, hurried straight back to camp for my camera.

Ted was on the hoist so I told him what I'd seen and that I was going back. He immediately thought I'd come back for my rifle and said, "Hang on a minute. Your two-two won't be much good against a king brown unless you hit him straight between the eyes. I'll get my shot-gun."

"I wasn't going to shoot it," I replied. "I only want to photograph it."

"That's as maybe," he retorted. "You get your picture and I'll finish him off. He's too near this camp for my liking."

With that he loaded his twelve bore and away we went.

We got to the spot but there was no sign of the snake. The situation was now rather tricky. Ted reckoned that they were rather slow at this time of year but, if we made too much noise trampling around in the grass, he would get away. On the other hand, it would be very dangerous to tread on him.

It is generally conceded that the average snake likes peace and quiet. That is why you seldom see one when you are walking normally in the bush. They don't attack unless surprised or cornered and provoked. They much prefer to get out of your way.

Much to his disgust, I had tied Jasper up to the Kombi but felt very uncomfortable prowling around trying to penetrate the long grass with my eyes and detect the excellent camouflage which these reptiles have.

Ted and I were about ten yards apart when I heard him call quietly, "There he is—coming towards you!"

By now I was really scared and remained so until I spotted his head coming in my direction about three yards away. Desire to get the picture overcame my fright and I focussed the camera and stood still. On it came towards me as Ted followed it with shot-gun poised.

At two yards my courage failed me. I hastily re-focussed, released the shutter and leapt backwards.

"Okay," I yelled to Ted as he closed in. Taking careful aim he called "Stand clear" and with a loud bang the gun discharged causing bits of snake's head to be scattered in all directions, whilst the long body thrashed and convulsed in its death throes.

Ted reckoned that the blast at that range had taken not only the head but almost a foot of the body as well. We took the remains back to camp and measured it. It was three-and-a-quarter inches in diameter by sixty-six inches long—without the head and neck!

I spent the rest of the morning doing my last bit of gouging. My efforts were not very productive, but Alan found a nice little 'nobby' with a good show of red and blue. It was not a very valuable stone, but encouraging. It looked as if they were on the right track and I felt pleased that I should be leaving them while their spirits were high.

The only thing I regretted was that I doubted if I should ever know if there really was opal where my divining wires had indicated. Had I had time, I would have cut that extra few feet of drive on my own.

Perhaps it's just as well because, had I found opal of any value there, I would surely have been 'hooked'.

In the afternoon I did all I had planned to do and when we returned for our last evening with these two excellent mates they had put on a special 'tea' in my honour. Ted had made a marvellous stew. I imagine it contained everything but the kitchen sink and it was delicious. Even Jasper had his share.

It was nearly midnight before the fire was allowed to die down and I turned in after having a bush bath with only the glow of the dying embers for illumination.

At 9.15 on Sunday morning I turned the key to start the Kombi. As a parting gift, these good mates of mine presented me with a small plastic bag full of black potch 'nobbies' to remember them by. I shall make a tie-bar from one of them even though it shows no colour. It will be useful and unobtrusive if I ever get around to wearing a tie again.

As I turned east down the bush track, I left a cloud of dust behind me, so that I couldn't take a last look at that camp by way of the rear vision mirror.

The sun was well up straight ahead of us and a fine day was promised.

By tomorrow afternoon, we should be back to where the trip had started from. I turned to Jasper and said, "We'll soon be . . ." I nearly said "home", but now, for the first time, I realised that we had no home apart from this Kombi where we had lived for sixteen months.

He had abandoned his position by the window and was sitting close and leaning against me.

As I put my arm around him, he turned and licked my face, then he, too, looked straight ahead towards the east.